ELEMENTS OF

CHINESE HISTORIOGRAPHY

ELEMENTS OF CHINESE HISTORIOGRAPHY

BY

HAN, YU-SHAN

中國史學綱要

韓玉珊

W. M. HAWLEY   HOLLYWOOD 46   CALIFORNIA   1955

Copyright 1955 - Yu-shan Han

Pronunciation of Chinese Words

The writing of Chinese words in Roman letters (called romanization) presents many difficulties and several different systems have been developed. The system invented by Sir Thomas Wade in the 1880s and modified by H. A. Giles in his Chinese-English Dictionary of 1912, though badly in need of revision, remains in use because of its widespread employment in modern Sinological works.

Many older, but still valuable reference works used the systems of the Morrison or Williams dictionaries and there are still others for foreign languages. The chart "Romanization of Chinese" by W. M. Hawley is a cross-reference conversion table of seven systems.

Some Chinese sounds cannot be correctly represented by the letters of the English alphabet. For instance, *j* should be pronounced somewhere between the soft French j and r, but to most American ears the j sound cannot be distinguished.

The use of an apostrophe in *ch'*, *k'*, *p'*, *t'*, *ts'*, *tz'* indicates that these letters retain their usual English sounds, while its absence denotes hardening of the sound. An instance of this is in the words *Tao*, *Tao*ism, which should be pronounced Dow, Dowism.

I by itself is ee; *in* as in pin; *ing* as in sing.

The Classic of Changes *I Ching* or in older texts *I King* is to be pronounced ee jing in the official Mandarin dialect.

Principle deviations from common English pronunciations —

a as in father	*hs* as s	*shih* as shir
e as o in wolf	*j* as r	*t* as d in din
ei as ay	*je* as ro	*t'* as in tin
er or *erh* as rrh	*jih* as rir	*ts* as ds
eng as ung	*k* as g in gun	*ts'* as ts
ch as j in jungle	*k'* as in king	*tzu* as dz
ch' as in child	*ou* as in dough	*tz'u* as tz
chih as jir	*p* as b in bin	*ui* as way
ch'ih as chir	*p'* as in pin	*ü* as ü in German

In older works, check spellings of all words before quoting.

PREFACE

Seventeen years have passed since the first work on Chinese historiography in English was published. The author of the present work hopes to add something to this fundamental presentation, by a bi-lingual approach, by emphasis on Chinese sources, and by an expansion of the subject in scope and in historical continuity.

Command of the Chinese language is no longer limited to the very few as it was seventeen years ago. New generations of sinologists carry advanced research studies in the original. With extensive references to Chinese works given, the student is able at once to grasp suggestive fields of intensive studies, and also the importance of individual works. Continuity, whether regarded as an element of weakness or of strength, is one of the characteristics of Chinese historiography. It is shown by the peculiar tradition of the Chinese historian, by the rich legacy that he left, and by his established fields of historical research and criticism. Chinese historiography, like Chinese life, exhibited a constant struggle to maintain a balance between the free and the required, variety and unity, the new and the continuous.

Chapter I attempts to show the strength of the historian in China. The chapter is supplemented by Appendix I in a chronological treatment of the offices and functions of the historian in government from 256 B.C. to 1911 A.D.. Chapter II reviews some of the problems that lie in the study of Chinese historiography. This is followed by classifications and types of Chinese histories (Chapters III. IV, V).

The next three chapters are devoted to the translation and illustration of 242 terms denoting types of historical writings, 413 descriptive terms used in Chinese history, and to a selection of 46 modern historians with their major works. Chapter IX illustrates traditional types of historical research. Chapter X deals with historical criticism in its disguised forms, in schools of thought, and as a whole in its continuity.

Chapter XI presents some historical geography in three aspects: national and local, official and private, and the changes of geographical names. The last chapter gives an analysis of the twenty-six dynastic histories in their compilations, divisions, and continuity. Comparative charts covering divisions, treatises, and biographies, give a ready reference to the variations in the twenty-six dynastic histories.

Since there is as yet no absolute standard of romanization of Chinese words, the author has followed the Wade system, not because it is better than other systems, but because of its continued employment in publications. All Chinese words in romanization are italicized. Well known place names are given in the common Chinese Postal romanization except where they occur as part of romanized book titles in which cases the Wade system is followed.

In the biographical data on Chinese historians, many dates of birth and death are lacking, in which cases dates when they received literary degrees or were appointed to official positions are given. In some cases only the approximate dates when they flourished are known.

I have made free use of the Chinese materials found in the *Chung-kuo shih-hsüeh-shih* 中國史學史 A History of Chinese Historiography, by *Chin Yü-fu* 金毓黻 and in the *Nien-wu-shih lun-kang* 廿五史論綱 Essentials of the Twenty-five Dynastic Histories, by *Hsü Hao* 徐浩, and of information in Eminent Chinese of the *Ch'ing* Period, edited by Arthur W. Hummel. To these authors I am indebted. I am also indebted to Miss Mabel E. Bennett for her constructive criticism as regards form and clarity.

Yu-shan Han

Los Angeles, California
   October 10, 1954

Table of Contents

I.	Role of the Historian in China	1
II.	Some Problems of Chinese Historiography	13
III.	Traditional Classifications of Chinese History	39
IV.	Development of General Histories	49
V.	Types of Specialized Histories	59
VI.	Terms Denoting Types of Historical Writings	77
VII.	Descriptive Terms of Historical Events	105
VIII.	Modern Historians and their Works	121
IX.	Traditional Types of Historical Research	147
X.	Continuity of Historical Criticism	161
XI.	Historical Geography	175
XII.	The Twenty-six Dynastic Histories	191
Appendix I.	Office and Function of the Historian	205
Appendix II.	*Nien-hao* or Year Titles	210
Appendix III.	A list of New Histories	213
Indexes —	General	221
	Translated Chinese Book Titles	223
	Romanized Chinese Book Titles	229
	Authors	240

Illustrations

Chen Yen Academy in *Hunan* province	END PAPERS
Portrait rubbing of *Ku Yen-wu*	FRONTISPIECE
A page from a *Sung* edition of the *Han-shu*	Page 11
Portrait of *Ch'ien Ta-hsin*	12
Portrait of *Hui Tung*	38
Examples of 4 successive styles of Chinese characters	47
Portrait of *Ssu-ma Kuang*	48
Portrait of *P'eng Ting-chiu*	58
A page from a *Sung* edition of the *T'ang-shu*	75
Portrait of *Ou-yang Hsiu*	76
Portrait of *Hung Liang-chi*	104
A document — the Veritable Records	119
Portrait of *Lu Lung-ch'i*	120
Rubbing from the Stone Classics cut in the *T'ang* Dynasty	145
Portrait of *Yu T'ung*	146
A document — Annals	159
Portrait of *Liang Chang-chü*	160
A Civil Service examination paper	173
Portrait of *Chen Hung-mo*	174
Portrait of *Chi Tseng-yün*	190
Portrait of *Chu Hsi* in the *Nan-hsi* Gazetteer	204

皇清處士顧公炎武

一代大儒
學貫天人
隱居求志
比跡河汾

Portrait rubbing of *Ku Yen-wu* (see p. 133)

Chapter I

THE ROLE OF THE HISTORIAN IN CHINA

The significance given to history by the Chinese people from the beginning until now is unique. It is characteristic of the Chinese not only that they have endured, but that they have consciously endured. Their experience of continuity has demanded both the methods of historiography and interpretive thought. Their earliest records reveal the high role of the historian.

Chinese passion for the written characters of their language furthered a desire to make records of men and events. This devotion had almost a religious nature; whether a Chinese could read or not the characters were sacred and even the use of modern newspapers for wrapping paper was frowned upon by the common people and scholars alike. "Heaven rejoiced" when the characters were invented since they "established contact between the human and the divine";[1] in like manner "Hades was made to tremble." As late as the 1930's men still went about the streets, gathering scraps of paper bearing any signs of writing or printing to be placed in bamboo baskets bearing the inscription, *Ching-hsi-tzu-chih* 敬惜字紙 (Reverence-love-charactered paper). Such papers were then burned at Buddhist, Taoist, or Confucian temples.

Because of this reverence for the printed word Oracle Bones found by farmers were preserved as something of value, and as a result historians found a great source for historical verification and revelation. By 1899 such men as *Lo Chen-yü* and *Wang Kuo-wei* had deciphered the bones. Because inscriptions dealt with divination they came to be known as Oracle Bones, but they authenticated Chinese history to a time 500 years earlier than had previously been accepted, 1600-1500 B.C. instead of 1100-1000 B.C.

According to an inscription on one of the Oracle Bones, the term history 史, etymologically, is a "hand holding records of events."[2] The pictograph for history also stood for events themselves; in other words, history became at once the records of events and the events themselves. From other inscriptions on Chinese bronzes, history 𢆶 or 𠧢, etymologically, was a "hand seizing the middle"; this character conveyed the meaning of "impartial narration of events." Or, as Wieger says, a hand holding a fountain pen enscribing characters. We are reminded of Polybius' concept, "Directly a man assumes the moral attitudes of an historian he ought to forget all considerations, such as love of one's friends, hatred of one's enemies.... He must sometimes praise enemies and blame friends."

The office of the historian as part of China's body politique began with the dawn of Chinese civilization, and his function played a unique role in China's intellectual and political history. A survey of the office and function of the historian indicates both the strength and the problems of Chinese historiography. Authentic titles for historians among the oracle bone inscriptions are given as *Ta-shih* 大史 grand historian; *Ch'ing-shih* 卿史 official historian; and *Yü-shih* 御史 imperial historian. The term *Ta-shih,* grand historian, and another, *Nei-shih* 內史, inner historian,[3] have been found on ancient bronzes. In accordance with the *Chou-kuan* 周官, Officers of *Chou,* there were six classes of historians, with the titles: *Ta-shih* 大史 grand historian, *Hsiao-shih* 小史 junior historian, *Nei-shih* 內史 inner historian, *Wai-shih* 外史 outer historian, *Tso-shih* 左史 left historian, and *Yu-shih* 右史 right historian.

The duties of historians during the *Chou* period were chiefly the interpretation of ancient documents[4] and the compilation and preservation of imperial charges and ordinances, of histories of the operations of the imperial government, and of records of various states. Since natural phenomena were regarded as closely related to human affairs, the historian performed the duties of the astrologer and the astronomer.

The grand historian during the pre-*Ch'in* period had a double duty. He saw and recorded natural happenings and human events. During the

THE ROLE OF THE HISTORIAN IN CHINA

Han period, observation of natural phenomenon was assigned to the Office of Sacrificial Worship, the *T'ai-ch'ang* 太常. *Ssu-t'ien-t'ai* 司天台 or Office of Uranography during the *T'ang* was a new name for the Office of the Grand Historian. This combination of offices in one man helps to explain why the earliest Chinese historical documents (down to 200 B.C.) include so many data on eclipses and other celestial phenomena. It was only natural for the concurrent duties of the historian to be delegated or subdivided later on when affairs of the state became more complex. Division of functions led to multiple designations for the historian as well as did the change of names under new political powers.

Chronologically, the essential functions of the historian were channelled into three distinct offices in the government; namely, (1) astronomy, (2) national history, (3) supervision and impeachment. Prior to the *Han* period, the first two were more closely related, but by the Christian era the latter two had become more closely associated.

Since time immemorial, man has watched the sky and observed the movements of the celestial bodies and their relative positions to one another. From the practical relationship between man and natural phenomena, a mystical or supernatural significance was bestowed upon them by the ancients; hence the pseudo science of astrology, but the faithful periodical or cylical movements of the sun, the moon, the planets, and the stars gave man the basis for the measurement of time and the making of calendars so astrology and astronomy went hand in hand for many centuries.

The making of a calendar (*chih-li,* 治曆), and the regulation of time (*shou-shih,* 授時 or *shih-ling,* 時令) were two of the most important functions of the government affecting public works, punitive expeditions, judicial hearings, hunting and fishing, festivals and religious sacrifices, planting and harvesting. Faithful recordings of natural phenomena were just as important as were faithful records of human events, if not more so, as the former often gave accurate forecast of natural occurrences.

By the time the first standard history, the Historical Memoirs, was written, the function of calendar-making, of astronomical observations and predictions, and of geography had become separate if not independent sciences or endeavors. What had been an almost hereditary official historian of multiple functions, disappeared since the astronomer, astrologer, censor, and historian, all performed distinct duties. However, belief in the intrinsic relationship between the ways of nature and the fortunes of man continued to dominate Chinese thought, and concurrency of official positions held sway for centuries.

Just as the combined duties of the astrologer and the historian gradually were separated, the concurrent function of the historian and the censor became distinct. The appearance of scientific historic writing and the elevation of the imperial historian to be censor came about the same time, namely, the first century before the Christian era. Under emperor *Wu-ti* (140-87 B.C.) the imperial historian was given the status of deputy prime minister vested with duties to receive memorials from high officials, to evaluate the services of officials, and to have impeachment power.[5] In the year 1 B.C. Emperor *Ai* (6-1 B.C.) extended the historian's powers of control and created a special seat in the Court for him, known as *Yü-shih-t'ai* 御史台 or Imperial Historian Pavillion. This marked the definite establishment of a censorate which lasted until 1912. This office was again restored to dignity and importance in *Sun Yat-sen's Wu-ch'üan-hsien-fa* 五權憲法 or Five Power Constitution exemplified in the Organic Law of the National Government of the Republic of China, Dec. 8, 1928. The office of the historian and that of the censor exemplified the same ideal in two distinct ways: the former through the might of his impartial brush, the latter, through fearless but just judgment. One left a mirror for future generations; the other, the goal of maintaining the operation of justice. It was the close association of these two offices that made the role of the Chinese historian, legendary and historic, meaningful, and despotic rules of

THE ROLE OF THE HISTORIAN IN CHINA

short duration.

As to the records concerning Chinese historians, some may be considered by modern scholars as forgeries, interpolations, or imaginative creations, but the influence of these records upon the course of history in China cannot be questioned, since they were for ages a part of the subject matter required of candidates taking imperial civil service examinations. One such record is the story of *Chung Ku* 終古, court recorder of Emperor *Chieh* 桀. *Chung Ku,* seeing that the Emperor was neglecting his duties, came before him, and with maps and national records in his hand knelt before the Emperor and wept. When the Emperor met this plea with indifference, *Chung Ku* went over to *Ch'eng T'ang* 成湯 as a protest, and the latter founded a new dynasty. Another story is about Court Historian *Hsiang Chih* 向摯 who escaped from the tyranical last Emperor of the *Shang* dynasty to the court of a new ruler with all the maps and records of the *Shangs.* Such traditions were taught for centuries to Chinese youths; they showed the importance of the historian throughout their history and established certain ideals. The historians of China, whether in the capacity of censor or historian, were often called upon to brave the wrath of unworthy rulers. Once in the 6th Century B.C., when a commander of the palace guard, named *Ts'ui Chu* 崔杼, killed the Prince of *Ch'i* for having deprived him of a beautiful woman, the official historian recorded the incident in one sentence: *"Ts'ui Chu* murdered Duke *Chuang,"* whereupon *Ts'ui Chu* took the tablet from the archives and had the historian executed. Then a brother of the historian renewed the record, only to suffer death himself. When a second brother presented himself, brush in hand, *Ts'ui* saw that he truly stood condemned, and the record was made.

The right of the historian to tell the truth and the censor to be outspoken about men in power became so fiercely guarded a tradition that even the most tyranical rulers had to accept it.

China suffered from "barbarian" rule at various times in her history. Such times were hard on her historians for they emphasized the conflict which always exists between official and private versions of events. China had little in the way of religious persecution, but her literary persecutions amounted at times to inquisitions. The worst of these persecutions came under the *Manchus*.

When a history begun by *Chu Kuo-chen* 朱國楨 " of the *Ming* Dynasty was brought up to date to include the invasion of the Manchus in 1644, the Chinese scholars who did the work presented a realistic account of the invasion. Seventy persons, among whom were several noted historians, were put to death, and their women banished. Another scholar of this time was *Tai Ming-shih* 戴名士. Though, unlike many of the scholars, he agreed to take the civil service examinations under the Manchus, in 1701 he published a history which gave a true account of the *Mings* and a preference for their rule. He collected fast disappearing records of the Southern Courts of the *Ming*, visited elder scholars in retirement, and sought out private histories of the period. The *Manchus* under *K'ang Hsi*, (scholar-emperor though he was), involved several hundred persons in punishment of *Tai Ming-shih* for this work. When *K'ang Hsi* was presented with the facts, he found many noted historians among the condemned. Later on he revised the judgment of the Grand Secretaries and most of the scholars were spared.

Chinese historians in the Court resisted interference from their *Manchu* rulers for ninety years, 1645-1735. Finally when they published the first edition of the *Ming* History (1368-1644) they continued to resist both imperial favors and displeasure concerning this work. The official edition, completed in 1739, listed twenty-five historians as having been directors in the compilation of the history. Concerning the writing of this *Ming* History four *Manchu* rulers issued seventeen edicts,[7] two of which are revealing: Emperor *K'ang Hsi* said "You failed to record the causes for the *Manchu* expeditionary forces against the *Ming*," by which edict he merely wished to have the invasion justified by his historians. In reply the historians said, "The causes for the *Manchu* expedition are recorded in the Annals of *T'ai Tsu* 太祖."

The historians went on to say that since *T'ai Tsu's* Annals were records of events prior to the entry through the Great Wall, they should not appear in the History of the *Ming*. The second edict by Emperor *Ch'ien Lung* 乾隆 (1736-1795), "I have just read the Annals of Emperor *Ying Tsung* 英宗 (1436-1449) of the *Ming* Dynasty with reference to the execution of Provincial Censor *Wang Ch'eng* 汪澄 and of the retired Censor *Ch'ai Wen-Hsien* 柴文顯 and two other censors. You have failed to record the crimes which brought their death and this failure might lead to misjudgment of the emperor," This edict was in reality a decree that the historians add records which would excuse the emperor and put the blame upon the censors who had paid with their lives, but the historians let the decree go unheeded.

What we have described is the spirit of the Chinese historian, upholding both political morality and intellectual integrity. We shall look now at his office in the government and the relationship between official and private historians.

The title *T'ai-shih* 太史, grand historian, continued until the beginning of the Christian era, though the function of this officer became more singular and independent as time passed. *Chu-tso* 箸作, compiler, was introduced to designate the historian at court in the reigns of *Chang-ti* 章帝, 76-88, and *Ho-ti* 合帝, 89-106. This designation was used until the middle of the fifth century. Then for a hundred years the term *Chuan-shih hsüeh shih* 撰史學士, compiler of history, signified the court historian. *Chuan*, to compile, characterizes the function; *hsüeh-shih*, learned scholar, the historian.

During the next fourteen hundred years new titles were introduced as it became necessary to establish new bureaus of government. Among these are *Hsiu chuan* 修撰 senior compiler; *Pien-hsiu* 編修 junior compiler; *T'ung-hsiu* 同修 co-compiler; and *Chien-t'ao* 檢討 research fellow.

A persistent office under a single name for twenty centuries was that of *Ch'i-chü-chu* 起居注, which had the function of recording "the activity and repose" of the sovereign. These records are generally known as "diaries" of the emperor, and upon them the *Shih-lu* 實錄, the Veritable Records, were based. The office of the historian in government. with titles and duties, are presented chronologically in appendix 1.

History writing in China was taken up not only by those employed specially for the purpose but also by scholars engaged in other pursuits both in and out of government. The chief concern of the scholar class in China was always the nation's political heritage, the fundamental pronouncements of her great rulers, principles of human relations, the achievements in her economic programs, and victories in her military expeditions, often referred to as "liberations" of peoples from evil rulers or cultural submissions. Available sources for intellectual discipline were records of the State and accounts of scholars. Ancestor veneration had become a national cult which embraced the realm of biological ancestors, political ancestors and intellectual ancestors. History developed into that of a mirror, a judge, a manifestation of eternal principles from which no one escapes. Since this was the ideal of all learned men, the only difference between official and private historians lay in whether or not they were holding office as such or were temporarily appointed for certain official compilations.

The demarcation between official compilations and private compilations of a certain history was even less significant, as the number of the latter far surpassed that of the former. Furthermore, many private compilations served as the basis of official compilations. Sometimes, a worthy compilation was "converted" into an official one by imperial recognition by a special decree; also, often when an important compilation had to be made, historians both in civil service and in private life were summoned to do the work. It was perhaps through expediency gained by naming men for temporary concurrent posts that the practice of concurrent offices developed. Many "private" historians had compiled histories of the Later *Han*, the Three Kingdoms, the *Chin*, and the sixteen states of the *Chin* period, and official historians later did not hesitate to appropriate them. It has been estimated that during the

THE ROLE OF THE HISTORIAN IN CHINA 9

period 200 to 600 A.D. only one- or two-tenths of historical work was done by official historians. However, official compilation was important because it was done through the permanent office, through continuous records of the affairs of State in imperial libraries and with archives as primary sources of historical data. Then, the mobilization of those interested in and able to carry on historical works, satisfied both the demand of the imperial court for monuments of their rule and the objective of the scholar for intellectual "immortality." Finally, it often happened that results of individual historical research were scattered or lost simply for lack of funds for publication, or for lack of prestige on the part of the compilers.

Official compilations generally covered the following types of history: (1) *Ch'i-chü-chu* 起居注 or Diaries of Activity and Repose of the emperor, (2) *Shih-lu* 實錄 or Veritable Records written at the end of each reign, (3) *Cheng-shih* 正史 or Standard Histories, (4) *Tien-li* 典禮 or Institutes of Rites, (5) *Fang-chih* 方志 or Official Gazetteers. The first type naturally constituted the best primary source of historical materials as it was made up of eye-witness accounts and of official documents. Various emphases occurred at different periods of Chinese history on account of varying types of mind of both the emperors and the historians, the trends of events, and the fashions obtaining in intellectual pursuits. Many were lost because their purposes may have been served in some systematic historical compilation, they were summarized in separate works, or they were too bulky to survive time. Definite form for the "veritable record" began with the *Liang* emperors;[8] as an institution it began with the *Tang*.

Regarding the *Tien-li* 典禮, it has not received as much attention until very recently for the simple reason that priority was given to the demand for standard histories and for historical criticism. However, the historical deposit of political institutions is rich in China; the landmarks are monumental.

Private compilation of historical works of both individual and cooperative production may be classified by the nature and the extent of their creativity into the following: (1) initiating new fields, (2) new approach to unprecedented works, (3) advancement made by new emphases. The pioneering work may be termed creative production (創修); the remaining, revision (改修), in various forms: (a) general revision of a single historical work (修訂), (b) enlargement of a sectional study into an independent piece of work (分撰), (c) reconstruction of several works into a unified whole (總輯), (d) supplements in additions (補闕), (e) in annotations (補注), (f) notes on combined works (合鈔), (g) restoration of scattered or lost works (輯逸).

NOTES FOR CHAPTER I.

1. *Hsü Ch'ieh* 徐鍇 (920-974), *Shuo-wen-hsi-chuan* 說文繫傳 or Annotated Edition of the *Shuo-wen* (in Chinese), 1839 edition, the Preface.
2. *Lo Chen-yü, Yin-hsü-shu-ch'i* 殷虛書契 Records of the Ruins of *Yin*, Vol. V, p. 39.
3. *Wang Kuo-wei* 王國維, *Shih-shih* 釋史 Explanations of History, cited in *Wei Chü-hsien's Shih-hsüeh-shih* 史學史 or History of Chinese Historiography, p. 88.
4. James Legge, Chinese Classics, Vol. III, Pt. I, pp. 10, 11, citing *K'ang-hsi-tzu-tien*.
5. *Kao I-han* 高一涵, *Chung-kuo yü-shih-chih-tu-ti yen-ko* 中國御史制度的沿革 The Development of the Chinese Censorate, (Shanghai, 1933), pp. 6-10.
6. *Chu Kuo-chen* 朱國楨 (1557-1632) compiled a general history of the *Ming* Dynasty, entitled *Huang Ming shih-kai* 皇明史概 printed 5 of 10 parts in 1632.
7. *Li Chin-hua* 李晉華, A History of the Compilation of the *Ming* Dynasty History, Yenching Journal of Chinese Studies, Monograph 3, (Peiping 1933) pp. 1-9.
8. *Liang-huang-ti shih-lu* 梁皇帝實錄 The Veritable Record of the *Liang* Emperor by *Chou Hsing-ssu* 周興嗣, recording major events under Emperor *Wu-ti* (502-549); another one of the same title by *Hsieh Wu* 謝吳, events under *Yüan-ti* (552-554).

高帝紀第一上

漢書一

漢 護軍班固撰

唐 議大夫行秘書少監琅邪縣開國子顏師古集註

高祖

荀悦曰諱邦字季邦之字曰國國之字曰邦張晏曰禮諡法無功最高而爲漢帝之太祖故特起名馬師古曰讳邦之字曰國者臣下所避以相代也

沛豐邑中陽里人也

應劭曰後沛爲縣而豐爲沛之聚邑耳方言高祖稱豐公蓋是氏其鄉里之者也臣瓚曰高祖,本豐人徙沛豐者,沛之鄉也師古曰沛者,本秦泗水郡之屬縣豐者,沛之聚邑耳此下言縣邑鄉里者所生故舉其本稱以繫於縣也○劉𥤙

師古曰紀理也統理衆事而繫之於年月者也

A page from a *Sung* edition of the *Han-shu* (p. 31)

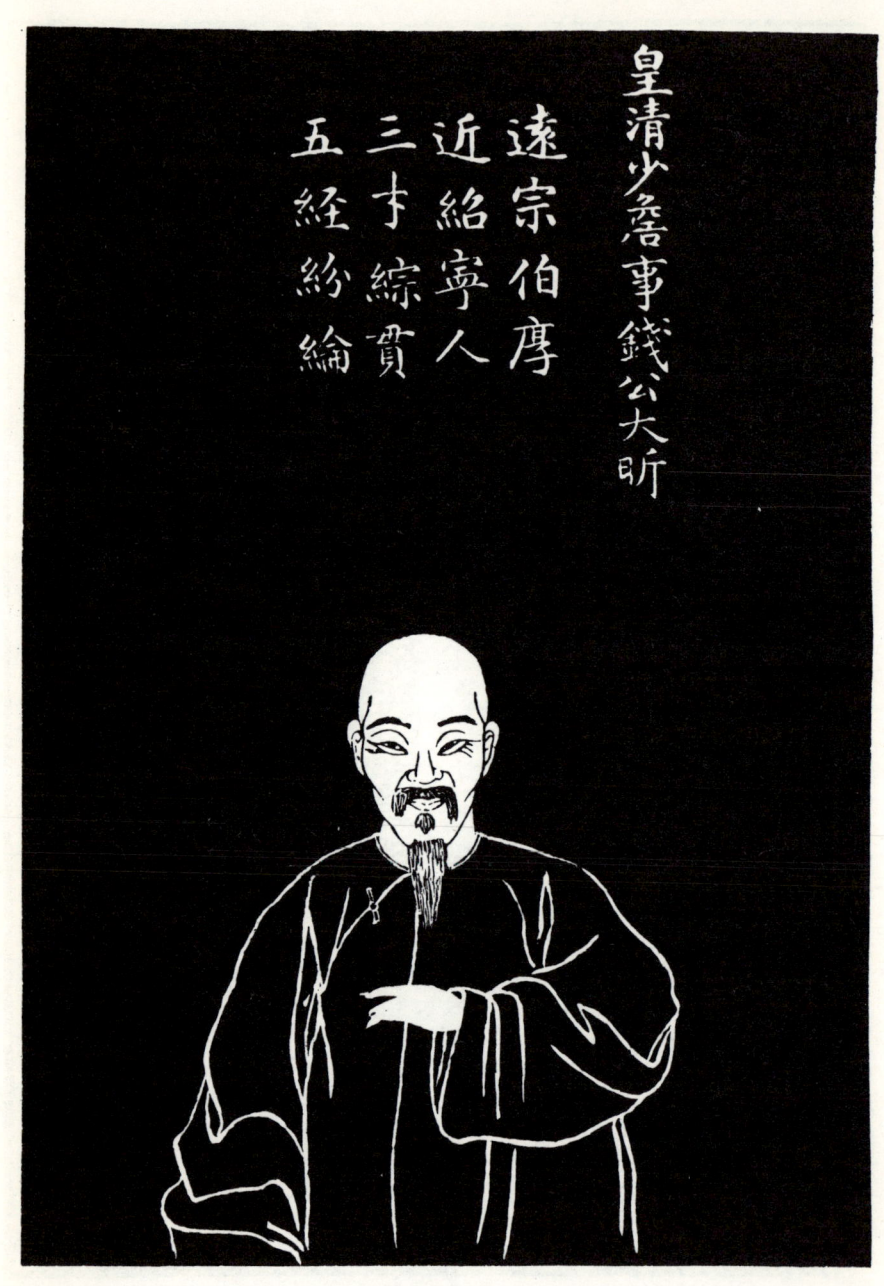

Portrait of *Ch'ien Ta-hsin* (p. 126)

Chapter II

PROBLEMS OF CHINESE HISTORIOGRAPHY AND HISTORICAL STUDIES

This chapter is intended to survey some of the basic problems in Chinese historiography. Many of the difficulties of the subject are common with those of Sinology. Problems which might seem to present obstacles for Western scholars only, do so for native students as well, except that their language problem is comparatively easier.

The basic problems of Chinese historiography have long been recognized by the Chinese. In former days some of them were even welcomed, since drudgery was approved and cherished as something of value, but in our own times the way of life has changed, our ideals are different, and few modern scholars can afford the loss of time which arises from these basic difficulties.

However, Chinese history is a legacy without which the Chinese people cannot properly be understood or evaluated. The road of Chinese historiography and of Chinese historical studies may be so rugged and the accumulated records so enormous that we can hardly see the forest for the trees, but it is a road that has both necessity and rewards.

CONFUSION OF NAMES

The mutilation of Chinese names (of both persons and places) by radio-broadcasters, and the errors in these names which constantly appear in magazines and books indicate a problem of nomenclature for the historian. An even more serious aspect—one which plagues Chinese as well as Western scholars—is the multiplicity of names by which a scholar or person of importance may be known. There are four or five names which he may acquire in his life-time, and two which may be added after his death.

The child is known first by a "milk" name, *ju-ming* 乳名 until he receives his "book" name *shu-ming* 書名, upon entering school. This latter is analogous to the Christian name of the West; it is his legal name. *Chiang Kai-shek* signs every document with the name, *Chiang Chung-cheng; Kai-shek* is his "courtesy" name *tzu* 字, one given at a capping ceremony *Kuan-li* 冠禮 when a man reaches the age of twenty. This name is often a literary, ethical, geographical, historical, or philosophical derivative of his book name. A second courtesy name, used as commonly as the first, is given by a friend or chosen by the person himself. Giles calls it a fancy name, *hao* 號. Further, if a man achieves any real scholarship he is given a name to convey the character of this work. For example, *Yüan Chen* 元眞 (779-831) is referred to as *Yüan Ts'ai-tzu* 袁才子, or *Yüan*, the Talented One, for his great achievement in music. Madam *Sung* 宋 (3rd century), mother of *Wei Ch'eng* 魏逞, received the name of *Hsüan Wen-chün* 宣文君, Princess of Cultural Dissemination, because of her success in phonetics and etymology. On the other hand, both the founder of a school of thought, and the school itself may be given a name indicating the region where the philosopher lived and the school originated. *K'ang Yu-wei* 康有爲 (1858-1927) is sometimes referred to as *K'ang Nan-hai, Nan-hai* 南海 being the name of his birth-place in *Kwang-tung* province. *Wang Yang-ming's* 王陽明 book name is *Wang Shou-jen* 王守仁 (1472-1528); *Shou-jen* 守仁, literally, "Abide by Benevolence." *Yang-ming* 陽明, meaning "Sun Brightness," is *Wang's* second courtesy name by which he is better known both in China and abroad. The *Yang-ming* school of thought is also known as *Yao-chiang* school, *Yao-chiang* 姚江 being the native place of *Wang Yang-ming*. *Sun Yat-sen* 孫逸仙 is known in the West by his courtesy name, but in China he is best known by two names: *Sun Wen* 孫文, book name, and *Chung-shan* 中山, second courtesy name. A posthumous title is often given to a great man and it is this name that is most frequently used in publications. Though the practice of conferring posthumous titles has been abolished since the founding of the Chinese Republic, the use of such titles in publications continues. Fortunately the fad of adding a foreign name has lost favor.

Inasmuch as dynastic histories constitute the main portion of Chinese traditional history, their system of chronological designation often causes confusion. For example, the founder of the *Ming* dynasty was *Chu Yüan-chang* 朱元璋; his courtesy name was *Kuo-jui* 國瑞, but he is often referred to by his *nien-hao* 年號 "year title," *Hung-wu* 洪武. In addition to the foregoing, an emperor received a canonized name after his death: that of *Chu Yüan-chang* was *Hsiao-k'ang* 孝康. Also, he received a temple name, *T'ai-tsu* 太祖, Great ancestor. This name usually designated his genealogical position.

The system of *nien-hao*, or year title, began with *Han Wu-ti* (140-87 B.C.) in 140 B.C.; as a rule, there are two characters in each *nien-hao* with four sources for their selection: (1) phrases which suggest good fortune, such as *Yung-p'ing* 永平 or Perpetual Peace; (2) unusual events, such as *Yüan-ting* 元鼎 or Commemorating a Tripod; (3) observance of the Five Elements of *Wu-hsing* 五行, such as *Huang-ch'u* 黃初 or Yellow (earth) Beginning; (4) ideals of the Imperial Court, such as *Ch'ung-ning* 崇寧 or Devotion to Peace. Prior to the *Ming* dynasty, each emperor might change his *nien-hao* several times; frequent references were made in publications to the *Miao-hao* or temple names to avoid confusion resulting from the use of too many *nien-hao* for one emperor.

American geographers now appreciate the importance and difficulty of Chinese geographical names. "The principal difficulties with Chinese names arise from transcription of different systems and from multiplicity of names for the same place."[1] The publication of the *Chung-kuo ti-ming ta-tz'u-tien* 中國地名大辭典 in 1930, and of the *Chung-kuo ku-chin ti-ming ta-tz'u-tien* 中國古今地名大辭典 in 1931 now furnishes scholars with a central reference. The numerous editions of the China Postal Atlas, *Chung-hua min-kuo yu-cheng yü-t'u* 中華民國郵政輿圖, and the Guide to Geographical Names in China by the Board on

Geographical Names of the U. S. Department of the Interior, have all been useful in bringing Chinese geographical names into unity of transcription. Several valuable Japanese works,[2] notably *Shina ritai chimei Yoran,* 支那歷代地名要覽 are available. Other aids are being produced.[3]

LACK OF TIME-SAVING DEVICES

To the classical scholar of China there was no such thing as a time-saving device. He simply did not care for it; even if he felt the need of it, he did not wish to use a short-cut as he firmly believed that his position as a scholar depended upon the tenacity he maintained over his difficulties. Very few of the old publications had simplified versions[4] or marked-off references; none of them had an index. As a rule there was no punctuation at all.

In his valuable little book, Chinese Traditional Historiography, Charles Gardner says, "Certain features of modern writing are conspicuously absent in the traditional product of Chinese historians. Perhaps none is more sadly lacking than bibliography and reference. Not only is no effort whatever made to indicate the sources open to the enquiring reader who would go further, or even, save in exceptional cases, to substantiate with a list of titles consulted, the conclusions of the author; but individual statements are ordinarily made ex cathedra without any reference documentation. Long and arduous systematic research sometimes fails to reveal the source for perfectly well-founded assertions."[5] However, we do often find aids for the discovery of sources in prefaces which usually give a history of various editions and sources for current publications. The practice of preserving prefaces by the author and his contemporary scholars has made up for certain lack of reference. Good tables of contents often served to a large extent the purpose of indices. Collected gems or *Ch'iung-lin* 瓊林 (Jade Forest) was first the name of a famous garden constructed in 963; later, the name of the Imperial Treasury; and then, the name of reference books on numerous practical subjects. *Chi-chü* 集句, collected quotations, *hui-hsüan* 彙選, classified selections, and *shih-i* 拾遺 supplements, are also time-saving tools. *Ching-chi chih* 經籍志, treatises on the classics, and *i-wen-chih* 藝文志, treatises on literature, both in the dynastic histories, and the various *ts'ung-shu* 叢書 collected works, have served as time savers.

"The unalphabetical nature of the language is responsible for much acknowledged clumsiness in Chinese works of reference, and for the lack of proper indices to names, places, events, and institutions recorded in literature."⁶ As the modern scholar has an imperative need of time-saving devices, their requirement is slowly being met. In China some publications of serious nature now furnish references, including those in foreign languages, and good bibliographies. Numerous ways have been employed to furnish indices: by topics, system of rhymes, radicals contained in the characters, number of strokes contained in each character. Knowledge of the system of rhymes was among the first requirements of a student prior to 1904; therefore classified index or reference by rhyme furnished a tool. The best example is found in *Shih-hsing yün-pien* 史姓韻編, surnames in the Twenty-four Histories by the syllabary rhymes of *Wang Hui-tsu* 汪輝祖 (1731-1807). The classical syllabary still has to be learned because most of the characters cannot be found by following the contemporary pronunciation. There are 214 radicals (roots) in the Chinese language, ranging from 1 to 17 strokes. Some characters have more than one radical in appearance, making it difficult to determine the real one. Chinese dictionaries and encyclopedic works usually use this method of arrangement, supplemented by the number of strokes added to the radical. Of these four methods, those of topics and number of strokes are most successful. The best example of the topical method is the excellent publication of the Legislative *Yüan* of the National Government of China, Constitutions of the World,⁷ in two volumes. The first contains 1085 pages of which 123 pages are an index by topics; the second has 1307 pages of which 301 pages make the index. Chinese telephone books are good examples of the index shown by the number of strokes in the characters. Hummel, of the Library of Congress, regards the "promising solution" to be found "in the direction of some numeral system, whereby ideographs can be assigned a number which, when filed in order, can be traced perhaps as easily as in an alphabetical language."[8] *Wang Yün-wu*, a contemporary lexicographer, initiated a numerical system more than twenty years ago, generally referred to as the "four-corner" system[9] Numerous publications, both in China and abroad, have given this system a trial; it is, perhaps, too early to say which system will win general acclaim. A system developed by W. M. Hawley through long experience arranges characters by radical, then by the number of additional strokes, then by the radical of this additional portion. This has the advantage of having the fewest number of characters in any one category, and permits of conversion to a numbering system for indexing which requires no code or other artificial aid beyond knowing the radicals by number which is almost indispensable in any use of Chinese dictionaries. The work of recent decades in making available indices of standard histories of China is a definite step forward in time-saving devices.

PROBLEM OF INACCURACIES

The most evident possibility of inaccuracy is found in the traditions which had to be observed. The scholar labored to pack each paragraph with historical and literary allusions as a mark of distinction. *Liu Chih-chi* 劉知幾 661-721, a prominent historical critic who completed his *Shih-t'ung* 史通 revolted against the evil of inaccurate references and obsolete expressions, yet he packed his own paragraphs with allusions which are not only difficult to understand but also contain inaccurate allusions in the nature of generalities. Recently, a scholar by the name of *Liu Hu-ju* 劉虎如, published an abridged edition of *Shih-t'ung* 史通 (selections and annotations). Each page of *Liu's* text requires an average of from twenty to twenty-five footnote explanations. The habit of beginning every problem of historical study with allusions from great antiquity such as the "Canons of *Yao* and *Shun*," and Spring-Autumn Annals of Confucius, and tracing historical examples down to the author's time often defeated his intended accuracy. Each reference had its particular import of time and place; therefore linking seemingly similar events, passages, and problems furthered the chance of inaccuracies.

Making separate occasions appear almost identical is another source of inaccuracy. Two frequently used allusions to injustice, "no rain for three years" and "heavy snow in the month of June," refer to these reported unjust acts and penalties. Madam *Tou* 竇, a filial widow of the first century B.C., was unjustly put to death by the magistrate, and within his district there was a drought for three years after the act. *Tsou Yen* 鄒衍, fourth century B.C., a native of *Ch'i*, unjustly imprisoned by Prince *Hui* 惠王 made supplications to heaven, and heavy snow fell in June. Though the Chinese have a deep-seated belief that human injustices always cause natural catastrophies, the allusions given above eliminate the types as well as the degrees of injustices done and make instances of injustice appear identical. Unless readers are extremely careful, and, are familiar with the entire historical episode, the concluding impression might be quite inaccurate.

A more serious source of inaccuracy was an arbitrary selection of documents, though documentary sources were highly respected by Chinese historians. When documents recorded the same event, arbitrary choice was usually made, and the selected one became the "authentic" record. The discarded documents not only sometimes supported but often articulated the causal relationship of the event and its antecedent. The rejected sources were at times taken up later by a new group or school having enough force to challenge the selection. In using Chinese sources, the historian must constantly keep this practice in mind and search for the "rival," "heretical" or "discarded" documents. Some material of this abandoned or suppressed nature appeared in private diaries in total or fragmentary form; also, each succeeding dynasty made it a practice to collect and restore taboo documents, since they no longer meant anything "dangerous" to the ruling Court.

Another source of inaccuracy is in the determination of dates. In the Chinese calendar, each year is identified by one of the twelve symbols of the zodiac: the rat, ox, tiger, rabbit, dragon, snake, horse, sheep, monkey, chicken, dog, pig, One year follows another in this order. Since 25 A.D. the years have been further identified by combining these twelve zodiac symbols with another set of ten symbols. The combination of the two sets of symbols gives a sixty-year cycle. In computing time in the sixty-year cycle the twelve zodiac symbols are represented by the numbers 1, 2, 3, 4, 5, 6, 7, 8, 9, 10, 11, and 12. These symbols are known as branches, signifying earth. The ten symbols, known as stems, signifying heaven, are represented by A, B, C, D, E, F, G, H, I, and J.

Combining the first stem and the first branch and each succeeding stem and branch in turn gives A 1, B 2 ... J 10, A 11, B 12, C 1 ... J 12. After sixty such combinations, the series repeats. A new cycle begins. Each combination thus recurs every sixty years.

Therefore no combination of symbols can identify a year unless the cycle also can be placed. For example, when we read the famous poetic essay of *Su-shih* 蘇軾, 1036-1101, "The Pleasure Trip to Red Cliff," the first phrase in the essay gives the time, "In the autumn of *Jen-hsü* ..." *Jen-hsü* is I 11, but since this combination appears twice in the lifetime of the author it is difficult to decide which *Jen-hsü* he means without his biographical record before us.

To take another example, it is not sufficient to know in what dynasty I 11, D 2, or any other year may fall, for in any dynasty of more than sixty years, each combination of symbols appears more than once. *Jen-hsü*, I 11, appears six times in the *Sung* period, first in 962, last in 1262.

The year any event occurs can be placed if the *nien-hao* of the ruling emperor is known in addition to the year identified by any of the sixty symbols A 1 to J 12.

The difficulty in determining dates correctly lies not in conversion to the Western calendar, for manuals of comparative chronology are available. It lies, rather, in the information available in Chinese literature. Chinese vital statistics are inadequate. Individual biographies give complete chronologies, but such books are not generally available. *Chung-kuo jen-ming ta-tz'u-tien* 中國人名大辭典 falls short of giving complete information. The *Li-tai ming-jen nien-p'u* 歷代名人年譜 of *Wu Jung-kuang* gives vital statistics of famous men, but to transcribe them accurately according to the Western calendar requires more information than *Wu* gives. The dates on which scholars took their hightest civil service examinations are ordinarily given, but these allow only a rough estimate of the dates of birth for some took the examination by the time they were twenty, others not until they were thirty or more. Fortunately, centers of Sinological studies both in Europe and in America have begun to publish much better biographies of noted Chinese.

Care must be taken in calculating dates of birth. Many errors that have been made have arisen from the Chinese custom of counting a child as a year old on the date of his birth and distinguishing between the number of birthdays and the number of years of his life. A child is said to be a year old at birth and two years old on the first New Year in his life, New Year being a kind of universal birthday.

PROBLEMS OF THE SIZE OF SOURCES

The humanistic approach of China to the whole of life has made her an extremely history-conscious people; thus, she has enormous literary deposit in general, and historical deposit in particular. *Wei Chü-hsien* 衛聚賢 in his *Chung-kuo shih-hsüeh-shih* 中國史學史, Survey of the historical works of the last six dynasties, from 589 to 1911, shows the imposing number of 137,162 *chüan*.

It is impossible for any one historian to master all the material, but if one wishes to accept the life-long work of research into even one particular time or period, or into one special aspect of the historical process, he must still have command of the materials concerned. The tremendous size of source materials and the limitations of libraries, public and private, have added much to the hardships of research work in modern times. With the new interest of the Western world in Sinology, bringing an ever-increasing number of specialists into the field plus the facility of microfilming, the problems of size do not now appear quite so vast. Sometimes a scholar must wait to publish until he finds more reference works if he demands perfection or full completion.

PROBLEM OF OVER-SIMPLIFICATION

In the writing of Chinese histories we find many illustrations of over-simplification. An important event can be dismissed with as few as eleven words, as happened in an account made by *Ssu-ma Ch'ien*, on the pacification of *Shu* 蜀 in the period of the Warring States (403-221 B.C.): "6th year, (of) Duke *Hui, Shu* rebelled; *Ssu-ma Ts'uo* pacified *Shu*." Another example shows how *Chu-ko Liang* (181-234) made his conquest of the *Man* 蠻 tribes: *Ch'en Shou* 陳壽, historian of the 3rd Century, expended forty-four words on this event in one passage and twenty in another. The former tells of the annexation of *Szechuan* province; the latter of the conquest of the aborigines in the southwestern provinces. The entire history of the relationship of China to the great area of southwest China is covered in some sixty-four words in the *San-kuo-chih* 三國志. The over-simplification may be due to the attitude of political and cultural superiority which the Chinese, in general, held for these areas. However, when we consider the space allotted to **Asiatic** history in Western world histories, or even that given to the histories of American Indians and western states in American histories, we can understand that Chinese historians shared in a common failing.

Liang Ch'i-ch'ao points out that records of the influence of Buddhism on Chinese ideas and institutions show over-simplification.[10] Buddhistic influence in China can hardly be over-estimated, yet the histories of *Sui* and *T'ang,* written when Buddhism was at its highest peak in China give no clear impression at all of this fact. Though several Buddhist monks of the *Sui-T'ang* period occupied leading places in scholarship, it was the Confucianists who manned the government and compiled the histories. Furthermore, socially the monks were restricted. A majority were monks only because of poverty or illness, and they were disciplined in but a few liturgies. Moreover, Buddhism, in the eyes of Chinese scholars, was an imported idea or institution and their own Chinese humanism in its highest form seemed to them to create the greatest values. Similarly, historians of the *Mongol* and *Ming* periods omitted almost altogether the epoch-making creative works in drama[11] and fiction[12] at the time. Supremacy of classical literature over folk literature was, in a way, the result of deep admiration for the disciplined and controlled way of life. The low status of actors, playwrights, fiction writers, and of fiction itself was due to Chinese fear of the free flow of human emotions and flattering of the senses. It was the custom, therefore, for unusual genius to hide "creative" expressions behind an assumed name or anonymity.

PROBLEM OF OVER-OBJECTIVITY

Originally, historians were merely scribes transmitting imperial commands and recording state affairs; gradually, they became keepers of national records. When state affairs grew more complex, a division of labor was made: the historian 'at the left' recorded the utterances of the ruler and the 'one at the right' the deeds of the ruler. Uranography and astronomy were mixed with astrology; prayers and divination, and especially, the recording of occurrences of natural phenomena which were deemed to be closely related to human fortunes and misfortunes were functions of the historian. Gradually the dignity of the historian was enhanced when he developed and controlled state records and often state destinies. As time went on bureaus of astrology, historiography, and a court of censors were created, but the name *T'ai-shih* or Grand Historian was used for all functionaries.

The ideal of the classical historian was "impartial narration of events." A reader of history was to draw his own conclusions and let the moral speak for itself. Interpretation of history was regarded as too subjective; it must be as little in evidence as possible. Professor Homer H. Dubs says that "the practice of separating interpretations from actual accounts has been a constant feature of Chinese histories."[13] The Chinese historian stands with Leibniz in agreeing that documents should be collected and preserved as they are instead of being mutilated by scholars. Necessarily this practice cannot be taken too literally, since selection of documents and arrangement of them imply judgment and interpretation. The failure of the attempt to be objective lay in eliminating all but a minimum of the original documents without giving correlation and interpretation. Objectivity thus obtained fails to meet the function of both historian and archivist.

Furthermore, the objectivity of Chinese historians has been limited by traditional philosophical currents and by the Chinese moral concept of history. The rivalry between the utilitarian legalist 法家 and the Confucian moralist 儒道 in the early period of Chinese history, and between the *Ch'eng Chu* 程朱[14] or *Ko-wu* 格物 "investigation-of-things" school and the *Lu Wang* 陸王[15] or creative intuition-of-"innate ideas" 致良知 school in the later period inevitably affected objectivity in the selection of documents and interpretation of historical continuity. While the slogan of the legalists was *fu-kuo-ch'iang-ping* 富國強兵, or "prosperity of the nation and strength in military defense," the Confucianists insisted upon *wei-cheng-i-te* 爲政以德, or "moral example, the core of good government." The former stressed government by law and prosperity by state control; the latter, the goodness of man 性善, who was to find discipline by making the most of the least. The Chinese people had learned to distrust "unusual men," or men who offered glowing promises; legalists were regarded as being in this category. The Confucianists in the main controlled national policy and wrote the histories and because of this, as we have seen, objectivity was vindicated in a peculiar way.

Among Confucian scholars as a whole the difference in methodology tended to obscure objectivity. The *Ch'eng-chu* school proceeded from the particular to the universal in a scientific approach, while the *Lu-Wang* or the intuitive school began with definite assumptions of "innate ideas." In historiography both schools stressed objectivity but in the last analysis they reached the same over-objectivity in making history a documentary compilation.

As a rule, objective detachment has been more pronounced among Chinese historians than it has elsewhere in the world. One reason for this characteristic is that the Chinese historian had a deep-seated belief in a humanistic "immortality." The *San-pu-hsiu* 三不朽 or Three Avenues to Immortality (first found in the *Tso-chuan* 左傳), taught that moral character, service to the community or state, and publications were the three roads by which a man could climb to a place of lasting worth. The historian was expected to be both judicious and objective. He believed that he must keep his mind constantly on the causes of individual, social and national failures and successes, but he was not to make a digest of official records nor to gear his knowledge for a history of his own creation, though it might be supported by scrutinized sources. Objectivity was regarded as equivalent to impartiality, and the Chinese historian labored to keep pure records of events as primary-source materials and these materials to be so selected that they lent criteria for human conduct. To render service to the community, local or national, was to keep the "mirror of human events" polished and objective by keeping impartial personal records of great events and by careful compilation of local and national histories.

PROBLEM OF INTERPOLATION AND DELETION

Textual criticism has long been a favorite study, even a recreation, of Chinese scholars in general, and of Chinese historians in particular. The destruction of the Classics during the *Ch'in* period, and subsequent destruction and mutilation of books for various reasons, made it necessary to establish the authenticity of documents and to seek to verify the meanings of words and phrases. Wieger, in the "Vicissitudes of Books," gives a very useful account of the fate of books in the long history of China, listing numerous tragic occurrences in which whole libraries were lost and repeated efforts were made to restore them.

Scholars of the *Han* period made such great advance in their methods of textual criticism, that when the late *Ming* and early *Ch'ing* scholars reacted against the *Sung* school for its rationalism and against the *Ming* school for its intuitionism, they established a school of textual criticism and called it *Han Hsüeh* 漢學, the *Han* school.

Textual problems found in Chinese historical works arise from mistakes made when copying documents or books or when repairing a text partially destroyed by fire, by insects, or by weather. Further, through change in the meaning of characters or through ignorance of the meaning of characters no longer in current use the original meaning could be lost. Studies in philology, phonetics, and grammar corrected wrong transcriptions, alterations, mistaken meanings, and eliminated extraneous characters, phrases, and sentences.

The *K'ao-chü* 考據, search-for-evidence school, reached its fruitful period in the "new" historical scholarship by the end of the eighteenth century with leaders such as *Wang Nien-sun* 王念孫, 1744-1832; his son, *Wang Yin-chih* 王引之, 1766-1834; and *Sun Hsing-yen* 孫星衍, 1753-1818. By this scientific method of textual criticism, annotations and emendations of ancient dictionaries and difficult passages of ancient texts have been made. Numerous classics and ancient texts have also been re-examined and analyzed; forgeries, interpolations and plagiarisms have been corrected. From the middle of the 19th century to the present time, Chinese scholars have deepened their spirit of historical criticism. Analyses of spurious historical writings from the standpoint of their genesis 偽史源, their comparative study 偽史例, and the principles that underlie them 偽史封鞠, have been made by men such as *Liang Ch'i-ch'ao, Ch'en Yüan,*[16] *Hu Shih, Ch'ien Hsuan-t'ung,*[17] *Wang Kuo-wei,*[18] and *Ku Chieh-kang.*[19] Meanwhile, Western sinologists have played an important role in their tireless efforts, through scholarship in etymology and phonetics[20] as well as in archaeology;[21] these men include Karlgren, Chavannes, Pelliot, and Duyvendak.

The problem of interpolation and omission originated from many sources, both intentional and unintentional. Prior to the second century of the Christian era there had been no method of differentiating the text from the comments. To mark off the parent from the child has long been a problem for Chinese scholars. *Ma Jung*[22] first used the method of smaller characters for comments arranged in a double column within the space normally occupied by a single column of text (See illustration on page 11).

No system of quotation marks was used, so direct references were often indiscernible unless the author was cited by name. Often an idea was well known while the originator of it was not, and this because of the practice of using phrases such as "The Ancient said," "As the Proverb says," or "So recorded the Classics," etc.

Though Chinese scholarship has been highly regarded by Western sinologists for its respect for established texts and for scrupulous fidelity in reproduction, the process of copying done by professional copyists, and the process of printing by means of wood blocks inevitably caused omissions, alterations, substitutions, and additions. Also, Chinese scholars often relied upon their discipline of memory as one of the main sources for quotations; they often combined similar ideas and statements of different sources into one. For example, the Chinese National Anthem, *San Min Chu I* 三民主義, contains only forty-eight characters but with two references from the Book of History,[23] one from the Book of Rites,[24] and one from the Book of Poetry.[25] The ability to combine extensive sources to evidence similar ideas constituted one of the requirements of civil service examinations. As a result of these possibilities of textual problems, rigid discipline of collation and emendation led to the development of lexicography, etymology, textual and historical criticism.

Interpolation or deletion has been a serious problem for historical criticism. There was the insertion of extraneous matter into a genuine document on account of ignorance or carelessness of the copyist, the scholar's vanity, jealousy, party interest, or imperial interference. For example, even the reasonably authentic twenty-four *pien* 篇 of the fifty-three *p'ien* of *Motzu* still contain many later insertions.[26] More than thirty per cent of the original confessions of *Li Hsiu-ch'eng*,[27] one of the *T'ai P'ing* leaders, was "trimmed away"[28] for reasons of party interests, scholar's vanity, and fear of imperial disapproval.

Toward the middle of the sixteenth century *Mei Tsu*[29] initiated a courageous step in historical criticism by his work, *Shang-shu k'ao-i* 尚書考異 or Discrepancies in the Classic of History. He was succeeded by a whole train of critics[30] down to our own times. The French scholar, Chavannes, following the work[31] of *Wang Ming-sheng* 汪鳴盛, 1722-1798, pointed out the interpolations made by *Chu Shao-sun* 朱紹蓀 in the Historical Memoirs of *Ssu-ma Ch'ien*. Without modern means of exchange of information, historians often were not benefited by the results of research done by specialists.

PROBLEMS OF RELATED FIELDS

Epigraphy has long been a field of historical studies in China. This field is known as *Chin-shih-hsüeh* 金石學 or "Metal and Stone Learning"; that is, studies of inscriptions on bronzes and on stone monuments.

Since the discovery of the Oracle Bones, there has been a new field of research, *Chia-ku-wen* 甲骨文, "Shell, Bone Inscriptions."

Metal was used in the form of bronze: bronzes for sacrifices, weapons, exchange, personal signatures, bells and utensils. Inscriptions on these bronzes and the artistry and symbolism employed gave records of the past. In connection with the study of inscriptions on bronzes, there have been numerous problems. First, archeology was in the past a more accidental than a regular channel for the extension of historical records. The work of excavation for such objects was for a long time limited because of the custom of holding tombs as sacred. There were discoveries through excavations of an accidental nature: digging of wells, making foundations for buildings, canals, etc. Often when floods came they revealed treasures of this type of the long-buried past. In recent times the digging into the ground necessitated by war has brought things to light; also cooperation on the part of the government for archeological expeditions has encouraged greater activity. For a long time when findings were uncovered accidentally by farmers the fact did not reach the knowledge of scholars before a great deal of harm had been done through injury to the articles and through scattering. Even precious patina was often scoured away including inscriptions in order that the finder laborer might see what his treasure was. Thus, not only was the progress for archeology delayed, but the material for correlated study of historical evidences was also limited. Further, there was the problem of assembly of the findings for study. After this difficulty was overcome, the historian met numerous obstacles in dealing with changes in types of Chinese characters in the inscriptions.

Regarding inscriptions on stone the history is much shorter than that of bronzes, though the number of stone inscriptions is far greater than that on bronzes. Stone monuments take the form of histories in themselves for the Chinese loved to build beautiful places and commemorate the building by inscribing upon marble gateways, bridges, and especially upon monuments; there were whole recordings concerning Buddhist and Taoist temples and the entire Confucian classics were written in stone. In Soochow we have today five hundred marble slabs on which are carved the pictures and biographies of five hundred scholars.[32] Rubbings are still made of these records. The ancient Stone Drums in the Peiping palace carry some of the oldest records of China. They relate the story of King *Hsüan's* hunting expedition. He lived between 827-782 B.C.; today scholars tend to date the drums in the third century B.C. Recently scholars have begun to publish inscriptions from rubbings in collected form, but without the original rubbing we miss the internal evidence of anthenticity of time and authorship, as there is no calligraphy or the condition of the monument to judge by. There are a number of schools of calligraphy by which the authenticity of a document can be established. Furthermore, the styles of writing of various periods of history are different; therefore they also serve as evidences for verification. Also, since much of the content is related to the history of temples, institutions, localities, and individuals, specialization and correlation of this content is necessary in order to enrich related historical studies.

Inscriptions on Oracle Bones have become a specialized research study and both Chinese and foreign scholars have made valuable published results. *Sun I-jang* 孫詒讓,[33] *Lo Chen Yü* 羅振玉,[34] *Wang Kuo-wei* 王國維, *Sun Hai-p'o* 孫海波,[35] *Tung Tso-pin* 董作賓,[36] *Jung Keng* 容庚, and James M. Menzies[35] are the main leaders in this field of research. They have done much to anthenticate ancient history and institutions of China.

PROBLEMS OF ESTABLISHED PATTERNS

Chinese philosophy of education held that wide learning was the foundation of any creative work. One must study masterpieces of literature, art, calligraphy, and music until they were familiar, understood, and digested before any creative work could be done in these fields. This was good, but there was the inherent danger of deadening patterns.

PROBLEMS OF CHINESE HISTORIOGRAPHY 31

Rigid forms and adherence to patronized schools of thought in the interpretation of the Classics were required of the candidates for civil service. They also must remember all the literary taboos (Published in two volumes by *Lung Kuang-tien* 龍光甸 about 1838, known as *Lin-wen pien-lan* 臨文便覽 (Convenient Guide for Literary Correctness). Examination of any branch of Chinese learning, whether it is in the humanities in general, or in history in particular, must lead any fair-minded person to a mixed appraisal: admiration and appreciation for the zeal, insight, pioneering and creative work, but regret and criticism for stilted forms and styles.

Ssu-ma Ch'ien made the first pattern of Chinese history in his *Shih Chi* or Historical Memoirs. This work came after a long period of evolution of the content of history and its divisions. He divided his Memoirs into five sections: (1) Imperial Annals; (2) Genealogy of Feudal Rulers; (3) Chronological Tables; (4) Treatises on Special Subjects (Rites, Music, Astronomy, Astrology, Rivers, Canals, Equalization, Standards); (5) Biographies of Great Persons.

The second dynastic history is *Han-shu,* the History of the Former Han Dynasty. *Pan Ku,* the author, wrote his history in four divisions, omitting the "genealogy of feudal rulers" found in the Historical Memoirs of *Ssu-ma Ch'ien.* Of the twenty-six dynastic histories, ten contain four divisions; seven, two divisions; seven, three divisions; and two, five divisions.

The divisions of treatises always has provided opportunity for an author to add new subjects. In the *Han-shu, Pan Ku* added four new subjects: laws and punishments, five elements, geography, and literature. In the twenty-four later histories, ten more subjects were added. Two of these are found only in the last of the dynastic histories, the Draft History of the *Ch'ing* Dynasty. One is "foreign relations," the other "legislation." (See pp. 199-201.)

Another large division of the dynastic histories is the biographies, as might be expected, since the Chinese favor "rule by men" rather than "rule by law." The *Ch'ing-shih kao* devotes 316 of its 536 *chüan* to biographies.[38] This division also gives opportunity for the presentation of diverse materials.

Limitations, however, provided serious shortcomings for true histories. Revolt against the limitations and suggested corrections began with *Liu Chih-chi* 劉知幾 (661-721) and has been continued to the present time. Established patterns tended toward the use of cryptic statements and descriptions which were difficult for later generations to understand in full. Classical expressions were employed at the expense of current language; consequently, contemporary thought, feelings, and pulse of the time were colored or blurred. Further, established patterns neglected folk songs, folk ways and festivals; hence the life of any generation was only partially recorded in "official" histories. Finally, historians needed new classifications for newly developed human activities and achievements on the one hand, and a clear perspective on the other.

Whatever applied to the standard national histories applied also to the writing of local histories. In 1933 the National Library of Peiping published a "Catalogue of Local Records" listing 3,800 titles. Two years later the Library of Congress in the U.S.A. published the "Union List of Chinese Local Records" enumerating 5,832 editions.[39]

The large majority of prefects or magistrates were scholars who had a great interest in bringing local history up to date, as well as in doing the writing. Recognition of the importance of local gazetteers was first given in the Book of *Chou* Rites when the "External Historian" 外史 under the Ministry of Spring 春官 had charge of local records. The earliest local gazetteer was done by *Chao Ch'i* 趙岐 (d.201), magistrate of *P'i Shih* 皮氏, (near *Ho Chin, Shansi*) in the year 153 A.D. His work is known as *San-fu chüeh-lu* 三輔決錄, meaning Verified Record of Three Cities.[40] This work was annotated by *Chih Yu* 贄尤 (died in 311). The original work was lost but a restored edition was made.[41]

More freedom obtained in the writing of local histories in that the number of divisions of materials was never rigidly set. Divisions usually contained the following: 1—History of the founding of the district; 2—Mountains and streams; 3—City walls; 4—Bridges; 5—Public offices; 6—Schools of all types; 7—Census and revenue; 8—Temples and shrines; 9—Monuments and tombs; 10—Successful candidates in civil service; 11—Scholars; 12—Outstanding loyal and faithful men and women; 13—Publications; 14—Local products.

Changes were recorded only within the scope of any of the divisions; the growth of the district as a whole, economically, socially, intellectually was sadly neglected. Interpretation of development was entirely lacking.

Other types of history written about economics, the law, philosophies, literature, and art exhibited the same defects as dynastic histories with regard to established patterns. China has a rich deposit of histories of special subjects, but still lacks general histories of these subjects. For example, histories of education, medicine, transportation, music, architecture, printing, irrigation, religion, and industries, are more in the nature of individual records of certain periods rather than of connected histories in the true sense of the word. In other words, here again patterns have destroyed free and faithful genetic presentation of changing ideas and institutions. During the last fifty years[42] there has been conscious effort on the part of Chinese historians to reconstruct and to develop general histories of these individual histories and to keep free of the old patterns.

CONCLUDING REMARKS

Chinese historical science received the Western impact at first in a spirit of pride and an attempt at isolation, but it was not long before apology and capitulation followed. Now new understanding and appreciation for Chinese historiography from both Chinese and Westerners is beginning to accord it its proper value. Western Sinologists

34   ELEMENTS OF CHINESE HISTORIOGRAPHY

used to depend upon long years of study of the language or upon interpreters or both. Today modern methods of language study, library facilities and aids to research make the task less gruelling. The amount of Chinese historical material in translated form has been estimated to be less than one per cent.

On the other hand, the Chinese historian of today feels a much greater freedom, because the old patterns no longer hold; he has greater aids in archeology, anthropology, and geography, and he has a combined discipline of native tradition and of the West. With all this he believes he is creating a new methodology of historical research. An examination of Chinese publications on this subject during the last thirty years shows good promise of the continuance of what has been called the rugged strength of Chinese historical scholarship, and of China's age-long insistence on intellectual integrity.

NOTES FOR CHAPTER II.

1. Meredith F. Burrill, "Reorganization of the United States Board on Geographical Names", Geographical Review, 35 (Oct. 1935), 652.
2. *Shina chimei shusei* 支那地名集成 Collection of Chinese Place Names, compiled by the intelligence office of the Japanese Foreign Mimistry, (Tokyo, 1937).
3. Han Yü-shan, 韓玉珊 "A historical survey of some geographical names of China" Sinologica, 1 (November 1947), 152-170.
4. In 1711, *Wu Ch'eng-ch'üan* 吳乘權 published the *Kang-chien-i-chih-lu* 綱鑑易知錄 or History-made-easy, a summary of the following works: *Tzu-chih-t'ung-chien* 資治通鑑, a comprehensive history by *Ssu-ma Kuang* (1019-1086), and *T'ung-chien-kang-mu* 通鑑綱目 by *Chu Hsi* (1130-1200). See section on general histories.
5. Charles S. Gardner, op. cit., p. 75.
6. Arthur W. Hummel, The Autobiography of a Chinese Historian (Leyden, 1931), xxxiii.
7. *Hsien-fa hui-pien* 憲法彙編, Constitutions of the World, (Shanghai, 1933-34).
8. Hummel, ibid. xxxiv.
9. *Wang Yün-wu* 王雲五 (1889-   ).
10. Liang Ch'i-ch'ao, 梁啓超 *Chung-kuo li-shih yen-chiu-fa* 中國歷史研究法 Methods of research in Chinese history, *pu-pien* 補編, 6.

11. *Wang Che-fu* 王哲甫, *Chung-kuo hsin-wen-hsüeh yün-tung shih* 中國新文學運動史 History of modern Chinese literature, (Peiping, 1933).
    Chang Jo-ying 張若英, *Chung-kuo hsin-wen-hsüeh yün-tung shu-p'ing* 中國新文學運動述評, A critical account of the "new literature" movement in China, (Peiping 1935). See the section on Drama in the *Wen-hsüeh lun-wen so-yin* 文學論文索引, Index of articles on literature, published by the Library Association of China, 3 vols., (Peiping, 1932, 1933, 1936).

12. *Hu Shih* 胡適, *Pai-hua wen-hsüeh shih* 白話文學史, A history of the vernacular literature, (Shanghai, 1928).
    Lu Hsin 魯迅, *Lu Hsin san-shih-nien chi* 魯迅三十年集, Collected works of *Lu Hsin*, 1906-1936, (Shanghai, 1947).

13. Homer H. Dubs, "The reliability of Chinese histories", Far Eastern Quarterly, vi (November, 1946), 30.

14. *Ch'eng Chu hsüeh-p'ai* 程朱學派, the school of thought of the *Ch'eng* brothers, *Ch'eng Hao* 程顥 (1032-1083) and *Ch'eng I* 程頤 (1033-1083) and of *Chu Hsi* 朱熹 (1130-1200).

15. *Lu Wang hsüeh-p'ai* 陸王學派, school of thought of *Lu Hsiang-shan* 陸象山 (1139-1191) and *Wang Shou-jen* 王守仁 (1472-1528).

16. *Chen Yüan* 陳垣 (1880-), one time director of the Sinological Institute, Peking National University, chancellor *Fu Jen* University 輔仁大學, well known historian, has published numerous monographs of historical studies in addition to his *Yüan-lü tseng-hsiu* 元律增修 Corrected and supplemented texts of the code of the *Yüan* Dynasty, and *Chung-hsi-hui nien-li pi-chiao-piao* 中西回年歷比較表.

17. *Ch'ien Hsüan-t'ung* 錢玄同, an ardent proponent of the "literary revolution" of 1917, specialist in etymology, exerted great influence on historical research.

18. *Wang Kuo-wei* 王國維 (1877-1927) made a contribution in the source of materials in his publications: (1) *Sung Yüan hsi-ch'ü shih* 宋元戲曲史, A History of *Sung* and *Yüan* Drama, (2) *Yüan mi-shih shan ch'uan ti-ming so-yin* 元秘史山川地名索引, Index of geographical names in the *Yüan* secret history, (3) *Ch'ien-lung Chekiang t'ung-chih k'ao-i* 乾隆浙江通志考異, Discrepancies in the general gazetteer of *Chekiang, Ch'ien-lung* edition, (4) *Ku-shih hsin-cheng* 古史新證, New evidence for old history.

19. *Ku Chieh-kang* 顧頡剛 (1893-), gained a reputation as a scientific historian by his *Ku-shih pien* 古史辨, Symposium on ancient Chinese history, 4 vols., 1926-33. *Ku* also did an outstanding piece of work in editing and repunctuating the definitive edition of the *Ts'ui Tung-pi i-shu* 崔東壁遺書 in 1936. The *Shih-chi* 記 was also edited and punctuated by *Ku*, Peiping, 1936.

20. B. Karlgren, "The Authenticity of Ancient Chinese Texts", Bulletin Museum of Far Eastern Antiquities No. 1, (Stockholm, 1929).

21. Sir Aurel Stein, Sand-buried Ruins of Khotan: Personal Narrative of a Journey of Archeological and Geographical Exploration in Chinese Turkestan, (London, 1903); On Ancient Central-Asian Tracks: A Brief Narrative of Three Expeditions in Inner-Most Asia and Northwestern China, (New York, 1933).

22. *Ma Jung* 馬融 (79-166 A.D.), a man of profound learning popularly known as "the universal scholar".

23. *I-hsin* 一心 or "one mind" and *I-te* 一德, "one truth" (in conduct) are both from the *Shu-ching* 書經 or Book of History.

24. *I-chin ta-t'ung* 以進大同 or "To advance world brotherhood", from the *Li-chi* 禮記 or Book of Rites.

25. *Su-yeh fei-hsieh* 夙夜匪懈, "vigilance day and night", from the *Shih-ching* 詩經 or Book of Poetry.

26. *Hu Shih* 胡適, *Chung-kuo che-hsüeh-shih ta-kang* 中國哲學史大綱 (Shanghai, 1919), 151; *Liang Ch'i-ch'ao* 梁啓超, *Mo-tzu hsüeh-an* 墨子學案 (Shanghai, 1921), 11-14.

27. *Li Hsiu-ch'eng* 李秀成 (1824-1864), comander-in-chief in the *T'ai-p'ing* revolution wrote the story of this revolution in the form of his confessions.

28. According to *Tseng Kuo-fan's* dairy, *Li Hsiu-ch'eng's* account was abridged by *Tseng* from more than 40,000 words to about 28,000. See *Lo Yung* 羅邕 in his *T'ai-p'ing t'ien-kuo shih-wen ch'ao* 太平天國詩文鈔 (Shanghai, 1931) *shang-tsè*, 60.

29. *Mei Tsu* 梅鷟 (*chü-jen* 舉人 of 1513) led a strenuous attack upon the spuriousness of the *ku-wen* 古文 or ancient script of this work.

30. Those that continued the work of *Mei Tsu* during the *Ch'ing* period: *Yen Jo-chü* 閻若璩 (1636-1704) wrote *Ku-wen shang-shu shu-cheng* 古文尚書疏證, Inquiry into the authenticity of the *Shang-shu* or Classic of history; *Hui Tung* 惠棟 (1697-1758) published *Ku-wen shang-shu k'ao* 古文尚書考, A critique of the ancient script edition of the Classic of history, *Chiu-ching ku-i* 九經古義, An exegesis of the difficult passages of the Nine Classics; *Ts'ui Shu* 崔述; see 26, 27.

31. *Wang Ming-sheng* 汪鳴盛 (1722-1798) made his major contribution to scholarship by his *Shih-ch'i shih shang-ch'üeh* 十七史商榷, published in 1787.

32. *Ku Yüan* 顧沅 collected portraits of old scholars and made sketches of them. The introduction written by *Liang Chang-chü* 梁章鉅 (1775-1849) contains an historical sketch of the attempt to collect and preserve portraits of great scholars. The first record appears in the *Sui-shu ching-chi-chih* 隋書經籍志. Another was written by *T'ang Chin-chao* 湯金釗 (1772-1856). (See illustrations.)

33. *Sun I-jang* 孫詒讓 (1848-1908) first made himself known for critical studies of the *Mo-tzu*, 墨子訓詁. His early training in epigraphy brought him unusual joy when he saw the facsimile of the Oracle Bone inscriptions made by *Liu E* 劉鶚 (1857-1909). *Liu* was first to identify the inscriptions and *Sun*, first to make good use of them for historical treatise.

34. *Lo Chen-yü* 羅振玉 (1866-1940) continued and excelled the work of *Liu E* and *Sun I-jang*. *Lo's* best publications are (1) *Yin-hsü shu-ch'i ch'ien-pien* 殷虛書契前編 (2) *Yin-hsü shu-ch'i hou-pien* 殷虛書契後編 Inscriptions from the ruins of *Yin* in two volumes, (3) *Yin-hsü ch'i-wen k'ao-shih* 殷虛契文考釋, divided into 8 *pien* as follows: capitals, rulers, individual names, geographical names, language, divination, rites, and method of divination.

35. *Sun Hai-p'o* 孫海波 published the *Chia-ku-wen pien* 甲骨文編 in 1934.

36. *Tung Tso-pin* 董作賓 (1895-   ), archaeologist. *Chia-ku-wen tuan-tai yen-chiu-li* 甲骨文斷代研究例, Essay in the Collected Essays in Celebrating the 65th Birthday of *Ts'ai Yuan-pei*, 1933; "Ten Examples of Early Tortoise-shell Inscriptions", Harvard Journal of Asiatic Studies, 11 (1948), 119-129.

37. James M. Menzies 明義士, Canadian scholarly missionary to China stationed in *An-yang, Honan* province, wrote Oracle Records from the Wastes of *Yin* 殷虛卜辭 (Shanghai, 1917). Menzies is regarded as one of the very few foreigners who have made real contributions to the study of the oracle bones.

38. *Ch'ing-shih-kao* 清史稿 *Ch'ing* dynasty history draft, under the editorship of *Chao Erh-hsun* 趙爾巽 and *K'o Shao-min* 柯劭忞 1927, (1942 edn. *Lien-ho* Book Co.).

39. *Fang-chih shu-mu* 方志書目 Catalog of local histories, National Library of Peiping 1933; *Chung-kuo ti-fang-chih tsung-lu* 中國地方志綜錄 Union list of Chinese local records, (Washington, 1935).

40. The three cities were *Ch'ang-an* 長安 the capital, *Feng-i* 馮翊 (*Ta-li, Shensi*), and *Fu-feng* 扶風 (*Hsien-yang, Shensi*).

41. The restored edition is by *Mao P'an-lin* 毛泮林 and *Chang Shu* 張澍 (*chin-shih*, 1799). See *Ch'ing-shih kao* 清史稿, *leih-chuan* 列傳, #272.

42. S. Y. Teng, "Chinese historiography in the last fifty years", Far Eastern Quarterly, 8 (February, 1949), 131-156.
    Chu Shih-chia, Chang Hsüeh-ch'eng, His Contributions to Chinese Local Historiography, (Doctoral Dissertation, Columbia University, 1950).

Portrait of *Hui Tung* (p. 126)

Chapter III

TRADITIONAL CLASSIFICATION OF CHINESE HISTORY

From the beginning of Chinese political history, *T'u-chi* 圖籍, maps and records, were held to be highly important (p. 175), almost as much so as sovereignty. The reason for this importance was both practical and ideal, as the *T'u-chi* recorded population and taxation, basic physical and economic geography, and human and heavenly conduct. They were kept in the imperial palace and guarded by imperial historians. An early intellectual achievement was the attempt to classify information as well as to classify records of events. This early classification was by subjects, by forms or styles, and by importance. Confucious edited the ancient records into six classics: Poetry, History, Philosophy, Rites, Music, and the Spring-Autumn Annals, a "local history." He also classified his disciples according to their aptitudes and fields of concentration in ethics, languages, politics, and literature.

The proto-type of historical classification is generally said to be the six classifications in the *Shih-pen,* Book of Generations,[1] of unknown authorship:
Annals of emperors, feudal families, biographies, chronological tables, political geography, and treatises of institutions. *Ssu-ma Ch'ien,* inspired by these patterns or divisions, constructed his own divisions in his *Shih-chi,* or Historical Memoirs. This internal division of a historical work marked the beginning of classification of historical writings.

Later, all written works of the empire were classified. Emperor *Ch'eng,* 32-7 B.C., ordered that all existing books be collected, and he appointed *Liu Hsiang* to study the collection. *Liu* placed these works under six headings: classics and commentaries, works of the philosophers, poetry and poetic prose, military works, divination, and medicine. Later *Liu's* son, *Liu Hsin,* added "general summary" as a seventh class."

Another classification of all works was made by *Hsün* (d. 289 A.D.), who initiated a lasting four-group classification: classics, histories, philosophies, and *belles lettres*.

Three centuries later, the question of classifications of history was discussed by *Wei Cheng* 魏徵, 580-643, who concluded his history section of the treatise on literature in the *Sui-shu*, the History of the *Sui* Dynasty, thus: *"Pan Ku* attached history under the Spring-Autumn Annals, but we have established an independent section of history with thirteen classifications." Other historians saw need for a different number of classifcations: *Chang T'ing-yü* 張廷玉, editor of the *Ming* history, said the number was ten; *Ch'ien Ta-hsin* 錢大昕 thought fourteen was right; *Chia Hung* 賈鴻, 1541-1620, fifteen; *Ch'en Chen-sun* 陳振孫, fl. 1225-1240, sixteen; and *Lu Wen-ch'ao* 盧文弨, 1717-1796, eighteen.

Here we describe twenty-seven types of history. They include all classifications that have been used in one way or another.

1. *Pien-nien* 編年, Annals or Chronicles.

As the term shows, the sequence of time is important, *Pien-nien*, meaning "strings the events of the year" and "strings together the years."

2. *Chi-chuan* 紀傳, Essentials and Biographies.

Chi 紀 gives the general picture; *chuan,* 傳 the detailed. *Shih-chi* 史記, the first example.

3. *Chi-shih pen-mo* 紀事本末, Narratives from Beginning to End, making the sequence of events supreme.

T'ung-chien chi-shih pen-mo 通鑑紀事本末 General History in Narratives from Beginning to End was the first of this kind.

In Chinese, these three forms are distinguished in simple terms as (1) *Nien-pieh,* 年別, Chronological treatment, (2) *Jen-pieh* 人別, Biographical treatment, (3) *Shih-pieh* 事別, Genetic topical treatment.

4. *Cheng-shih* 正史, Standard Histories — commonly known as Dynastic Histories. These are basically in the *Chi-chuan* form though the chronological aspect is included. Each was recognized by the central

authorities.

The term, *Cheng-shih*, was first used in the introduction to the treatise on classics and literature in the *Sui-shu*. The selection of materials was exceedingly rigid, excluding almost all except official documents.

5. *Pieh-shih* 別史, Separate Histories.

Inclusive term or type of histories other than the above four types. The position of *Pieh-shih* is below *Cheng-shih* and above *Tsa-shih*.

Pieh-shih is neither *Pien-nien* nor *Chi-chuan*, but treats diverse subjects of one or more dynasties. It is very difficult to distinguish *Pieh-shih* from *Tsa-shih*, but *Pieh-shih* generally deals with the important political affairs of a dynasty either in official publications or revised editions of dynastic histories, and *Tsa-shih* deals, in small scope, with affairs of small concern from private records by private historians.

Further information on the distinction between these types can be found in *Ch'ien-ch'ing-tang shu-mu* 千頃堂書目 Book List of Ten-Thousand-Acre Hall, by *Huang Yü-chi* 黃玉箕, 1629-1691, and in *Shu-mu ta-wen* 書目答問 Queries and Answers Regarding Lists of Books, by *Chang Chih-tung* 張之洞, 1837-1909, and *Miao Ch'uan-sun* 繆荃孫, 1844-1919.

6. *Tsa-shih* 雜史, Miscellaneous Histories.

Usually these had a much smaller scope than that of the standard or the separate histories.

7. *Pai-shih* 稗史 Minor Histories.

Records of the folkways of a particular area or a particular period.

8. *Pa-shih* 霸史. Histories of States Ruled by Force.

The states were rivals, real or nominal, of the central authorities. First termed, *Wei-shih* 偽史, History of the Usurper by *Juan Hsiao-hsü* 阮孝緒 in his Seven Records. (See p.60). Changed to *Pa-shih* in the *Sui-shu ching-chi-chih* 隋書經籍志. Both terms were used by *Ma*

Tuan-lin 馬端臨.

9. *Shih-p'ing* 史評, Historical Criticism.

Criticism may be (1) on great events in history, (2) method of historical approach, (3) the entire historical work. Though *Tso's* Commentary and the Historical Memoirs of *Ssu-ma Ch'ien* had made a beginning, historical criticism on historiography reached a new height only in *Liu Chih-chi's Shih-t'ung* 史通, Historical Perspectives, and in *Chang Hsüeh-cheng's Wen-shih t'ung-i* 文史通義, Fundamental Principles of Cultural History. (See pp. 162-166.)

10. *Shih-ch'ao* 史鈔, Historical Excerpts.

These were selected verbal transcriptions from historical works to establish certain precedent and significance. Two kinds of historical excerpts: (1) Excerpts from one particular history, (2) Excerpts from numerous histories. Such classification first appeared in the Treatise on Literature of the *Sung-shih*.

11. *Yeh-shih* 野史, Private Histories.

These were written accounts of events as recorded by private individuals instead of official historians. (*Yeh* 野, literally wilderness or farm, antonym of *Ch'ao* 朝, the imperial court. Historical records kept not by court historians.) This classification has not been used by authorities in their general classifications of history. First appearance of such a designation was in the Treatise on Literature of the *T'ang* history, *T'ai-ho yeh-shih* 太和野史, or Private History of Emperor *Wen-tsung* to Emperor *Chao-tsung*, 827-889, by *Kung-sha Chung-mu* 公沙仲穆.

12. *Ku-shih* 古史 Ancient Histories.

It was a term used in the *Sui-shu ching-chi-chih* referring to the *Pien-nien* form, which came earlier than the *Chi-chuan* form (p. 40).

Ku-shih is a term used in the *Sui-shu ching-chi-chih* to denote *Pien-nien*. *Chi-chuan*, a later form, he called *Cheng-shih*, standard history. (See nos. 1, 2, and 4 above.) *Ku-shih* is not again employed until *Ch'ien Ta-hsin* (p. 126) used it in his *Yüan-shih i-wen-chih*, the treatise on literature in the *Yüan-shih.*

13. *Shih-hsüeh* 史學, Historical Studies, or Historiography.

Records say that during the *Chin* period an office in the government in charge of historical studies was created, but this was not until Emperor *Mu-tsung* (821-824), when historical discipline became a universal requirement in all civil service examinations. *"Shih-hsüeh"* was not included in general classification of history until *Lu Wen-ch'ao* 盧文弨, for the reason that it was included in *Shih-p'ing* or Historical Criticism.

14. *Chao-ling tsou-i* 詔令奏議, Mandates, and Memorials.

Collectively, these were state papers; severally, *chao-ling* were issued by the sovereign in many forms: (1) *Kao* 誥, to enjoin upon (*Kao-feng* 誥封 to ennoble; *kao-ming* 誥命, to commission); (2) *Chao* 詔, a royal proclamation or a mandate; (3) *Ling* 令, to command; (4) *Yü* 諭, edict (usually prefixed with the word, *shang* 上, or *sheng* 聖, meaning his Majesty's commands); (5) *Hsi-shu* 璽書, documents bearing imperial seal; (6) *Ch'ih-ming* 勅命, to bestow honors by imperial order; (7) *Ts'e-ming* 策命, imperial instructions.

Tsou-i 奏議, memorials to the throne with recommendations or without imperial command.

15. *Chuan-chi* 傳記, Biographical Memoirs.

Under this classification, *Nien-p'u*, chronological biographies, counsels and exhortations of high-minded men, and significant achievements of statesmen.

Earlier term was *Tsa-chuan* 雜傳, miscellaneous biographies; after *Sung*, *"Chuan-chi"* was in use.

16. *Tsai-chi* 載記, "Contemporaneous" Records.

Histories of contemporary states, usually smaller in area and shorter in duration, and as a whole viewed as illegitimate—assertion of power bordering the frontiers.

17. *Ch'i-chü-chu* 起居注, "Diary of Activity and Repose."

Records of "daily word and deed", of an emperor attending

public functions or other occasions. Court historians began their duties with such records as early as the *Han* period. During the *Ch'ing* period there was a detailed prescription for the recording of these Diaries.

18. *Shih-lu* 實錄, "Veritable Record."

Shih lu records were prepared at the end of each reign, based chiefly upon the "Diaries" though not limited to them. Lists of Veritable Records can be easily secured, though most of the earlier ones, with a few exceptions, were lost.

19. *Cheng-shu* 政書, Political Treatises.

Ordinances, institutes, regulations, and precedents governing governmental machinery, describing the changes in organization and in regulation.

Nung-cheng-ch'üan-shu 農政全書 (Agricultural Administration) by *Hsü Kuang-ch'i* 徐光啓 (1562-1633) *Hsüeh-cheng-ch'üan-shu* 學政全書 (Educational Administration), decreed in 1767.

20. *Chih-kuan* 職官, Functions and Officers.

Records of names, functions, and changes of offices and their officials, both civil and military. *Chin-shen-lu* 搢紳錄 Directory of Officials.

21. *Ti-li* 地理, Geography.

Includes three main types: historical, national, and local. Each records topography, economics, distinguished personalities, religions, temples, and literary productions, in the nature of local gazetteers, thus furnishing a real treasury of information.

22. *Shih-ling* 時令, Regulation of Time.

"Time" was important to ancient Chinese for two main reasons: practically, seasons and farming had a close relationship; theoretically, natural phenomena foretold fortunes of the dynasty. Time had a threefold function: Political, economic, and religious.

23. *Hsing-fa* 刑罰, Laws and Punishments.

Though the political ideal was not to resort to law and punishments, they were found to be necessary. Origin and objective of laws, codification and revision of laws, procedure of trial and the method of inflicting punishments, as well as ways to avoid or to correct injustices, constituted a special class of histories. Sometimes, instead of *"Hsing-fa"* the term, *fa-ling* 法令 or Laws and Ordinances was used.

24. *Shih-huo* 食貨, Food and Commodities.

Every treatise in the standard histories had a section on food and commodities. Some historians stressed the importance of the subject and made a separate classification.

25. *P'u-tieh* 譜諜, Genealogical Registers.

These registers were genealogies of the imperial clan and its collateral relations. *Ssu-ma Ch'ien* stated that he had made use of these genealogical registers for his Historical Memoirs. Some historians used the term, *P'u-hsi* 譜系, Genealogical Continuity while others used *Shih-tsu* 氏族, or Clan and its Kinsmen.

26. *Mu-lu* 目錄, Itemized Records or Catalogues.

Bibliographical guide including epigraphical records. Earlier efforts were directed to extensive inventory of published works; in the modern period *Mu-lu* includes a critical estimate of the contents and their approach. *Po-lu* 薄錄 Record List, or *Shu-mu* 書目, Book List, was sometimes used in place of *Mu-lu*.

27. *Chiu-shih* 舊事, Ancient Affairs.

A modern student finds it difficult to distinguish between this classification and the *Tsa-shih* or Miscellaneous Histories. Every *Chih* or Treatise contains this classification whether in the terms, *Ku-shih* 故事, *Tien-ku* 典故, or *Chiu-shih,* with the exception of four important works: (1) *Ch'ung-wen shu-mu* 崇文書目, (2) *Chün-chai shu-chih* 郡齋書志, (3) *Ssu-k'u shu-mu* 四庫書目, and (4) *Shu-mu ta-wen* 書目答問.

NOTES FOR CHAPTER III.

1. *Shih-pen* 世本 lost during the Northern *Sung* period, but numerous restored editions were made during the *Ch'ing*, the best of which were by *Mao P'an-lin* 茆泮林 and *Chang Shu* 張澍 of late *Ch'ing*. *Chang Ping-lin* 章炳麟 (1868-1936) agrees with *Yen Chih-t'ui* 顏之推 (531-595) that the *Shih-pen* was probably the work of *Tso-ch'iu Ming* 左丘明, of the 4th century B.C. This was supported by the Biography of *Pan Piao* 班彪 (3-54 A.D.) in the *Hou-han-shu* 後漢書.

2. *Tsien Mu* 錢穆, *Liu Hsiang Hsin fu dz nien-pu* 劉向歆父子年譜, Yenching Journal, VII (June 1930), 1189-1318.

3. *Ch'ung-wen* General Catalog 崇文總目 by *Wang Yao-ch'en* 王堯臣, *Chün-chai* Book List 郡齋書錄 by *Ch'ao Kung-wu* 晁公武 (Prefect of *Shensi* in 1165), *T'ung-chih* 通志 by *Cheng Ch'iao* 鄭樵 (1104-1162).

甲骨	小篆	隸字	楷書
Chia-ku	*Hsiao-chuan*	*Li-tzu*	*K'ai-shu*
Shell and bone characters	Lesser seal form of the *Han* Dynasty	Official script at end of *Han*	Brush written style used
c. 1200 B.C.		c. 200 A.D.	400 A.D. on

Examples of 4 successive styles of Chinese characters

Portrait of *Ssu-ma Kuang* (p. 50)

Chapter IV

T'UNG SHIH 通史 GENERAL HISTORIES

T'ung-shih (General History) as an independent form of history began with the lost work of *Wu Chün* 吳均, decreed by *Hsiao-yen* 蕭衍 (464-549), though *Ssu-ma Ch'ien's* Historical Memoirs may be regarded as the first successful general history covering more than a single dynasty. To achieve *hui-t'ung* 會通, interrelatedness or synthesis, was the criterion of a general history. In the *hsü* 序, preface to the *T'ung-chih* 通志, *Cheng Ch'iao* 鄭樵, 1104-1162, summarized his entire historical method in *Hui-t'ung-chih-tao* 會通之道.

Chang Hsüeh-ch'eng 章學誠 champion of general history, deliberated in his *Wen-shih-t'ung-i* 文史通義, on the "genetic view of history." He listed the merits as follows: (1) *Mien-ch'ung-fu* 免重復, "avoidance of duplication or repetition," treating, for example, the fall of one dynasty and the rise of another as a continuous succession; (2) *Chün-lei-li* 均類例, "balance of classified general information and actual institutions," giving the sources of ideas and institutions, their developments, and new tendencies; (3) *Pien-ch'üan-p'ei* 便銓配, "convenient for selection and distribution of historical records," affording good opportunity for proper proportion in historical perspectives; (4) *P'ing-shih-fei* 平是非, "judgment of right and wrong," basing upon documentary evidences instead of governmental wishes; (5) *Ch'ü-ti-wu* 去牴牾, "elimination of inconsistencies and contradictions" as found in dynastic histories; (6) *Hsiang-lin-shih* 詳鄰事, "explicit accounts of the affairs of contemporary and co-existing kingdoms and neighboring countries." This sixth merit of general history appears in the history of the Northern and Southern dynasties and in the history of the Five Dynasties. In the first, Later *Liang* and Northern *Wei* are properly dealt with, and in the latter *Wu* 吳, *Ching* 荊, and *T'an* 潭, (*T'an-chou* 潭州, *Ch'ang-sha, Hunan*) received a complete account. In addition to these advantages (便), *Chang Hsüeh-ch'eng* further discussed two special merits of this approach: (1) *Chü-chien-ts'ai* 具剪裁: it affords greater freedom for the selection of essential details; (2) *Li-chia-fa* 立家法: it establishes a special technique of research and a special method of approach. Though an ardent advocate for general history, the historian was not unaware of its pitfalls, which he summarized into three groups: (1) *Wu-tuan-ch'ang* 無短長, over equalization of space at the expense of sequence and comparison; (2) *Jeng-yüan-t'i* 仍原題, copying the original terminology and classification at the expense of new and creative designations and descriptions; (3) *Wang-piao-mu* 忘標目, neglecting topical notations for convenient reference and omitting seemingly independent and isolated personalities and events.

The first attempt to write general history was made in the early sixth century by *Wu Chün*. Five-hundred years later *Tzu-chih-t'ung-chien* appeared and was followed by many annotations and supplements, the chief of which are listed below. Then came *Tzu-chih-t'ung-chien kang-mu* (p. 53), followed by works of like pattern and many supplements. A representative selection is given. Finally, this chapter lists works representing a new approach to general history.

I. *Tzu-chih-t'ung-chien* 資治通鑑
    Comprehensive Mirror for Aid in Government
    Ssu-ma Kuang 司馬光 1019-1086.

The author covered 1,362 years from the *Chan-kuo* 戰國 period, 402-221 B.C., to the end of the Five Dynasties, 959 A.D. He worked nineteen years, assisted by *Liu Pin* 劉邠 1022-1088, *Liu Shu* 劉恕 1052-1078, and *Fan Tsu-hui* 范祖輝 1041-1098. They selected sources from more than 320 miscellaneous historical works.

The work consisted of 324 *chüan* and 30 *chüan* of *K'ao-i* 考異, Investigation of Discrepancies.

GENERAL HISTORIES

A. ANNOTATIONS OF THE COMPREHENSIVE MIRROR

1. *Tzu-chih-t'ung-chien yin-chu* 資治通鑑音注
   Annotations of the phonological problems found in the Comprehensive Mirror:
   Hu San-hsing 胡三省 1230-1287
   His work was further corrected and collated by *Ch'ien Ta-hsin* (See p. 126) in his *T'ung-chien-chu-pien-cheng* 通鑑注辨正 (printed in 1792) and by *Ku Kuang-ch'i* 顧廣圻, 1776-1835, and *P'eng Chao-sun* 彭兆蓀, 1769-1821, in their collation of Hu's Annotated edition of the Comprehensive Mirror (published in 1817 under the name of *Hu K'o-chia* 胡克家, 1757-1816.).

2. *T'ung-chien shih-wen pien-wu* 通鑑釋文辨誤
   Explaining terms and correcting mistakes in the Comprehensive Mirror
   Hu San-hsing 胡三省 1230-1287

3. *T'ung-chien ti-li t'ung-shih* 通鑑地理通釋
   General Explanation of Geographical Aspects in the Comprehensive Mirror
   Wang Ying-lin 王應麟 1223-1296

4. *T'ung-chien ta-wen* 通鑑答問
   Answers and Questions on the Comprehensive Mirror
   Wang Ying-lin 王應麟 1223-1296

5. *T'ung-chien wen-i* 通鑑問疑
   Inquiry on the Doubtful in the Comprehensive Mirror
   Liu Hsi-chung 劉羲仲 son of *Liu Shu* 劉恕

6. *Tu T'ung-chien lun* 讀通鑑論
   Discourse on Reading the Comprehensive Mirror
   Wang Fu-chih 王夫之 1627-1679

B. SUPPLEMENTS TO THE COMPREHENSIVE MIRROR

1. *T'ung-chien wai-chi* 通鑑外紀
   Supplements to the Comprehensive Mirror

52   ELEMENTS OF CHINESE HISTORIOGRAPHY

Literally, *wai-chi* means "additional history."
Another term, *ch'ien-chi* 前紀 or "prior history" might have been used, but *Liu Shu* showed respect for his master and wished to convey only the idea of some "extra records."
Liu Shu 劉恕 1052-1078.

2. *Hsü Tzu-chih-t'ung-chien ch'ang-pien* 續資治通鑑長編
Supplements (in the sense of continuation) to the Comprehensive Mirror in a chronological form.   The "Continuation" consisted of records of 166 years of the Northern *Sung* under nine emperors.
Li T'ao 李濤 1115-1184.

3. *Sung t'ung-chien-ch'ang-pien chi-shih-pen-mo* 宋通鑑長編紀事本末 *Sung* Comprehensive Mirror Chronological History from Beginning to End
Yang Chung-liang 楊仲良   c. 1241-1271

4. *Chien-yen i-lai hsi-nien yao-lu* 建炎以來繫年要錄
Primary Records Chronologically arranged since *Chien-yen,* 1127
This is a continuation of *Li Tao's* work
Li Hsin-ch'uan 李心傳 1166-1243

5. *Tzu-chih-t'ung-chien ch'ien-pien* 資治通鑑前編
Pre-Comprehensive Mirror History
This general history of early China covers the days of Emperor *Yao* down to the point where the Comprehensive Mirror began.
Chin Lü-hsiang 金履祥 1232-1303

6. *Sung Yüan tzu-chih-t'ung-chien* 宋元資治通鑑
Comprehensive Mirror (general history) of *Sung* and *Yüan* Dynasties to Aid in Government
Wang Tsung-mu 王宗沐 fl. 1530-1560

7. *Hsüeh Ying-ch'i* 顧廣圻 contemporary of *Wang Tsung-mu* wrote a similar work under similar title, *Sung Yüan tzu-chih-t'ung-chien.*

8. *Tzu-chih-t'ung-chien hou-pien* 資治通鑑後編
Post-Comprehensive Mirror History   This supplement is superior to all those attempted after *Liu Shu* but *Pi Yüan's* Supplement

to the Comprehensive Mirror was equally good.
Hsü Ch'ien-hsüeh 徐乾學 1631-1694 assisted by *Wan Ssu-t'ung*, *Yen Jo-chü*, and *Hu Wei*.

9. *Hsü tzu-chih-t'ung-chien* 續資治通鑑
   Supplement to the Comprehensive Mirror
   Pi yüan 畢沅 1730-1797
   This supplement extended the history from the beginning of the *Sung* dynasty to the end of the *Yüan*. *Pi* having died before the printing was done it was completed by *Shao Chin-han* 1743-1796, and *Ch'ien Ta-hsin*, 1728-1804.

10. *Ming Chi* 明紀
    Essentials of *Ming* History
    Ch'en Ho 陳鶴 (進士 1796) flourished 1800-1825, and his grandson, *Ch'en K'o-chia* 陳克家 *chü-jen*, 1850

11. *Ming t'ung-chien* 明通鑑
    Comprehensive Mirror of the *Ming* Dynasty
    Hsia Hsieh 夏燮 latter half of 19th century

12. *Tzu-chih-t'ung-chien pu-cheng* 資治通鑑補正
    Additions and Corrections of the Comprehensive Mirror
    Yen Yen 嚴衍 1574-1645

13. *Hsü t'ung-chien-ch'ang-pien shih-pu*
    Additional Notes to the Comprehensive Mirror Supplements
    Huang I-chou 黃以周 flourished 1865-1895
    Ch'in Hsiang-yeh 秦湘業 1813-1883

II. *Tzu-chih-t'ung-chien kang-mu* 資治通鑑綱目
    Abridged View of the Comprehensive Mirror for Aid in Government   *Chu Hsi* 朱熹 1131-1200
This is generally known by the shorter name, *Tung-chien kang-mu*, Abridged View of the Comprehensive Mirror. The aim of the author was to eliminate unnecessary details in reporting causes and consequences and to vivify the basic unities and diversities. His treatment

was, nevertheless, chronological. His view of history was well expressed in his preface and in his explanation of basic principles, the *fan-li* 凡例. We select seven of the many related works.

Numerous historical works followed this one:
1. *Tzu-chih-t'ung-chien kang-mu hsü-pien* 資治通鑑綱目續編
   Supplement to the *T'ung-chien-kang-mu*
   Shang Lo 商輅 1414-1486
2. *Tzu-chih-t'ung-chien kang-mu ch'ien-pien* 資治通鑑綱目前編
   Pre-*T'ung-chien kang-mu* History
   Nan Hsüan 南軒 Flourished 1526-1566
   Chin Lu-hsiang's early history served as a supplement to *Ssu-ma Kuang's* 司馬光 Comprehensive Mirror as *Nan Hsüan's* did to *Chu Hsi's* abridged view.
3. *Tzu-chih-t'ung-chien kang-mu san-pien* 資治通鑑綱目三編
   The Third Supplement to the Comprehensive Mirror
   Shen Te-ch'ien 沈德潛 1673-1769, Compiler
   Ch'i Chao-nan 齊召南 1706-1768, Compiler
   Shang Lu's Supplement covered the *Sung* and *Yüan* periods; this Third Supplement, the *Ming period*, 1368-1644.
4. *T'ung-chien chi-lan* 通鑑輯覽
   A Synoptic View of the Comprehensive Mirror
   Fu Heng 傅恆 d. 1770, Director-general, assisted by *P'eng Yüan-jui* 彭元瑞 1731-1803, *Chao I* 趙翼 1727-1814, *Lu Hsi-hsiung* 陸錫熊 1734-1792, *Juan K'uei-sheng* 阮葵生 1727-1789, *Chao Wen-che* 趙文哲 1725-1773, *Yen Ch'ang-ming* 嚴長明 1731-1787, *Pi Yüan* 畢沅 1730-1797, *Chi Yün* 紀昀 1724-1805.

This general history of China attempted to correct the mistakes and omissions of *T'ung-chien-tsuan-yao* 通鑑纂要 Essentials of the Comprehensive Mirror by *Li Tang-yang* 李蕩陽, 1447-1516. His work covers the time from antiquity to the end of the *Ming* dynasty.

GENERAL HISTORIES   55

5. *San-ch'ao pei-meng hui-pien* 三朝北盟彙編
Chronological History of Negotiations with the Kingdom of *Chin* during the Three Reigns.   (Placed here because of its pattern after the *T'ung-chien-kang-mu.*)
Hsü Meng-hsin 徐夢莘 d. 1205.

6. *T'ung-chien hsü-pien* 通鑑續編
Supplement to the *T'ung-chien*
Ch'en Ching 陳桱 flourished 1340-1370.
A supplement to the *T'ung-chien-kang-mu* in the *kang-mu* style rather than a supplement to the original *T'ung-chien,* though it bears the name of *T'ung-chien-hsu-pien.*

7. *LiaoChin cheng-shih kang-mu* 遼金正史綱目
Fundamental Elements of the Standard Histories of *Liao* and *Chin*
Yang Lu-jung 楊陸榮 end of 17th century
This is still in manuscript form, preserved in the *Seikado* 靜嘉堂 collection of the *Iwasaki Yanosuke* 岩崎彌之助 (1851-1908) private library near *Tokyo.*

III. *Chi-shih-pen-mo* 紀事本末 (New approach to general history)

Every historical event involves time, place, and persons but in antiquity what happened was more important than the time element and much less important than where it happened; thus legends and lore accumulated without regard for time or place. Gradually those who caused events and those who were affected by the events took on importance, and records of time and of men developed. This simple description affords a summary of the development of Chinese historiography with its inscriptions on Oracle Bones and bronzes, the later chronological treatment of history, its biographic emphasis and the re-emergence of emphasis upon events in change and significance.

This last stage in the development of history represents an effort to write a general history of the growth of human ideas and institutions. Such a history has a unity of events, not a unity imposed by the limits of a dynastic period or the life span of a ruler. This unity is expressed by the term *Chi-shih-pen-mo* 紀事本末, meaning narration of events from beginning to end, and this term becomes the name of a type of general history. Three stages in the development of this type of writing are revealed in three books: *Shang-shu* 尚書 Classic of History, *K'o-lu* 科錄 Classified History, *Tung-chien chi-shih-pen-mo* 通鑑紀事本末 Comprehensive Mirror of Narration of Events from Beginning to End. Though some critics regard the last work as only a revision of the Comprehensive Mirror to show causal relations, it brought to full stature a type of general history represented by the works listed below.

1. *T'ung-chien-chi-shih-pen-mo* 通鑑紀事本末
   Comprehensive Mirror of Narration of Events from Beginning to End
   Yüan Shu 袁樞 fl. 1165-1205.
2. *T'ung-chien-chi-shih-pen-mo pu-hou-pien* 通鑑紀事本末補後編
   Supplements to the Comprehensive Mirror in Narratives
   Chang Hsing-yüeh 張星曜 b. 1633— d. after 1711.
3. *Sung-shih chi-shih-pen-mo* 宋史紀事本末
   Sung History in Narratives of Events
   Feng Ch'i 馮琦 fl. 1590-1610, and
   Ch'en Pang-chan 陳邦瞻 fl. 1590-1621.
4. *Yüan-shih chi-shih-pen-mo* 元史紀事本末
   Yüan History in Narratives of Events
   Ch'en Pang-chan 陳邦瞻 fl. 1590-1621
5. *Hsi-hsia chi-shih-pen-mo* 西夏紀事本末
   Narration of Events of Western *Hsia*
   Chang Chien 張鑑 fl. 1532-1566.
6. *Tso-chuan chi-shih-pen-mo* 左傳紀事本末
   Narration of Events of the *Ch'un-ch'iu* Period
   Kao Shih-ch'i 高士奇 1645-1703.
7. *Liao-shih chi-shih-pen-mo* 遼史紀事本末

Narration of Events of the *Liao* Period
Li Yu-t'ang 李有棠, fl. 1875-1900.
8. *Chin-shih chi-shih-pen-mo* 金史紀事本末
Narration of Events in the *Chin* Period
Li Yu-t'ang 李有棠, fl. 1875-1900.
9. *Ming-shih chi shih-pen-mo* 明史紀事本末
Narration of Events of the *Ming* Period
Ku Ying-t'ai 谷應泰 *Chin-shih*, 1647; d. after 1689.
10. *Hsü Ming chi-shih-pen-mo* 續明紀事本末
Supplement to the History of the *Ming* Dynasty
Ni Tsai-t'ien 倪在田 *Ch'ing* period
11. *Ming-ch'ao chi-shih-pen-mo pu-pien* 明朝紀事本末補編
Supplement to the *Ming* History
Sun I-jang 孫詒讓 1848-1908.
12. *San-fan chi-shih-pen-mo* 三藩紀事本末
Narration of Events of the Three Frontier Princes
Yang Lu-jung 楊陸榮. fl. 1680-1710.
13. *Hsü tzu-chih-t'ung-chien chi-shih-pen-mo* 續資治通鑑綱目紀事本末
Narration of Events of the Supplement of the Comprehensive Mirror.
Li Ming-mo 李銘模 fl. 1885-1905; Date of publication, 1903.
14. *I-shih* 繹史
Historical "Filature"
Ma Su 馬驌 1621-1673.
Though the author did not employ the designation, *chi-shih-pen-mo*, the word *I* 繹, to reel the thread," suggests that from a mass of source materials the individual threads from beginning to end must be traced. The work is an encyclopedic history consisting of extracts from many sources under various topics, arranged chronologically from antiquity to the end of the Ch'in dynasty, 206 B.C.

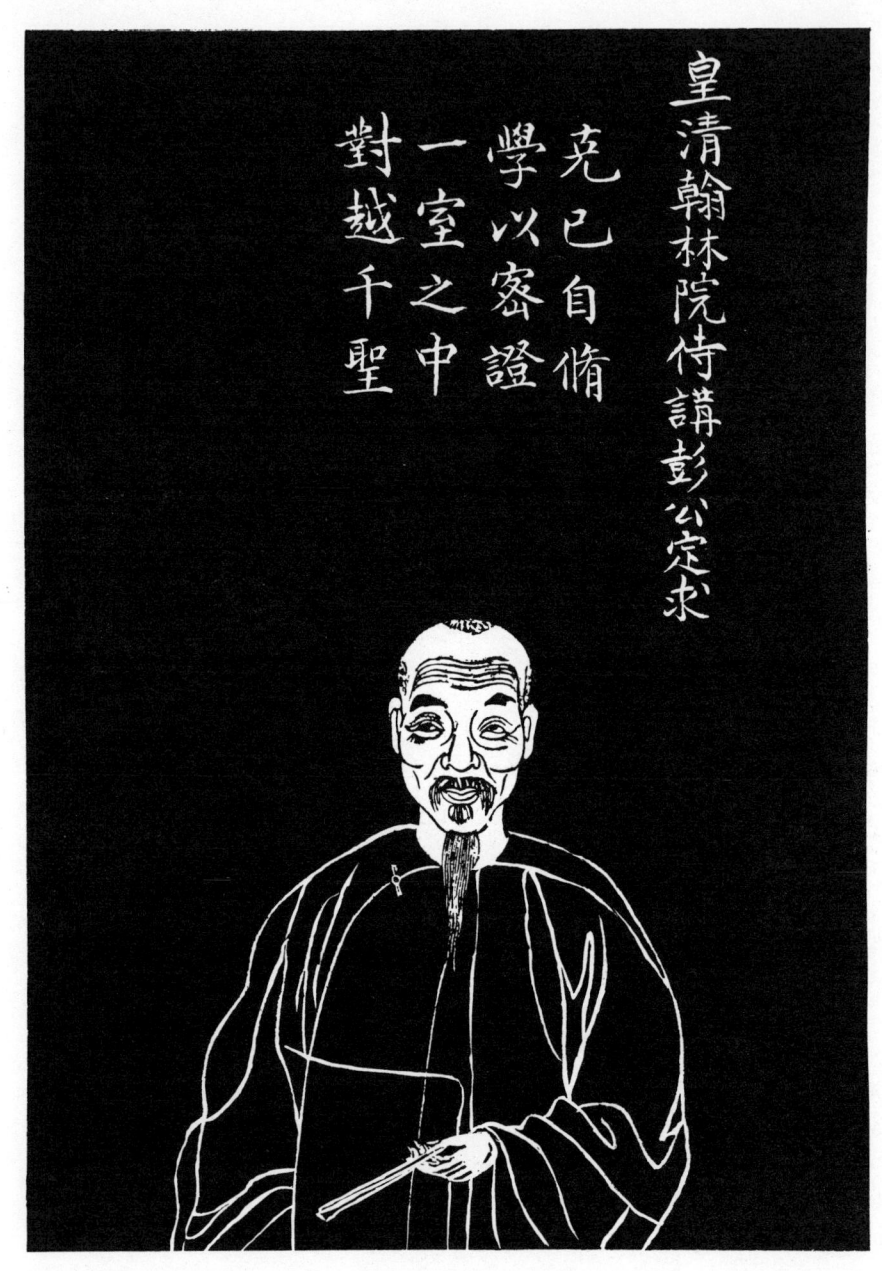

Portrait of *P'eng Ting-chiu* (p. 80)

Chapter V

TYPES OF SPECIALIZED HISTORIES

Of the twenty-seven categories of Chinese histories, *Pieh-shih* 別史 separate history, comes closest to *Chuan-shih* 專史, specialized history, which we outline here. This unique type of history arose from an interest in and an attempt to classify records for current and future reference. It is topical, as are the treatises in the dynastic histories (p. 199), but the topics are discussed more thoroughly than in the treatises. Not being limited to one dynastic period, specialized history treats topics genetically. Thus the dominant, and unique, characteristic of specialized history is *Shih-pieh* 事別, a genetical topical treatment. In these specialized histories we find a true picture of China's past.

There are two distinct types of specialized histories, the comprehensive and the individual. The latter treats of one subject only; the former, of many. The topics covered in the comprehensive histories are shown for each history we list. The individual type histories are listed under the single topic they cover.

A. COMPREHENSIVE TYPE OF SPECIALIZED HISTORIES

1. *Pieh-lu* 別錄 Separate Records
   Surviving works of classics, commentaries, philosophies, and poetry classified according to contents
   Liu Hsiang 劉向 80-9 B.C.
2. *Ch'i-lüeh* 七略 Seven Summaries
   Liu Hsin 劉歆 c. 46 B.C. - 25 A.D.

Chi-lüeh	輯略	Restored summaries
Liu-i	六藝	Six arts
Chu-tzu	諸子	Philosophers
Shih-fu	詩賦	Poetry and rhymed prose
Ping-shu	兵書	Military books

60 ELEMENTS OF CHINESE HISTORIOGRAPHY

    Shu-shu 術數 Divination
    Fang-chi 方計 Method for abundant life.
3. *Ch'i-chih* 七志 Seven Treatises
   Wang Chien 王儉 452-489
    Ching-tien 經典 Classics and institutes
    Chu-tzu 諸子 Philosophers
    Wen-han 文翰 Literature
    Chün-shu 軍書 Military books
    Yin-yang 陰陽 Astronomy
    Shu-i 術藝 Technology and arts
    T'u-p'u 圖譜 Maps and catalogs
4. *Ch'i-lu* 七錄 Seven Records
   Juan Hsiao-hsü 阮孝緒 479-536
    Ching-tien 經典 Classics and institutes
    Chi-chuan 紀傳 Chronology of men and events
    Tzu-ping 子兵 Philosophies and strategies
    Wen-chi 文集 Poetry and prose
    Chi-shu 技術 Techniques of divination
    Fo 佛 Buddhism
    Tao 道 Taoism
5. *Ch'i-lu* 七錄 Seven Classifications of Books
   Cheng Yin 鄭寅 fl. 1230-40
    Ching 經 Classics
    Shih 史 History
    Tzu 子 Philosophy
    I 藝 Arts
    Fang-chi 方技 Method and technique
    Wen 文 Literature
    Lei 類 Bibliography
6. *T'ung-tien* 通典 Comprehensive Institutes
   Tu Yu 杜佑 735-812

TYPES OF SPECIALIZED HISTORIES

Shih-huo	食貨	Food and commodities
Hsüan-chü	選舉	Civil service examinations
Li	禮	Rites
Yüeh	樂	Music
Ping-hsing	兵刑	Defense and justice
Chou-chün	州郡	Provinces
Pien-fang	邊防	Defense of frontiers

Tu Yu added Rites and Music of the *K'ai-yüan* period 開元 (713-755) to *Cheng-tien* 政典 Political Institutes by *Liu Chih* 劉秩 fl. 725-755 and renamed the work *T'ung-tien*.

(a) *Hsü t'ung-tien* 續通典 Supplement to the *T'ung-tien*

This was decreed by *Ch'ien-lung* in 1767. The period of the Supplement covers 888 years from Emperor *Su-tsung* (756-762) of the *T'ang* dynasty to the end of the reign of Emperor *Ch'ung-chen* (1628-1644) of the *Ming* dynasty. The 144 *chüan* follow the pattern of the *T'ung-tien*, except that the history of military affairs and judicial affairs are treated separately.

(b) *Ch'ing t'ung-tien* 清通典 Comprehensive Institutes of the *Ch'ing* dynasty.

This was also decreed in 1767. *Tu Yu's T'ung-tien*, with a few alterations, was the model. There were 100 *chüan* dealing with basic human affairs, prior to *Ch'ien-lung*.

6. *T'ung-chih* 通志 Comprehensive Treatises

Cheng Ch'iao 鄭樵 1104-1162

Consisting of 200 *chüan*, 51 of which were given to "Twenty Summaries" (Cf. *Liu Hsin's* "Seven Summaries"):

Shih-tsu	氏族	Families and clans
Liu-shu	六書	Six forms of Chinese characters
Ch'i-yin	七音	Seven musical notes
T'ien-wen	天文	Astronomy
Ti-li	地理	Geography
Tu-i	都邑	Capitals and cities

Li-shih	禮諡	Rites and posthumous titles
Fu-ch'i	服器	Costumes and utensils
Yüeh	樂	Music
Chih-kuan	職官	Officials and functions
Hsüan-chü	選舉	Civil service examinations
Hsing-fa	刑法	Punishments and laws
Shih-huo	食貨	Food and commodities
I-wen	藝文	Arts and literature
Chiao-chou	校讐	Textual criticism
T'u-p'u	圖譜	Maps and catalogs
Chin-shih	金石	Inscriptions on metal and stone
Tsai-hsiang	災祥	Misfortune and fortune
Ts'ao-mu	草木	Plants and trees
K'un-ch'ung	昆蟲	Insects

8. *Wen-hsien t'ung-k'ao* 文獻通考
   Comprehensive History of Civilization.
   Ma Tuan-lin 馬端臨 cir. 1250-1325.

The author explains the meaning of *wen* as culture of the past and present; *hsien,* documentary evidences of great projects and pronouncements. This comprehensive historical survey of cultural achievements is often referred to as an "Encyclopedia of Culture." There were 348 *chüan,* reconstructing the eight classifications of the *T'ung-tien* into 19, and creating 5 new divisions, thus making a total of 24 classifications:

T'ien-fu	田賦	Land tax
Ch'ien-pi	錢幣	Currencies
Hu-k'ou	戶口	Population
Chih-i	職役	Conscript services
Cheng-ch'üeh	征榷	Taxation and monoply
Shih-ti	市糴	Grain market
T'u-kung	土貢	Tributes
Kuo-yung	國用	National resources

TYPES OF SPECIALIZED HISTORIES

Hsüan-chü	選舉	Civil service examinations
Hsüeh-hsiao	學校	Schools
Chih-kuan	職官	Functions and offices
Chiao-she	郊社	Heaven and earth sacrifices
Tsung-miao	宗廟	Ancestral temples
Wang-li	王禮	Imperial rites
Yüeh	樂	Music
Ping	兵	Military
Hsing	刑	Punishments
Ching-chi	經籍	Classics and literature
Ti-hsi	帝系	Imperial genealogy
Feng-chien	封建	Feudal system
Hsiang-wei	象緯	Divination
Wu-i	物異	Unusual happenings
Yü-ti	輿地	Geography
Ssu-i	四裔	Frontier regions

(a) *Hsü wen-hsien t'ung-k'ao* 續文獻通考   254 *chüan*

Wang Ch'i 王圻 (fl. 1540-1550) attempted to supplement *Ma Tuan-lin's* work by bringing it up to *Wang's* time. He followed the model of the *Wen-hsien t'ung-k'ao* and added six divisions as follows:

Chieh-i	節義	The chaste and the righteous
Shu-yüan	書院	Academies
Liu-shu	六書	Six fundamentals of language
Shih-fa	諡法	Regulation of posthumous honors
Tao-t'ung	道統	Succession in Confucianism
Fang-wai	方外	Buddhism and Taoism

(b) *Ch'ing wen-hsien t'ung-k'ao* 清文獻通考   226 *chüan*

Decreed by *Ch'ien-lung* in 1747, originally to be published with the *Hsü wen-hsien t'ung-k'ao,* but it finally became a separate set. Final edition added one division, namely, *Ch'ün-miao* or, Various temples, to the traditional twenty-four.

Wen-hsien t'ung-k'ao, Hsü wen-hsien t'ung-k'ao, and the *Ch'ing wen-hsien t'ung-k'ao* together are known as *San T'ung-k'ao* 三通考.

9. *Yü-hai* 玉海 Ocean of Jade
   Wang Ying-lin 王應麟 1223-1296.

   This encyclopedic work contains information on twenty-one subjects, with 240 subtopics, intended for the candidates for civil service examinations. The work is thorough and sound.

10. *T'ai-p'ing yü-lan* 太平御覽 Great Peace Imperial Reading
    Li Fang 李昉 925-996.

    So named because Emperor *T'ai-tsung* (976-997) read three *chüan* a day and finished the reading in a year. *"T'ai-ping"* makes up the first part of *T'ai-tsung's* reign title (*T'ai-p'ing hsing-kuo,* 976-983). 1,000 *chüan* with 1,600 items under 55 classifications.

11. *Yüan-chien lei-han* 淵鑑類函 Deep Mirror Classified Knowledge

    Extends the *T'ang lei-han* 唐類函, Classified Knowledge of *T'ang* by *Yü An-ch'i* 俞安期 (a friend of *Wang Shih-chen* 王士禎 1526-1593). Even though there are only about half of the number of *chüan* in the *T'ai-p'ing yü-lan,* the information contained in this work far surpasses that in the *Yü-lan.*

12. *Ku-chin t'u-shu chi-ch'eng* 古今圖書集成
    "Synthesis of Books and Illustrations of Ancient and Modern Times" *Ch'en Meng-lei* 陳夢雷 b. 1651 *Chin-shih,* 1670

    10,000 *chüan* divided into 6 sections and subdivided into 32 institutes dealing with 6,109 topics. *Ch'en Meng-lei* worked ten years to complete it, but Emperor *Yung-cheng* (1723-1735) ordered revision under *Chiang T'ing-hsi,* 蔣廷錫 1669-1732, whose three years on the work resulted in very little. Most of the terms remained the same, though new importance was brought to some divisions.

B. INDIVIDUAL TYPE OF SPECIALIZED HISTORIES

GEOGRAPHY

1. *San-fu chüeh-lu* 三輔決錄

TYPES OF SPECIALIZED HISTORIES

    Chao Ch'i 趙岐 d. 201 A.D.
Clarified Record of three Capital Cities (Published in 153 A.D. *Ch'ang-an,* the Capital; *Feng-yu,* City at the Right; *Fu-feng,* City at the Left.)

2. *I-chou chih* 益州志 Gazetteer of *I-chou, Szechuan*
    Ch'iao Chou 焦周 c. 200-270 A.D.

3. *Kuei-lin feng-t'u chi* 桂林風土記
    Mo Hsiu-fu 莫休符
Climate and Soil of *Kueilin* (Includes customs of people of *Kueilin,* as the term, *feng-t'u,* takes on the meaning of "people's spirit; local customs.")

4. *Ling-hai yü-t'u* 嶺海輿圖 Maps of *Liang Kwang* 兩廣
    Yao Yü 姚虞
Ling refers to *Wu Ling* in the north; *Hai,* to Sea in the south; i.e. *Kwangtung* and *Kwangsi.*

5. *Yün-nant'ung-chih* 雲南通志 General gazetteer of *Yünnan*
    Juan Yüan 阮元 1764-1849

6. *Ta-Ch'ing i-t'ung chih* 大清一統志
    Hsü Ch'ien-hsüeh 徐乾學 1631-1694,
A comprehensive geography of the Empire

PHILOSOPHY

1. *I Lo yüan-yüan lu* 伊洛淵源錄
    Chu Hsi 朱熹 1130-1200
Sources of Philosophy of the Two *Ch'eng* Brothers (*Ch'eng Hao* 程顥, 1032-1083; *Ch'eng I* 程頤, 1033-1107)

2. *Ming-ju hsüeh-an* 明儒學案
    Huang Tsung-hsi 黃宗羲 1609-1695
History of thought of the *Ming* period

3. *Han-hsüeh shih-ch'eng chi* 漢學師承記
    Chiang Fan 江藩 1761-1831
56 Biographies of scholars of the *Han* learning

4. *Chung-kuo lun-li-hsüeh shih* 中國倫理學史
   Ts'ai Yüan-p'ei 蔡元培 1867-1940
   Chinese history of ethics

GOVERNMENT

1. *Po-kuan-piao chu* 百官表注
   Hsün Ch'o 荀綽 fl. 300 A.D.
   Annotations to the table of government offices
2. *Han chih-k'ao* 漢制考 A history of *Han* institutes
   Wang Ying-lin 王應麟 1223-1296
3. *Li-tai tsai-fu hui-k'ao* 歷代宰輔彙考
   Wan Ssu-t'ung 萬斯同 1638-1702
   Comprehensive history of prime ministers throughout the ages
4. *Ta-Ch'ing hui-tien* 大清會典 Collected statutes of the Empire
   Huang Shao-chi 黃紹箕 1854-1908, and others
   5th edition, 100 *chüan* with *shih-li* or precedents, 1,220 *chüan*, and *t'u* or illustrations 270 *chüan*, was decreed in 1886 and completed in 1899.
5. *Chung-kuo yü-shih chih-tu* 中國御史制度
   Kao I-han 高一涵 1883-
   Institution of the censorate of China

EDUCATION

1. *Chin-ssu lu* 近思錄
   Chu Hsi 朱熹 1130-1200
   Chin-ssu, phrase from *Tzu Hsia,* disciple of Confucius, in the Analects, XIX, vi, where *Tzu Hsia* said, "Learn extensively with a sincere objective; inquire with earnestness; benevolence (head of all virtues) is naturally in the course."
   Chu Hsi's commentary on the Great Learning is perhaps the simplest treatise on classical Chinese education.
2. *Ch'uan-hsi lu* 傳習錄 (*ch'uan,* instructions; *hsi,* exercises)
   Hsu Ai 徐愛 fl. 1506-10, disciple of *Wang Shou-jen* 王守仁

TYPES OF SPECIALIZED HISTORIES

A collection of *Wang Yang-ming's* lectures, and answers to questions from his disciples.

The above two works represent the leading schools of thought in general, and of education in particular.

3. *Li-tai kung-chü chih* 歷代貢舉志 A history of civil service
   Feng Meng-chen 馮夢禎 1548-1595
4. *Hsüeh-cheng ch'üan-shu* 學政全書 Educational administration
   Compilation decreed by *Ch'ien-lung* in 1774
5. *Tsou-ting hsüeh-t'ang chang-ch'eng* 奏定學堂章程
   Chang Po-hsi 張百熙 1847-1907
   Chang Chih-tung 張之洞 1837-1909
   School regulations by Imperial authorization
6. *Chung-kuo chiao-yü shih* 中國教育史
   Huang Shao-chi 黃紹箕 1854-1908
   History of Chinese education

LITERATURE

1. *Wen-chang chih* 文章志 History of prose literature
   Chih Yü 執虞 fl.270-309
2. *Lieh-ch'ao shih-chi* 列朝詩集 Anthology of *Ming* verse
   Ch'ien Ch'ien-i 錢謙益 1582-1664
3. *Ku-wen yüeh-hsüan* 古文約選 Selected ancient essays
   Fang Pao 方苞 1668-1749
4. *Nü-shih shih-ch'ao* 女士詩鈔 Excerpts of poems by women
   Wu I-feng 吳翌鳳 1742-1819
5. *Kuo-ch'ao Chin-ling shih-ch'ao* 國朝金陵詩鈔
   Chu Hsü-tseng 朱緒曾 d. 1824
   Anthology of poems of the current dynasty
6. *Sung Yüan hsi-ch'ü shih* 宋元戲曲史
   Wang Kuo-wei 王國維 1877-1927
   History of *Sung* and *Yüan* dramatic literature

JURISPRUDENCE

1. *T'ang-lü shu-i* 唐律疏義 Annotations to the *T'ang* code
   Ch'ang-sun Wu-chi 長孫無忌 d. 689
2. *Chia-yu lü-ling* 嘉祐律令
   Chang Fang-p'ing 張方平 1007-1091
   Laws enacted during the *Chia-yu* period, 1056-1063
3. *Wen-hsing t'iao-li* 問刑條例 Criminal prosecution procedure
   P'eng Shao 彭韶 Minister of Justice, 1491-1493
4. *Hsi-yuan lu* 洗冤錄 (literally, 'washing away injustices record')
   Sung Tz'u 宋慈 fl. 1195-1225
   A history of the coroners' inquest
5. *Wu-shih-nien-lai Chung-kuo chih fa-lü* 五十年來中國之法律
   Chiang Yung 江庸 1887-
   Laws of China during a 50 year period (c. 1880-1930)

RELIGION

1. *Lieh-hsien chuan* 列仙傳 Biographies of Taoist divinities
   Liu Hsiang 劉向 80-9 B.C.
2. *Kao-seng chuan* 高僧傳 Biographies of famous monks
   Hui Chiao 慧皎 fl. 502-550
3. *Nan-hua-ching fa-yin* 南華經發隱
   Yang Wen-hui 楊文會 1837-1911
   Annotations to the *Nan-hua* Sutra of *Chuang Tzu* 莊子
4. *Mo-ni-chiao ju Chung-kuo k'ao* 摩尼教入中國考
   Ch'en Yüan 陳垣 1880-
   History of Monichæism in China

CALLIGRAPHY

1. *Fa-shu yao-lu* 法書要錄 Summary list of model calligraphy
   Chang Yen-yüan 張彥遠 fl. 870-880
2. *Shu-tuan* 書斷 A critique of types of calligraphy
   Chang Huai-kuan 張懷瓘 fl. 715-740

3. *Shu-shih* 書史 History of calligraphy
    Mi Fei 米芾 1051-1107
4. *Shu-fa ya-yen* 書法雅言 Fundamental technique of calligraphy
    Hsiang Mu 項穆 1570-1600, son of *Hsiang Yüan-pien* 項元汴
5. *Kuang i-chou-shuang-chi* 廣藝舟雙楫
    K'ang Yu-wei 康有爲 1858-1927
    An enlargement of *I-chou-shuang-chi* "Art-boat pair of oars", by *Pao Shih-ch'en* 包世臣 1775-1855, "two oars" being prose and calligraphy. *K'ang's* "enlargement" was on calligraphy.

ART OF PAINTING

1. *Ku-hua p'ing-lu* 古畫評錄 A critical list of ancient paintings
    Hsieh Ho 謝赫 fl. 479-501
2. *Hua-hsüeh pi-chüeh* 畫學秘訣 Fundamental painting technique
    Wang Wei 王維 699-759
3. *Li-tai ming-hua chi* 歷代名畫記 History of famous paintings
    Chang Yen-yüan 張彥遠 fl. 870-880
4. *Hsüan-ho hua-p'u* 宣和畫譜 *Hsüan-ho* painting catalog
    Author's name not given but carries a preface by Emperor *Hui-tsung*, one of whose reign titles was *Hsüan-ho* 1119-1225
5. *Shan-shui chüeh* 山水訣 Laws of landscape painting
    Huang Kung-wang 黃公望 1269-1354
6. *Kuo-ch'ao hua-cheng lu* 國朝畫徵錄 Early *Ch'ing* painters
    Chang Keng 張庚 1685-1760
7. *Chung-kuo hui-hua-shang-ti liu-fa lun* 中國繪畫上的六法論
    Liu Hai-su 劉海粟 1895-
    Six canons in the Chinese art of painting

MUSIC

1. *Chieh-ku lu* 羯鼓錄 Drums of *Chieh*, a barbarian tribe
    Nan Cho 南卓 Judicial Commissioner of *Kuei-chou* in 847
    History of both the drum and musical notes, often in sanscrit

2. *Ch'in-shih* 琴史 History of the lute
   Chu Ch'ang-wen 朱長文 1029-1098
3. *Yüeh-lü ch'üan-shu* 樂律全書 Musical measures complete book
   Chu Tsai-yü 朱載堉 fl. 1570-1620
4. *Yüeh-hsien k'ao* 樂縣考 Study of ancient musical instruments
   Chiang Fan 江藩 1761-1831
5. *Hsin shih-ko-chi* 新詩歌集 Songs from contemporary poems
   Chao Yüan-jen 趙元任 1892-

MILITARY

1. *Li-tai ping-chih* 歷代兵制 History of China's military system
   Ch'en Fu-liang 陳傅良 1141-1207
2. *Ma-cheng chi* 馬政紀 Management of military horses
   Yang Shih-ch'iao 楊時喬 fl. 1523-1555
3. *Sho-shu* 射書 History of archery
   Ku Yü 顧煜 fl. 1650-1670
4. *Li-tai chü-chan hsü-lüeh* 歷代車戰叙略 Chariot warfare history
   Chang T'ai-chiao 張泰交 *chin-shih* 1682, governor 1702-06
5. *Min-kuo chün-shih chin-chi* 民國軍事近紀
   Ting Wen-chiang 丁文江 1887-1936
   Recent history of military affairs of the Republic

POLITICAL PARTIES

1. *Ch'ing-yüan tang-chin* 慶元黨禁
   Ch'iao Sou 樵叟 c. 1200-1250
   Prohibition of political parties, 1195-1200
2. *Yüan-yu tang-jen-pei k'ao* 元祐黨人碑考
   Hai Jui 海瑞 1514-1587
   History of party members monument of the *Yüan-yu* period
3. *Tung-lin tien-chiang lu* 東林點將錄 *Tung-lin* party leaders
   Wang Shao-hui 王紹徽 fl. 1595-1625
   Modeled after the novel, *Shui-hu* 水滸, All Men are Brothers

TYPES OF SPECIALIZED HISTORIES

4. *Li-tai tang-cheng shih* 歷代黨爭史
   Wang T'ung-ling 王桐齡 1870-
   History of the struggles of political parties in China

FOREIGN RELATIONS

1. *San-ch'ao pei-meng hui-pien* 三朝北盟彙編
   Hsü Meng-hsin 徐夢莘 d. 1205
   Source materials of negotiations with the Northern Tatars (*Chin* 金) during the three reigns from 1101 to 1161
2. *Chao-hsien chi-shih* 朝鮮紀事 Chronological record of Korea
   Ni Ch'ien 倪謙 fl. 1436-1475
3. *Fan-pu yao-lüeh* 藩部要略 History of frontiers (Mongolia)
   Ch'i Yün-shih 祁韻士 1751-1815
4. *Keng-tzu hai-wai chi-shih* 庚子海外紀事
   Lü Hai-huan 呂海寰 1840-1927
   Chronology of the Boxer affairs as recorded from overseas

AGRICULTURE

1. *Nung-sang chi-yao* 農桑輯要
   Essentials of Agriculture and Silk Production
   Decreed by *Kublai Khan* in 1273
   Contains ten divisions: Regulations and instructions, tillage and colonization, seed-sowing, planting of mulberry-trees, rearing of silk-worms, fruits and nuts, bamboo and timber, medicinal herbs, and animal husbandry.
2. *Nung-cheng ch'üan-shu* 農政全書
   Hsü Kuang-ch'i 徐光啓 1562-1633
   Complete book on agricultural administration
3. *Shou-shih t'ung-k'ao* 授時通考
   General history of instruction on seasons and crops
   Decreed by *Ch'ien-lung* in 1737.
   78 *chüan,* divided into eight classifications: The climate, soils,

grain planting, application of labor, exhortation and encouragement, savings, subsidiary work, silk-worm raising.

4. *P'u-ts'un-ko nung-shu* 樸存閣農書 A treatise on agriculture
   Tso Tsung-t'ang 左宗棠 1812-1885
   P'u-ts'un, courtesy name of *Tso,* and his studio which was named *P'u-ts'un-ko,* meaning "Thrift Preservation Hall".

CURRENCY

1. *Ch'üan-shih* 泉史 History of currency
   Hung Tsun 洪遵 1120-1174
2. *Pao-ch'ao t'ung-k'ao* 寶鈔通考
   Wu Ch'i 武祺 middle of the 14th century
   Comprehensive history of paper currency
3. *Ming t'ung-pao i* 明通寶義 Analysis of *Ming* coinage
   Lo Ju-fang 羅汝芳 fl. 1550
4. *Ku-ch'uan hui* 古泉滙 General collection of ancient coins
   Li Tso-hsien 李佐賢, *chin-shih,* 1835, Prefect in *Fukien* 1846
5. *Tseng-kai tsui-chin Shang-hai chin-jung shih* 增改最近上海金融史 History of the *Shanghai* money market in recent times
   Hsü Chi-ch'ing 徐寄頤 1880-

INDUSTRY

1. *Tsao-chuan t'u-shuo* 造磚圖說
   Chang Wen-chih 張問之 fl. 1522-1550
   Illustrated history of the manufacture of bricks
2. *Ku-chin tao-chien lu* 古今刀劍錄 List of swords and daggers
   T'ao Hung-ching 陶宏景 452-536
3. *T'ao shuo* 陶說 Study of ceramics
   Chu Yen 朱琰 fl. 1760-1780
4. *Nan ch'uan chi* 南船紀
   Shen Chi 沈啓 fl. 1525-1565
   Narrative on the boats of the south

TYPES OF SPECIALIZED HISTORIES

5. *Ku-yü t'u-k'ao* 古玉圖考 Illustrated history of ancient jade
   Wu Ta-cheng 吳大澂 1835-1902
6. *Hsiu p'u* 繡譜 Patterns of embroidery
   Ch'en Ting-p'ei 陳丁佩 fl. 1800-1830
7. *Yü-shan p'u* 羽扇譜 History of feather fans
   Chang Yen-ch'ang 張燕昌 1738-1814
8. *Hu-ch'uan lu* 湖船錄 History of lake boats
   Li O 李鶚 1692-1752
9. *Ch'a ching* 茶經 Classic of tea
   Lu Yu 陸羽 d. 804
10. *Hsiang cheng* 香乘 A study of incense
    Chou Chia-chou 周嘉冑 Late *Ming* period
11. *Mo-chih* 墨志 History of ink
    Ma San-heng 麻三衡 fl. 1600-1646
12. *Yin-jen chuan* 印人傳 Biographies of famous seal engravers
    Chou Liang-kung 周良工 1612-1672
13. *Yü-shih* 語石 On stone
    Yeh Ch'ang-shih 葉昌熾 1849-1917
14. *T'ien-kung k'ai-wu* 天工開物 Exploiting natural resources
    Sung Ying-hsing 宋應星 fl. 1600-1650

CUSTOMS AND FOLKWAYS

1. *I-su chi* 夷俗記 Record of "barbarian" customs
   Hsiao Ta-heng 蕭大亨 fl. 1522-1566
2. *Shen-chou feng-t'u chi* 深州風土記 Folkways of *Shen-chou*
   Kung Ju-heng 弓汝恒 1842-1914
3. *Hsin-chiang li-su chih* 新疆禮俗志
   Wang Shu-nan 王樹楠 1851-1936
   Treatise on rites and customs of *Sinkiang*

MEDICINE

1. *Shang-han lun* 傷寒論 Dissertation on fevers

Chang Chi 張機 fl. 168-190
2. *Shih-ku* 釋骨 Explanations of human bones
   Shen T'ung 沈彤 fl. 1735-1775
3. *Nü-k'o* 女科 On gynecology
   Fu Shan 傅山 1607-1684
4. *Yen-ko-fang* 眼科方 Prescriptions for ophthalmology
   Yeh Kuei 葉桂 1666-1745
5. *I-tsung chin-chien* 醫宗金鑑 Golden mirror of medical works Decreed by *Ch'ien-lung* in 1749; 90 *chüan*, dealing with *Chang Chi's* medical works, prescriptions of famous physicians, on the pulse, treatment of bone and various other diseases

CONSTRUCTION

1. *Ying-tsao fa-shih* 營造法式 Method of architecture, pub. 1103
   Li Ch'eng 李誡 d. 1110
2. *Yüan-yeh* 園冶 Garden architecture
   Chi Ch'eng 計成 b. 1582
   A preface by *Juan Ta-ch'eng* 阮大誠 1587-1646, is dated 1634
3. *Kung-tuan ying-tsao lu* 工段營造錄
   Li Tou 李斗 latter half of the 18th century
   Survey of constructions of the Board of Public Works
   (*Li Tou's* famous work, *Yang-chou hua-fang lu* 楊州畫舫錄, Record of the prosperous conditions of *Yangchow*, (1736-1786), was printed in 1795.)
4. *Ch'ü-fu K'ung-miao-chih-chien-chu chi ch'i-hsiu-chi chi-hua*
   曲阜孔廟之建築及其修葺計劃
   Liang Ssu-ch'eng 梁思成 1901-
   Architecture of the Temple of Confucius, *Ch'ü-fu*, and plans for its restoration; in the Bulletin of the Society for Research in Chinese Architecture, Vol. VI, No. 1, September, 1935

本紀第一

翰林學士兼龍圖閣學士朝散大夫給事中判制誥充
史館脩撰判祕閣臣歐陽脩奉　敕撰

唐書

高祖神堯大聖大光孝皇帝諱淵字叔德姓李氏
隴西成紀人也其七世祖暠當晉末據秦涼以自
王是為涼武昭王暠生歆歆為沮渠蒙遜所滅歆
生重耳魏弘農太守重耳生熙金門鎮將戍武
川因留家焉熙生天賜天賜生虎西魏時
賜姓大野氏官至太尉與李弼等八人佐周代魏
有功皆為柱國號八柱國家周閔帝受魏禪虎已

A page from a *Sung* edition of the *T'ang-shu* (p. 192)

Portrait of *Ou-yang Hsiu* (p. 164)

Chapter VI

TERMS DENOTING TYPES OF HISTORICAL WRITINGS

The difficulty of mastering Chinese characters lies in the highly diversified meanings they have accumulated in their long history and in the multiplicity of characters used to express similar meanings. As an aid to Sinologists, we have therefore selected, chiefly from the title of works of historians of the modern period of China, 242 terms denoting types of historical writings; some of which may be identified by several different terms. Each Chinese term is given with literal translation. On the next line is the Chinese title containing the term and the English translation of the title, in which the term may be translated by an expression differing somewhat from the literal translation. These illustrations of the diverse meanings of a given character, or term, will give the student a familiarity with an aspect of the language that is difficult for Western scholars.

An 案 A record, a case or a draft
    Ming-shih an 明史案 A draft history of the *Ming* dynasty
        Huang Tsung-hsi 黃宗羲 1610-1695

Cha-chi 札記 Simplified notes
    Shuo-fang pei-sheng cha-chi 朔方備乘札記 Annotations to a work on northern frontiers
        Li Wen-t'ien 李文田 1834-1895

Cha-chi 劄記 Classified notes
    Nien-erh shih cha-chi 廿二史劄記 Notes on the 22 histories
        Chao I 趙翼 1727-1814

Chan-yen 詹言 Basic word
    Chao-mei chan-yen 昭昧詹言 A critique on poetry
        Fang Tung-shu 方東樹 1772-1851

Ch'ang-pien 長編 Comprehensive compilation
    Ch'ung-chen ch'ang-pien 崇禎長編 Reign data of 1628-1644
        Wan Yen 萬言 1637-1705

Ch'ao-lüeh 鈔略 Copied essentials
    Ming-shih ch'ao-lüeh 明史鈔略 Exerpts from *Ming* History
        Lü Pao-chung 呂葆中 died about 1708

Che-chung 折中 Eclectic view
    Miao-chih che-chung 廟制折中 An eclectic view of the Institute of Temples
        Mao Ch'i-ling 毛奇齡 1623-1716

Cheh-yao 摘要 Selected essentials
    Ho-fang cheh-yao 河防摘要 Essentials of flood control
        Ch'en Huang 陳潢 d. ca. 1688

Chen-wei 甄微 Investigating the subtle
    Liu-li chen-wei 六歷甄微 Research on ancient calendars
        Sun I-jang 孫詒讓 1848-1908

Cheng-i 正義 Rectified meanings
    Chou-i cheng-i 周易正義 Annotations to Classic of Changes
        Hui Tung 惠棟 1697-1758

Cheng-hsin-lu 徵信錄 Verified record
    Ting-chia cheng-hsin-lu 鼎甲徵信錄 A verified record of top candidates in the civil service examinations
        Yen Hsiang-hui 閻湘蕙 compiler; revised by *Chang Ch'un-ling* 張椿齡, in 1866

Cheng-lüeh 徵畧 Testimonial sketches
    Kuo-ch'ao shih-jen cheng-lüeh 國朝詩人徵畧 Biographical sketches of poets of the current dynasty
        Chang Wei-p'ing 張維屏 1780-1859

Chi 記 Record
    Meng-ku yu-mu chi 蒙古遊牧記 Topography of Mongolia
        Chang Mu 張穆 1805-1849

Chi 集 A collection
    Chi-chai wen-chi 緝齋文集 Collectanea of *Ts'ai's* prose work
      Ts'ai Hsin 蔡新 1707-1800?

Chi-ch'eng 集成 Collection complete
    Ku-chin t'u-shu chi-ch'eng 古今圖書集成 A synthesis of books and illustrations ancient and modern (1st edition, 5050 vols.)
      Ch'en Meng-lei 陳夢雷 b. 1651

Chi-ch'eng 紀程 Narrative journey
    Hsi-cheng chi-ch'eng 西征紀程 An expedition to the West
      Tsou Han-hsün 鄒漢勳 1805-1854

Chi-chu 輯注 Gathered explanations
    T'ao Yüan-ming chi chi-chu 陶淵明集輯注 Annotations to the writings of *T'ao* (365-427)
      T'ao Shu 陶澍 1779-1839

Chi-i 稽疑 Investigating the doubtful
    Han-shu ti-li chih chi-i 漢書地理稽疑 Studies on the geographical treatise in the *Han-shu*
      Ch'üan Tsu-wang 全祖望 1705-1755

Chi-lan 集覽 Collected views
    Hsi-hu chi-lan 西湖集覽 Views of the West Lake
      Ting Ping 丁丙 1832-1899

Chi-shih 紀事 Chronology of events
    Fu-sho chi-shih 復社紀事 Events of the *Fu-sho* political club
      Wu Wei-yeh 吳偉業 1609-1672

Chi-yao 輯要 Collected essentials
    Chin-tai Chung-kuo wai-chiao shih-liao chi-yao 近代中國外交史料輯要 History of foreign relations of modern China
      Chiang T'ing-fu 蔣廷黻 1895-

Chia-p'u 家譜 Family record
    Wan-shih chia-p'u 萬氏家譜 Genealogy of the *Wan* family
      Wan Ssu-ta 萬斯大 1633-1683

Chiang-i 講義 Explaining the meaning
    Hsi-ming chiang-i 西銘講義 Lectures on "curing the stupid"
        Lo Tso-nan 羅澤南 1808-1856

Chiao-pu 校補 Critically examined and supplemented
    Ch'ün-shu chiao-pu 群書校補 Criticism of 35 rare editions
        Lu Hsin-yüan 陸心源 1834-1894

Chiao-ting 校訂 Re-examining and editing
    Tuan-shih shuo-wen chiao-ting 段氏說文校訂 Supplement to *Tuan's Shuo-wen*
        Niu Shu-yü 鈕樹玉 1760-1827

Chieh 解 Interpretation
    Chuang-tzu chieh 莊子解 An interpretation of *Chuang-tzu*
        Wang Fu-chih 王夫之 1619-1692

Chieh-ku 解詁 Analysis of old sayings
    Ch'un-ch'iu ming-tzu chieh-ku 春秋名字解詁 Analysis of the personal names of the 'Spring and Autumn' period 722-481 B.C.
        Wang Fu-chih 王夫之 1619-1692

Chieh-shuo 解說 Analytical discourse
    Yüeh-pen chieh-shuo 樂本解說 Analytical discourse on music
        Mao Ch'i-ling 毛奇齡 1623-1716

Chieh-yao 節要 Simple essentials
    T'ang Ch'ien-an wen-chi chieh-yao 湯潛庵文集節要 Simplified version of the prose collection of *T'ang Pin* 湯斌
        P'eng Ting-ch'iu 彭定求 1645-1719

Chieh-yao 解要 Exposition of the essentials
    Pen-ts'ao ching chieh-yao 本草經解要 Exposition of the essentials of the fundamental herbal classic
        Yeh Kuei 葉桂 1666-1745

Chien-shih 簡史 Brief history
    Chung-kuo ch'u-pan-chieh chien-shih 中國出版簡史 A brief history of Chinese publishing enterprises
        Yang Shou-ch'ing 楊壽清 contemporary

TERMS OF HISTORICAL WRITINGS

Chien-ts'un kao 檢存稿 Selected and preserved draft
   Hu-pei t'ung-chih chien-ts'un kao 湖北通志檢存稿 Preserved manuscript of the General Gazetteer of *Hupeh*
      Chang Hsüeh-ch'eng 章學誠 1738-1801
Chih-chang 指掌 Pointing at the palm of the hand (a clear view)
   Yü-t'u chih-chang 輿圖指掌 Map of China clearly exhibited
      Wang Yüan 王源 1648-1710
Chih-i 志疑 Noting the doubtful
   Shih-chi chih-i 史記志疑 Historical Memoirs recorded doubts
      Liang Yü-sheng 梁玉繩 1745-1819
Chih-nan 指南 Magnetic needle pointing south (a guide)
   Hsia-hsüeh chih-nan 下學指南 A guide to human studies
      Ku Yen-wu 顧炎武 1613-1682
Chih-yen 卮言 Casual word
   Ching-hsüeh chih-yen 經學卮言 Remarks on classical studies
      K'ung Kuang-sen 孔廣森 1752-1786
Chin-chien 金鑑 Golden mirror (excellent guide)
   Hsing-shui chin-chien 行水金鑑 A guide to river systems
      Li Shih-hsü 李世序 1773-1824
Ching-hsüan 精選 Careful selection
   Ku-ch'üan ching-hsüan 古泉精選 Old coins careful selection
      Wang I-jung 王懿榮 1845-1900
Ching-yen 精言 Crystalized treatment
   Shu-fa ching-yen 書法精言 On calligraphy
      Wang Hsi-hou 王錫侯 1713-1777
Chiu-miu 糾謬 Correcting errors
   Tu-shih chiu-miu 讀史糾謬 Corrections of dynastic histories
      Niu Yün-chen 牛運震 1706-1758
Ch'ou-pi 籌筆 Planned brush strokes (record)
   Chin-yao ch'ou-pi 金軺籌筆 An account of conferences and negotiations between China and Russia in 1880-81
      Tseng Chi-tse 曾紀澤 1839-1890

Chu 注 Commentary
    Shui-ching chu 水經注 Commentary on the Water Classic
        Li Tao-yüan 酈道元 d. 527
Chu-chieh 注解 Commentary and explanations
    Tu-shih chu-chieh 杜詩注解 Explanations of *Tu Fu's* poems
        Ku K'uei-kuang 顧奎光 1719-1764
Ch'u-chieh 初階 First steps
    Hsi-suan ch'u-chieh 西算初階 Primer of Western mathematics
        Hua Hung-fang 華蘅芳 1833-1902
Ch'u-i 芻議 General proposals
    Ch'ou-yang ch'u-i 籌洋芻議 A discourse on foreign affairs
        Hsüeh Fu-ch'eng 薛福成 1838-1894
Chü-li 舉例 Classified examples
    Ch'i-wen chü-li 契文舉例 Classified studies of inscriptions
        Sun I-jang 孫詒讓 1848-1908
Chu-lu 著錄 List of publications
    Hsiao-shih-fan t'ing chu-lu 小石帆亭著錄 Works on poetry by *Wang Shih-chen* 王士禎 1634-1711
        Weng Fang-kang 翁方綱 1733-1818
Chü-yü 舉隅 Explaining the important angle
    Chung-kuo k'o-hsüeh-shih chü-yü 中國科學史舉隅 A new angle on the history of Chinese science
        Chang Meng-wen 張孟聞 contemporary
Ch'üan-chi 全集 Complete collected works
    Tseng-wen cheng-kung ch'üan-chi 曾文正公全集 Collectanea of *Tseng Kuo-fan's* writings
        Tseng Kuo-fan 曾國藩 1811-1872
Ch'üan-shu 全書 Complete books
    Ssu-k'u ch'üan-shu 四庫全書 Complete library in four classes of literature
        Chi Yün 紀昀 1724-1805; *Lu Hsi-hsiung* 1734-1792, editors

TERMS OF HISTORICAL WRITINGS

Chüeh 訣 Secret
    Hsien-cheng tu-shu chüeh 先正讀書訣 Method of study of the ancients
        Chou Yung-nien 周永年 1730-1791

Chui-yen 綴言 Additional notes
    Tung-hua lu chui-yen 東華錄綴言 Appendix to the archival records
        I-keng 奕賡 ca. 1810-1870

Ch'un-ch'iu 春秋 Spring-autumn (life or history)
    Yen-tzu ch'un-ch'iu 燕子春秋 An account of swallows
        Hao I-hsing 郝懿行 1757-1825

Chun-sheng 準繩 Rules for accuracy
    Ch'iang-fa chun-sheng 鎗法準繩 Guide to the use of firearms
        Wu Ta-cheng 吳大澂 1835-1902

Fa-t'ieh 法帖 Model calligraphy
    Yün-ch'ing-kuan fa-t'ieh 筠淸舘法帖 Stone monument rubbings
        Wu Jung-kuang 吳榮光 1773-1843

Fang-lüeh 方略 Policy and strategy
    P'ing-ting shuo-mo fang-lüeh 平定朔漠方略 History of the campaign against the Eleuths
        Chang Yü-shu 張玉書 1642-1711

Fu-lu 附錄 Additional notes
    Ching-k'ao fu-lu 經考附錄 Notes on the study of the classics
        Tai Chen 戴震 1724-1777

Ho 覈 Verified
    Ssu-shu tien-ku ho 四書典故覈 Annotations to the Four Books
        Liu Wen-ch'i 劉汶淇 1789-1856

Ho-pi 合璧 Matching pair (jade objects)
    Ch'in-p'u ho-pi 琴譜合璧 Joint text (Chinese-Manchu) on the music of the lute
        Ho-su 和素 1652-1718

Hsiao-chi 小記 Short treatise
    Feng-ya hsiao-chi 蜂衙小記 A short treatise on bees
      Hao I-hsing 郝懿行 1757-1825

Hsiao-chih 小志 Short history
    Nei-ko hsiao-chih 內閣小志 Short history of the *Nei-ko*
      Yeh Feng-mao 葉鳳毛 1709-1781

Hsiao-kao 小稿 Short account
    Lü-hsing hsiao-kao 旅行小稿 Short account of travels
      Ch'ien I-chi 錢儀吉 1783-1850

Hsiao-shih 小史 Small history
    Chung-kuo suan-hsüeh hsiao-shih 中國算學小史 A short history of Chinese mathematics
      Li Yen 李儼 20th century

Hou-yü 後語 Appended words
    Mo-tzu chien-ku hou-yü 墨子間詁後語 Appendix to the commentary on *Motze*
      Sun I-jang 孫詒讓 1848-1908

Hsiang-chieh 像解 Illustrated explanations
    Sheng-yü hsiang-chieh 聖諭像解 A pictorial Holy Edict
      Liang Yen-nien 梁延年 magistrate 1673-1681

Hsien-chieh 閒詰 Recreational inquiry
    Yung-lu hsien-chieh 廬甬間詰 A study of snuff and snuff-bottles
      Chao Chih-ch'ien 趙之謙 1824-1884

Hsien-hua 間話 Leisurely chats
    Lao-yü hsien-hua 老漁間話 The old fisherman's chats
      Chang Wei-p'ing 張維屏 1780-1859

Hsin-pien 新編 New edition
    Yüan-shih hsin-pien 元史新編 A new revision of the *Yüan* dynasty history
      Wei Yüan 魏源 1794-1856

Hsin-yen 心言 The heart speaks
    Ku-yü hsin-yen 古愚心言 Collection of official correspondence
        P'eng P'eng 彭鵬 1637-1704

Hsing-ts'un-lu 幸存錄 Fortunately preserved records
    Hsing-ts'un-lu 幸存錄 Records of a political party
        Hsia Yun-i 夏允彝 1596-1645

Hsüeh-an 學案 Sources of learning
    Ming-ju hsüeh-an 明儒學案 History of *Ming* philosophies
        Huang Tsung-hsi 黃宗羲 1610-1695

Hsün-tsan 訓纂 Verified edition
    Shan-hai-ching hsün-tsan 山海經訓纂 Annotations to the classic of mountains and waterways
        Hui Tung 惠棟 1697-1758

Hui-ch'ien 會箋 Comprehensive compilation
    Yü-kung hui-ch'ien 禹貢會箋 Notes on the *Yü-kung*
        Hsü Wen-ching 徐文靖 1667-1756

Hui-han 彙函 Classified compilation
    Ku-ching-chieh hui-han 古經解彙函 Annotations to the classics
        Ch'en Li 陳澧 1810-1882

Hui-k'ao 彙考 Classified treatises
    Wu-fu i-t'ung hui-k'ao 五服異同彙考 Collected treatises on mourning rituals
        Ts'ui Shu 崔述 1740-1816

Hui-kuan 彙觀 Classified examples
    Mo-yüan hui-kuan 墨緣彙觀 Annotated catalog of examples of paintings and calligraphy
        An Chi 安岐 b. 1683

I-cheng 義正 Meanings verified
    Ch'ün-ching i-cheng 群經義正 Commentary on the meanings of the classics
        Wang Nien-sun 王念孫 1744-1832

I-chi 遺集 Bequeathed collection
    Chang-wen-ta-kung i-chi 張文達公遺集 Collected works of
    Chang Chih-wan 張之萬 1811-1897

I-kao 遺稿 Bequeathed manuscripts
    T'ung-ku shu-t'ang i-kao 銅鼓書堂遺稿 Writings of *Ch'a Li*
    Ch'a Li 查禮 1715-1783

I-nien-lu 疑年錄 Doubtful year record
    I-nien-lu 疑年錄 A record of uncertain dates
    Ch'ien Ta-hsin 錢大昕 1728-1804

I-shih 遺事 Remaining events
    Sheng-ch'ao i-shih 勝朝遺事 Defeated dynasty remaining events
    Wu Mi-kuang 吳彌光 1789-1871

I-shih 逸史 Scattered history
    Nan-chiang i-shih 南疆逸史 History of the Southern *Ming*
    Wen Jui-lin 溫睿臨 *chu-jen,* 1705

I-shu 遺書 Bequeathed books (literary remains)
    Lu-tzu i-shu 陸子遺書 Publications of *Lu-tzu*
    Shen Chin-ssu 沈近思 1671-1728

I-shu 翼疏 Extended explanations
    Ch'un-ch'iu Tso-chuan i-shu 春秋左傳翼疏 Annotations to the
    Ch'un-ch'iu Tso-chuan
    Ch'eng Chin-fang 程晉芳 1718-1784

I-t'ung 異同 Differences and similarities (a comparative study)
    Ching-tzu i-t'ung 經字異同 Characters of the classics compared
    Chang Wei-p'ing 張維屏 1780-1859

I-wen 遺文 Bequeathed prose work
    Wei-hsi i-wen 位西遺文 Prose work of *Shao I-ch'en*
    Shao I-ch'en 邵懿辰 1810-1861

I-wen 佚聞 Pleasant memories
    Ssu-ch'ao i-wen 四朝佚聞 Pleasant stories of the four reigns
    Chin Liang 金梁 contemporary

Jih-ch'ao 日鈔 Daily notes
    Chu-tzu yü jih-ch'ao 朱子語日鈔 Notes on sayings of *Chu Hsi*
      Ch'en Li 陳澧 1810-1882

Jih-chi 日記 Daily record (diary)
    Shih Ta-k'ai jih-chi 石達開日記 Dairy of *Shih Ta-k'ai*
      Shih Ta-k'ai 石達開 1821-1863

Ju-men 入門 Entering gate (introduction)
    Ching-hsüeh ju-men 經學入門 Introduction to classical studies
      Chiang Fan 江藩 1761-1831

Kai-lun 概論 General discussion
    Ch'ing-tai hsüeh-shu kai-lun 清代學術概論 An introduction to the learning of the *Ch'ing* period
      Liang Ch'i-ch'ao 梁啓超 1873-1929

K'ai-meng 開蒙 Removing obscurity
    Hsiao-hsüeh k'ai-meng 小學開蒙 Introduction to elementary education
      Tseng Ching 曾靖 1679-1736

K'an-wu 刊誤 Printing errors
    Su-shu k'an-wu 俗書刊誤 Common errors in characters
      Chiao Hung 焦竑 1541-1620

K'ao 考 Investigation (historical survey)
    Ta-ming shui-tao k'ao 大名水道考 History of river control at *Ta-ming* (in *Hopei* province)
      Ts'ui Shu 崔述 1740-1816

K'ao-i 考異 Examining discrepancies
    Kuo-shih k'ao-i 國史考異 Discrepancies in national history
      P'an Sheng-chang 潘檉章 1626-1663

Kou-ch'en 鉤沉 Rescue the lost
    Ku-ching chieh kou-ch'en 古經解鉤沉 Fragments of commentaries on the classics
      Yü Hsiao-k'o 余蕭客 1729-1777

Kuan-chien 管見 Viewing through a tube (narrow vision)
  I-li kuan-chien 儀禮管見 Personal view of the Classic of Rites
    Chu Yin-liang 褚寅亮 1715-1790
Kuang-chi 廣記 Extensive notes
  I kuang-chi 易廣記 Annotations to the Classic of Changes
    Chiao Hsün 焦循 1763-1820
Kuang-chu 廣註 Extensive notes
  Shan-hai-ching kuang-chu 山海經廣註 Extensive notes on the Mountains and Waterways Classic
    Wu Jen-ch'en 吳任臣 ca. 1628-1689
Kuang-yao 廣要 Elaborating essentials
  Mao-shih Lu-shu kuang-yao 毛詩陸疏廣要 Elaboration of Lu-chi's commentary on *Mao-shih*
    Mao Chin 毛晉 1599-1659
Kuei-fan 規範 Principles and models
  Lan-t'ai kuei-fan 蘭台規範 Collection of model prescriptions
    Hsü Ta-ch'un 徐大椿 1693-1771
Kung-an 公案 Judicial cases
  Shih kung-an 施公案 Judge *Shih's* famous cases
    Shih Shih-lun 施世綸 1659-1722
Kung-tu 公牘 Official correspondence
  Fu-wu kung-tu 撫吳公牘 Official papers during governorship at *Kiangsu*
    Ting Jih-ch'ang 丁日昌 1823-1882
Lei-han 類函 Book of classified knowledge
  Yüan-chien lei-han 淵鑑類函 Classified encyclopedia
    Wang Shih-chen 王士禎 1634-1711, editor
Lei-kao 類稿 Classified manuscript
  Wei-ching-wo lei-kao 味經窩類稿 Literary works of *Ch'in Hui-t'ien*
    Ch'in Hui-t'ien 秦蕙田 1702-1764

TERMS OF HISTORICAL WRITINGS 89

Lei-pien 類編 Classified collectanea
   Yüan-shih lei-pien 元史類編 Collectanea on *Yüan* history
     Shao Yüan-p'ing 邵遠平 *chin-shih*, 1669

Lei-tsuan 類纂 Classified compilation
   Pei-yang kung-tu lei-tsuan 北洋公牘類纂 Classified official correspondence from North China between 1894 and 1907
     Yüan Shih-k'ai 袁世凱 1859-1916

Li-an 例案 Precedents
   Ming-shih li-an 明史例案 *Ming* history precedents
     Liu Ch'eng-kan 劉承幹 fl. 1880-1936

Lüeh 略 or 畧 Projects; strategies
   Chih-p'ing lüeh 治平略 Principles of peace and security
     Shao T'ing-ts'ai 邵廷采 1648-1711

Lüeh-chi 畧記 Brief account
   Weng-shih chia-shih lüeh-chi 翁氏家事畧記 An account of the *Weng* family
     Weng Fang-kang 翁方綱 1733-1818

Lun 論 Discussion
   Ku-shih p'ing-tso lun 古詩平仄論 Discourse on rythm in ancient poetry
     Wang Shih-chen 王士禎 1634-1711

Man-kao 漫稿 Spontaneous notes
   Yün-ch'uang man-kao 雲窗漫稿 *Lo's* miscellaneous notes
     Lo Chen-yü 羅振玉 1866-1940

Man-pi 漫筆 Free brush (in painting)
   Yü-ch'uang man-pi 雨窗漫筆 Ten rules of painting
     Wang Yüan-ch'i 王源祁 1642-1715

Mu 目 List
   T'ao-chai ts'ang-shih mu 陶齋藏石目 Catalog of *Tuan Fang's* collection of inscriptions from stone monuments
     Tuan Fang 端芳 1861-1911

Mu-lu 目錄 Item record; catalog
 Ch'ung-pien Ning-po Fan-shih tien-i-ko t'u-shu mu-lu 重編寧波范氏天一圖書目錄 The *Fan* family library catalog, 1930
Nei-p'ien 內篇 Basic edition
 Kuan-ts'un wen-ch'ao nei-p'ien 管村文鈔內篇 Original edition of the prose works of *Wan Yen*
  Wan Yen 萬言 1637-1705
Nien-p'u 年譜 Yearly biographical record
 Ting wen-ch'eng kung nien-p'u 丁文成公年譜 Chronological biography of *Ting Pao-chen* 丁寶楨 1820-1886
  T'ang Chiung 唐烱 1829-1909
Ou-pi 偶筆 Occasionally brushed (written)
 Yün-lang ou-pi 筠廊偶筆 Miscellaneous writings of *Sung Lo*
  Sung Lo 宋犖 1634-1713
Ou-p'ing 偶評 Occasional criticism
 Tu-shih ou-p'ing 杜詩偶評 Critical notes on *Tu Fu's* poems
  Shen Te-ch'ien 沈德潛 1673-1769
Ou-shih 偶識 Occasional notations
 Tu-shu ou-shih 讀書偶識 Occasional notes from reading
  Tsou Han-hsün 鄒漢勳 1805-1854
Ou-tan 偶談 Occasional remarks
 Ch'ih-pei ou-tan 池北偶談 Travel in *Ch'ih-chou, Anhui*
  Wang Shih-chen 王士禎 1634-1711
Ou-ts'un 偶存 Duplicate filed
 Tien-tu ou-ts'un 滇牘偶存 Official correspondence in *Yünnan*
  Ho Shao-chi 何紹基 1799-1873
Ou-wen 偶聞 Occasionally heard
 K'o-she ou-wen 客舍偶聞 Learned during a stay in *Peking*
  P'eng Sun-i 彭孫貽 1615-1673
P'ang-cheng 旁證 Extended evidence
 Wen-hsüan p'ang-cheng 文選旁證 Further studies of prose
  Liang Chang-chü 梁章鉅 1775-1849

Pao-fa 寶筏 Precious raft
    Sheng-p'ing pao-fa 昇平寶筏 Precious peace vessel (a play)
       Chang Chao 張照 1691-1745

Pei-sheng 備乘 Ready conveyance
    Shuo-fang pei-sheng 朔方備乘 An historical source book of the Northern Regions
       Ho Ch'ang-ling 何長齡 1785-1848

Pen-cheng 本證 Root evidences
    Yüan-shih pen-cheng 元史本證 Yüan history basic evidence
       Wang Tsu-hui 汪祖輝 1731-1807

Pen-mo 本末 Roots and branches
    Ming-shih chi-shih pen-mo 明史紀事本末 Narrative *Ming* history
       Ku Ying-t'ai 谷應泰 died after 1689

Pi-chi 筆記 Brush record
    Po-t'ang tu-shu pi-chi 柏堂讀書筆記 Notes from studies at the Cedar Hall (exegetical notes)
       Fang Tsung-ch'eng 方宗誠 1818-1888

Pi-chi 祕笈 Rare books
    Pao-yen-t'ang pi-chi 寶顏堂祕笈 Rarities in *Pao-yen* Library
       Ch'en Chi-ju 陳繼儒 1558-1669

Piao 表 Table
    Ch'un-ch'iu ta-shih piao 春秋大事表 Table of important events in the Spring and Autumn Annals
       Ku Tung-kao 顧棟高 1679-1759

Peih-lu 別錄 Additional notes
    I-i pei-lu 易義別錄 Added notes on the Classic of Changes
       Chang Hui-yen 張惠言 1761-1802

Pien 辨 To discriminate
    Hsüeh-pien 學辨 On knowledge
       Chang Erh-chi 張爾岐 1612-1678

Pien-fei 辨非 Distinguishing the wrong
    Chou-kuan pien-fei 周宮辨非 Mistakes in the *Chou* institutes
        Wan Ssu-ta 萬斯大 1633-1683

Pien-huo 辨惑 Distinguishing the doubtful
    I-hsüeh pien-huo 易學辨惑 Discussion of the doubtful in the philosophy of changes
        Huang Tsung-hsi 黃宗羲 1610-1695

Pien-i 辨疑 Explaining the doubtful
    Han-shu pien-i 漢書辨疑 Critical annotations to the *Han-shu*
        Ch'ien Ta-chao 錢大昭 1744-1813

Pien-o 辨訛 Distinguishing mistakes
    Jung-ts'un tzu-hua pien-o 榕村字畫辨訛 A list of characters written in mistaken forms
        Li Kuang-ti 李光地 1642-1673

P'ing-i 平議 Critical discussion
    Chu-tzu p'ing-i 諸子平議 Critical notes on ancient philosophers
        Yü Yüeh 俞樾 1821-1907

P'ing-yü 評語 Critical statements
    T'ung-chien p'ing-yü 通鑑評語 Comments on the Comprehensive Mirror
        Shen Han-yü 申涵煜 1628-1694

Pu 補 Supplement
    Ch'a-shih pu 茶史補 Supplement to the History of Tea
        Yü Huai 余懷 1616-1696

P'u 譜 A treatise or list
    Yang-chü p'u 洋菊譜 A treatise on foreign chrysanthemums
        Tsou I-kuei 鄒一桂 1686-1772

Pu-cheng 補正 Supplemented and corrected
    Tsao-ch'iang hsien-chih pu-cheng 棗強縣志補正 Revision of the *Tsao-ch'iang* county gazetteers
        Fang Tsung-ch'eng 方宗誠 1818-1888

Pu-chih 補志 Supplementary treatise
   Nan-pei-shih pu-chih 南北史補志 Supplement to the Southern and Northern histories
      Wang Shih-to 汪士鐸 1802-1889

Pu-chu 補注 Supplementary annotations
   Tso-chuan pu-chu 左傳補注 Annotations to *Tso's* commentary
      Shen Ch'in-han 沈欽韓 1775-1832

Pu-i 補遺 Restoring omissions
   Chiang-chai wen-chi pu-i 薑齋文集補遺 Supplement to the collected works of *Wang Fu-chih*
      Wang Fu-chih 王夫之 1619-1692

Shang-chüeh 商榷 Discussion and evaluation
   Shih-ch'i shih shang-chüeh 十七史商榷 A critical study of the 17 Dynastic Histories
      Wang Ming-sheng 王鳴盛 1722-1798

Shang-tui 商兌 Consultation
   Han-hsüeh shang-tui 漢學商兌 Discussions of *Han* learning
      Fang Tung-shu 方東樹 1772-1851

Shen-lun 申論 Extensive discussion
   Fang-ch'eng shen-lun 方程申論 Discussion of mathematics
      Ch'en Shih-kuan 陳世倌 1680-1758

Sheng-i 賸義 Added meanings
   Chou-i chi-chieh sheng-i 周易集解賸義 Notes on the *Chou-i*
      Li Fu-sun 李富孫 1764-1843

Sheng-kao 賸稿 Additional notes
   I-man an sheng-kao 憶漫庵賸稿 Literary notes of *Yü Chi*
      Yü Chi 余集 1739-1823

Shih-i 拾遺 Restoring the lost
   Chou-i shih-i 周易拾遺 Study notes on the philosophy of the Book of Changes
      Hsü Wen-ching 徐文靖 1667- after 1756

Shih-i 釋義 Meaning explained
    Su-wen shih-i 素問釋義 Notes on an ancient medical work
      Chang Ch'i 張琦 1765-1833

Shih-kai 史概 History in general
    Huang-Ming shih-kai 皇明史概 General *Ming* history
      Chu Kuo-chen 朱國楨 1557-1632

Shih-li 釋例 Explaining precedents
    Li-ching shih-li 禮經釋例 Precedents on the Classic of Rites
      Ling T'ing-k'an 凌廷堪 1757-1809

Shih-liao 史料 History materials
    Chung-wai chiao-t'ung shih-liao 中外交通史料 Source materials for the history of Chinese foreign relations
      Chang Hsing-lang 張星烺 1887-

Shih-lu 實錄 Veritable records
    Jen-tsung shih-lu 仁宗實錄 Records of the reign of *Jen-tsung*
      Wang Yin-chih 王引之 1766-1834

Shih-lüeh 事畧 Outline of events
    Hsi-ch'ui tsung-t'ung shih-lüeh 西陲總統事畧 Accounts of administration in the western frontiers
      Ch'i Yün-shih 祁韻士 1751-1815; *Hsü Sung* 徐松 1781-1848

Shih-lüeh 識畧 General knowledge
    Hsin-kiang shih-lüeh 新疆識畧 Local history of *Sinkiang*
      Begun by *Wang T'ing-k'ai* 汪廷楷 between 1802 and 1809; continued by *Ch'i Yün-shih* 祁韻士 1751-1815; completed by *Hsü Sung* 徐松 1781-1848

Shih-piao 史表 Historical tables
    Li-tai shih-piao 歷代史表 Topical arrangement of events
      Wan Ssu-t'ung 萬斯同 1638-1702

Shih-pu 拾補 Gathered supplements
    Ch'ün-shu shih-pu 群書拾補 Notes on 38 literary works
      Lu Wen-ch'ao 陸文超 1717-1796

Shih-ti 釋地 Explanations of geographical terms
    Ssu-shu shih-ti 四書釋地 Place names in the Four Books
        Yen Jo-chü 閻若璩 1636-1704

Shih-tz'u 釋詞 Explanations of words and phrases
    Ching-chuan shih-tz'u 經傳釋詞 Philological explanations of terms in the classics and commentaries
        Wang Yin-chih 王引之 1766-1834

Shou-cha 手札 Personal letters
    Weng Sung-ch'an shou-cha 翁松禪手札 Collection of Weng's correspondence
        Weng T'ung-ho 翁同龢 1830-1904

Shu-cheng 疏正 Explanation and rectification
    Meng-tzu tzu-i shu-cheng 孟子字義疏正 Annotations to the works of Mencius
        Tai Chen 戴震 1724-1777

Shu-cheng 疏證 Critical comments
    Han-shu shu-cheng 漢書疏證 Analysis of the *Han-shu*
        Shen Ch'in-han 沈欽韓 1775-1832

Shu-hou 書後 Notes and comments
    Tu Ching-chiao-pei shu-hou 讀景教碑書後 A note on the Nestorian monument
        Li Chih-tsao 李之藻 d. 1630

Shu-lu 書錄 Book records
    Hsi-pao hsüan shu-lu 惜抱軒書錄 Bibliography of old books
        Yao Nai 姚鼐 1732-1815

Shu-mu 書目 Book list
    Shui-hsi shu-wu shu-mu 水西書屋書目 Catalog of a library
        Chou Yung-nien 周永年 1730-1791

Shu-wen 書問 Written inquiries
    Yu-p'eng shu-wen 友朋書問 Letters from friends
        Lu Hsin-yüan 陸心源 1834-1894

Shu-wen 述聞 Relating acquired knowledge
    Ching-i shu-wen 經義述聞 Philological notes on the meaning of the classics
        Wang Yin-chih 王引之 1766-1834

So-chi 瑣記 Fragmentary notes
    Kuei-t'ien so-chi 歸田瑣記 Studies during retirement
        Liang Chang-chü 梁章鉅 1775-1849

So-i 瑣憶 Minor reflections
    Wei-lu so-i 圍爐瑣憶 Notes from the fireside
        Hsieh Chang-t'ing 謝章鋌 1820-1903

So-yin 索隱 Explaining the obscure
    Shih-chi so-yin 史記索隱 Hidden meanings in the Historical Memoirs explained
        Ssu-ma Chen 司馬貞 8th century

So-yü 瑣語 Minor statements
    Sung so-yü 宋瑣語 Notes on the *Sung* dynasty history
        Hao I-hsing 郝懿行 1757-1825

Sui-pi 隨筆 Guided by the brush
    Ku-chung sui-pi 菰中隨筆 Miscellaneous notes
        Ku Yen-wu 顧炎武 1613-1682

Sui-yü 脺語 Finished notes
    Shih-shuo sui-yü 詩說脺語 Notes on literary criticism
        Shen Te-ch'ien 沈德潛 1673-1769

Ta-chih 大旨 Great objectives
    Tui-i ta-chih 讀易大旨 Fundamentals for the study of the Classic of Changes
        Sun Ch'i-feng 孫奇逢 1585-1675

Ta-ch'üan 大全 Most complete
    Ssu-shu ta-ch'üan 四書大全 Complete edition of the *Ssu-shu*, the Four Books with annotations
        Tai Ming-shih 戴明世 1653-1713

Ta-i 大義 Great significance
    Ch'un-ch'iu Tso-shih-chuan ta-i 春秋左氏傳大義 The significance of *Tso's* Commentary on the *Ch'un-ch'iu*
      Liu Yü-sung 劉毓崧 1818-1867

Ta-wen 答問 Answers and questions
    Ching-shih ta-wen 經史答問 Dialogue on classics and histories
      Ch'üan Tsu-wang 全祖望 1705-1755

Tai-ting-lu 待定錄 Unevaluated notes
    Tai-ting-lu 待定錄 Notes on classical and philosophical topics
      Fang Tung-shu 方東樹 1772-1851

T'an-yüan 探源 Searching for sources
    Shih-chi t'an-yüan 史記探源 Searching for the sources of the *Shih-chi*
      Ts'ui Shu 崔述 1740-1816

Tao-ch'ing 道情 Expressed feeling
    Hui-hsi tao-ch'ing 洄溪道情 Poems in folksong style
      Hsü Ta-ch'un 徐大椿 1693-1771

T'ao-yüan 討原 Expedition to the sources
    Hsüeh-chin t'ao-yüan 學津討原 Sources of streams of learning
      Chang Hai-p'eng 張海鵬 1755-1816

T'i-pa 題跋 Comments at the beginning and the end
    Pan-t'an-chai t'i-pa 半氈齋題跋 Bibliographical and epigraphical notes
      Chiang Fan 江藩 1761-1831

T'i-pi 題壁 Writing on the wall
    Su Pao-chi t'i-pi 宿寶鷄題壁 Record of famine at *Pao-chi*
      Chang Wen-t'ao 張問陶 1764-1814

T'i-yao 提要 Singling out the most essential
    K'ao-hsin-lu t'i-yao 考信錄提要 A summary of seven verified records
      Ts'ui Shu 崔述 1740-1816

T'iao-chi 條記 Itemized notes
    Tu kang-mu t'iao-chi 讀綱目條記 Notes on the Mirror of History
        Li Chao-lo 李兆洛 1769-1841

Tien-ku 典故 Canons of old
    Huang-ch'ao tz'u-lin tien-ku 皇朝詞林典故 Compendium on the *Hanlin* Academy
        Wang Yin-chih 王引之 1766-1834

Ting-pen 定本 Concluded edition
    Yang-cheng shu-wu ch'üan-chi ting-pen 養正書屋全集定本 Final edition of the collected literary works of *Min-ning*
        Min-ning 旻寧 1782-1850

Ting-pu 訂補 Edited supplements
    Shih-chi ting-pu 史記訂補 Supplements to the *Shih-chi*
        Li Li 李笠 20th century

Tsa-ch'ao 雜鈔 Miscellaneous notes
    Te-shu-lou tsa-ch'ao 德樹樓雜鈔 Notes from life-long studies
        Ch'a Shen-hsing 查慎行 1650-1727

Tsa-chih 雜誌 Miscellaneous notes
    Tu-shu tsa-chih 讀書雜誌 Miscl. notes on research studies
        Wang Nien-sun 王念孫 1744-1832

Tsa-chu 雜箸 Miscellaneous writings
    Mei-chuang tsa-chu 梅莊雜箸 Miscellaneous writings from the Village of the Plum Tree
        Hsieh Chi-shih 謝濟世 1689-1756

Tsa-p'ei 雜佩 Miscellaneous gems
    Ch'iu-yüan tsa-p'ei 秋園雜佩 Subjects from Autumn Garden
        Ch'en Chen-hui 陳貞慧 1605-1656

Tsai-pi 載筆 Carrying the brush (notes and memoranda)
    Huai-t'ing tsai-pi 槐庭載筆 Notes from Locust-tree Courtyard
        Fa Shih-shan 法式善 1753-1813

TERMS OF HISTORICAL WRITINGS

Ts'o-yao 撮要 Gathered essentials
    Sheng-wu-chi ts'o-yao 聖武記撮要 An abridged history of His Majesty's military operations
        Wei Yüan 魏源 1794-1856

Tsou-shu 奏疏 Memorial draft
    Sung-pi tsou-shu 松璧奏疏 Memorial of "Pine Jade"
        Kuo Hsiu 郭琇 1617-1684

Tsou-tu 奏牘 Memorials and reports
    Yü-shan tsou-tu 于山奏牘 Memorials and reports of *Yü*
        Yü Ch'eng-lung 于成龍 1617-1684

Tsuan-ku 纂詁 Edited and explained
    Ching-chi tsuan-ku 經籍纂詁 Dictionary of the classics
        Juan Yüan 阮元 1764-1849

Ts'un-chen 存眞 Preserved authentically
    Yeh-an ts'un-chen 葉案存眞 Authentic prescriptions of *Yeh*
        Yeh Kuei 葉桂 1666-1745

Ts'un-mu 存目 Preserved list
    Han-shih ts'un-mu 漢石存目 List of *Han* stone inscriptions
        Wang I-jung 王懿榮 1845-1900

Tsung 綜 Anthology
    Ming-shih tsung 明詩綜 Anthology of *Ming* poets
        Chu I-tsun 朱彝尊 1629-1709

Ts'ung-ch'ao 叢鈔 Miscellaneous notes
    Shu-ku ts'ung-ch'ao 述古叢鈔 Notes on the ancients
        Kuo Shang-hsien 郭尚先 1785-1833

Ts'ung-k'ao 叢考 Miscellaneous research studies
    Kai-yü ts'ung-k'ao 陔餘叢考 Notes of investigation
        Chao I 趙翼 1727-1814

Ts'ung-k'o 叢刻 Published collectanea
    Cheng-chüeh-lou ts'ung-k'o 正覺樓叢刻 A literary collectanea
        Hsü Ta-ch'un 徐大椿 1693-1771

Tsung-li 綜例 Comprehensive examples
    Chin-shih tsung-li 金石綜例 Epigraphy on metal and stone
    Feng Teug-fu 馮登府 1783-1841

Ts'ung-shu 叢書 Collectanea of books
    Ssu-ming ts'ung-shu 四明叢書 A collectanea from *Ningpo*
    Chang Huang-yen 張煌言 1620-1664

Ts'ung-t'an 叢談 Various chats
    Wei che ts'ung-t'an 尾蔗叢談 Short stories
    Li T'iao-yüan 李調元 1734-1803

T'u-chih 圖志 Maps and gazetteers
    Ch'in-ting Huang-yü hsi-yü t'u-chih 欽定皇輿西域圖志
    Official work on Chinese Turkestan (1756-1782)
    Fu Heng 傅恒 d. 1770

T'u-shuo 圖說 Maps and explanations
    Kuang-tung t'u-shuo 廣東圖說 Topography of *Kuangtung*
      Tsou Po-ch'i 鄒伯奇 1819-1869 and *Chao Ch'i-ying* 趙齊嬰
    1826-1865 maps, *Kuei Wen-ts'an* 桂文燦 1823-1884 expositor

T'ung-chien 通檢 Comprehensive critique
    Shang-shu t'ung-chien 尚書通檢 A critical examination of the Classic of History
    Ku Chieh-kang 顧頡剛 1893-

T'ung-chu 通注 Comprehensive commentary
    I-ching t'ung-chu 易經通注 Commentary on the *I-ching*
    Fu I-chien 傅以漸 1609-1665

T'ung-i 通義 General significance
    Han-ju t'ung-i 漢儒通義 *Han* philosophical writings
    Ch'en Li 陳澧 1810-1882

T'ung-k'ao 通考 Comprehensive history
    Hsü Wen-hsien-t'ung-k'ao 續文獻通考 Supplement to the cultural encyclopedia
    Ch'i Chao-nan 齊召南 1706-1768 compiler

T'ung-kuei 通軌 Universal orbits
    Shu-hsüeh t'ung-kuei 數學通軌 General mathematical rules
        K'o Shang-ch'ien 柯尚遷 fl. 1536-1566

T'ung-shih 通史 General history
    Ch'ing-tai t'ung-shih 清代通史 *Ch'ing* period general history
        Hsiao I-shan 蕭一山 1902-

T'ung-yen 通言 General introduction
    Tu-i t'ung-yen 讀易通言 On the study of the *I-ching*
        Wang Yüan 王源 1648-1710

Wai-chi 外紀 External or additional notes
    Tung-shan wai-chi 東山外紀 Notes on the Eastern Hills
        Ch'a Chi-tsuo 查繼佐 1601-1676

Wai-kao 外稿 Additional manuscripts
    P'u-shu-t'ing chi wai-kao 曝書亭外稿 Additional writings in prose and verse
        Chu I-tsung 朱彝尊 1629-1709

Wei-ch'eng-kao 未成稿 Incomplete draft
    Hu-pei t'ung-chih wei-ch'eng-kao 湖北通志未成稿 Fragments of the manuscript for the *Hupeh* Gazetteer
        Chang Hsüeh-ch'eng 章學誠 1738-1801

Wei-ting-kao 未定稿 Unedited manuscript
    Chan-yüan wei-ting-kao 湛園未定稿 Collected essays
        Chiang Ch'en-ying 姜宸英 1628-1699

Wen-ch'ao 文鈔 Prose exerpts
    Chung-shan wen-ch'ao 中山文鈔 Prose works of *Hao Yü*
        Hao Yü 郝浴 1623-1683

Wen-hsien 文獻 Cultural contributions
    Sung-ling wen-hsien 松陵文獻 Biographical sketches of famous persons in *Sung-ling*
        P'an Ch'eng-chang 潘檉章 1626-1663

Wen-hui 文滙 Prose collectanea
    Lu-chiang Ch'ien-shih wen-hui 廬江錢氏文滙 Collectanea of prose works of the *Ch'ien* family
        Ch'ien I-chi 錢儀吉 1783-1850

Wen-kao 文稿 Prose manuscripts
    Tung-ch'ien wen-kao 東潛文稿 Articles in prose
        Chao I-ch'ing 趙一淸 ca. 1710-1764

Wen-nan 問難 Inquiring into difficult questions
    Mao-shih wen-nan 毛詩問難 An inquiry into the problems regarding *Mao-shih*
        Ma Kuo-han 馬國翰 1794-1857

Wen-ts'ui 文粹 Literary excellence
    Yang-chou wen-ts'ui 揚州文粹 Anthology of literary works of *Yangchow*
        Chiao Hsün 焦循 1763-1820

Wen-ts'un 文存 Prose work preserved
    Ch'eng-huai-yüan wen-ts'un 澄懷園文存 Collected works in prose of the "Pure Heart Garden"
        Chang T'ing-yü 張廷玉 1672-1755

Yao-i 要義 Fundamental meaning
    Ou-mei cheng-chih yao-i 毆美政治要義 The fundamentals of European and American politics
        Tuan Fang 端芳 1861-1911

Yao-lan 要覽 Basic view
    Yü-t'u yao-lan 輿圖要覽 Essential collection of atlases
        Ku Tsu-yü 顧祖禹 1631-1692

Yao-lu 籥錄 Basic records
    I-yü yao-lu 易餘籥錄 Basic passages from the *I-ching*
        Chiao Hsün 焦循 1763-1820

Yao-lüeh 要略 Essential account
    Hsi-ch'ui yao-lüeh 西陲要略 Outline history of *Sinkiang*
        Ch'i Yün-shih 祁韻士 1751-1815

Yao-yen 要言 Urgent words
   Hsing-shih yao-yen 醒世要言 Urgent exhortation to awaken the world
      Ho-su 和素 1652-1718

Yao-yen 藥言 Healing word
   Tso-chih yao-yen 佐治藥言 Indispensable guide to political administration
      Wang Hui-tsu 汪輝祖 1731-1807

Yen-chiu 研究 Research
   Li-tai t'un-k'en yen-chiu 歷代屯墾研究 A study of frontier colonization throughout the dynasties
      T'ang Ch'i-yu 唐啓宇 contemporary

Yin-te 引得 Index
   San-shih-san chung ch'ing-tai chuan-chi yin-te 三十三種淸代傳記引得 Union Index of 33 Biographies of the *Ch'ing* period
      Harvard-Yenching Institute, Sinological Index, Series 9, Peiping, 1932

Yü-shuo 隅說 Illustrative discourse
   Yen-fa yü-shuo 鹽法隅說 On salt administration
      Sun K'uo-t'u 孫擴圖 1717-1787

Yüan-chien 淵鑑 Source mirror
   Ku-wen yüan-chien 古文淵鑑 Annotated anthology of ancient essays
      Hsü Ch'ien-hsüeh 徐乾學 1631-1694

Yüeh-fu 樂府 Music palace (store of musical literature)
   Ming yüeh-fu 明樂府 Collection of *Ming* musical compositions
      Wan Ssu-t'ung 萬斯同 1638-1702

Portrait of *Hung Liang-chi* (p. 130)

Chapter VII

SOME DESCRIPTIVE TERMS IN CHINESE HISTORIES

The terms in chapter VI indicate types of historical writings, different in scope, in emphasis, and in subject matter. In this chapter the terms are those frequently employed by writers in all types of histories. The criteria for selection of these terms are their frequent use, the significance of the meaning they convey, and the difficulty they present to the Western scholar.

TERMS OF HISTORICAL AND RELATED STUDIES

Chan-ch'i	展期	Extending time; postponement
Ch'an-lin	禪林	Buddhist temples
Chan-wang	瞻望	Watching but not advancing
Ch'an-yen	讒言	Whispering criticism of others
Ch'ang-chien	長箋	Determination of the most authentic version after comparative criticism
Ch'ang ch'üeh	猖獗	Ravaging disturbance
Chang-ku	掌故	Record of past events
Ch'ao-pen	抄本	Hand copied edition
Chao-ling	詔令	General term for all forms of imperial decrees
Chao-shih	肇始	Marking the beginning
Chao-shu	詔書	Command from the emperor to the people
Chao-ya	爪牙	Claws and teeth; agents of defense
Cheng-cha	爭扎	Struggle for supremacy
Ch'eng-chi	乘機	To embrace an opportunity
Ch'eng-chiao	呈繳	To proffer
Cheng-ch'uan	爭權	Struggle for power
Ch'eng-ho	呈核	To submit for perusal
Cheng-hsiung	爭雄	Struggle for supremacy
Cheng-li	爭立	Struggle for succession to the throne

Ch'eng-li 成立		Complete establishment; inauguration
Ch'eng-se 成色		Quality of things
Ch'eng-shih 乘時		To embrace an opportunity
Ch'eng-yü 成語		Established words; familiar quotations
Ch'i-chia 起家		Raising the family status
Chi-chung 集中		Gathered to the center; concentration
Ch'i-i 起義		To start a revolution
Chi-lü 紀律		Written rules; discipline
Chi-pi 積弊		Accumulation of evils
Chia-p'u 家譜		Family record; genealogical record
Chia-se 稼穡		Agricultural affairs
Chia-chao 矯詔		A forged edict
Chiao-ch'eng 交呈		To submit to a superior
Chiao-ch'üeh 交卸		To resign
Chiao-k'an 校勘		Comparative criticism to establish authenticity
Chiao-tai 交代		To hand over things to one's successor
Chiao-t'i 交替		Exchange or replacement
Chiao-tien 交點		Point of intersection
Chiao-tien 焦點		Focal point
Chiao-tzu 交子		Means of exchange; first paper currency under government administration (1023 A.D.) after private issuance failed
Chieh-chü 結局		Conclusion
Chieh-sheng 結繩		To tie knots in a rope; recorded events
Ch'ien-chü 前車		The cart ahead; warning from others' experience
Ch'ien-hsü 遣戍		Sent to guard frontiers; banishment
Ch'ien-k'un 乾坤		The universe
Ch'ien-lung 潛龍		Hidden dragon; retreat for a better opportunity
Chien-pen 監本		Publications by the *Kuo-tzu-chien* (National Academy)
Chien-sho 建設		Establishment or construction
Ch'ien-sheng 千乘		A thousand chariots; status of a feudal kingdom

Chien-tieh	間諜	A spy
Chien-tieh	簡牒	A memorandum
Chien-wei	僭位	Usurpation
Chien-yen	踐言	To carry out one's word
Chien-yüeh	僭越	To go beyond what is lawful
Chih-chiao	至交	Very intimate friends
Chih-ling	指令	Order in response to inquiries from inferior offices
Chih-ming	誌銘	To carve an inscription on stone
Chih-wu	支吾	Confused
Chih-yüan	紙鳶	Paper hawk; a kite
Chin-chi	緊急	Emergency
Chin-chung	禁中	Forbidden Center, or residence of the emperor
Chin-kuo	巾幗	Literally, head ornaments of women; women
Ch'in-ming	欽命	By imperial order
Chin-pu	進步	Advancing steps; progress
Chin-shih	近勢	Recent tendencies
Ch'in-ting	欽定	Published after imperial approval
Chin-ts'ui	盡瘁	To serve to the end
Ching-chi	經紀	A broker
Ch'ing-i	清議	Public opinion
Ching-kuo	經過	That which has transpired
Ch'ing-liu	清流	Clear stream; persons of high character seeking neither power nor wealth
Ching-tien	經典	Classical allusions
Ching-ying	經營	Planning and building
Chiu-ching	究竟	Exhaustive effort
Ch'iu-hsin	秋汛	Autumn overflow; The Yellow River rises during autumn
Ch'iung-t'u	窮途	End of the road; blind alley
Ch'ou-hsiang	抽象	Abstraction
Ch'ou-jen	疇人	Family-specialized work in succession; applied to mathematicians and astronomers

Chü-chia	舉家	The whole family
Chu-ch'ih	住持	Head priest
Chü-i	舉義	To uphold righteousness; revolution
Chu-kuan	主觀	Subjective view
Ch'u-pan	初版	First edition
Chü-pen	局本	Edition from official publication bureau
Chü-pien	遽變	Dramatic change; sudden change
Ch'u-p'in	處貧	To be in poverty
Ch'u-shen	出身	Qualification
Chü-shih	舉世	The whole world
Ch'u-shih	處士	A private gentleman
Ch'ü-t'i	取締	To repress
Ch'uan-chi	傳奇	A story book
Chuan-chih	專制	Dictatorial administration
Ch'üan-chin	勸進	Urging an advance (to the throne)
Ch'üan-chü	全局	General situation
Ch'uan-ming	傳名	To become famous
Ch'uan-p'iao	串票	Tax receipt
Ch'üan-pien	權變	Acting according to circumstances
Ch'uan-wen	傳聞	Hearsay
Chuang-p'iao	莊票	Local banknotes
Ch'üeh-hsia	闕下	At the foot of the Palaces; the Capital
Chüeh-pan-pen	絕版本	Out of print
Chüeh-pen	絕本	The only copy extant
Chüeh-tui	絕對	Absolute
Chüeh-wang	絕望	End of hope; hopeless
Chüeh-wu	覺悟	Realization
Chui-feng	追封	To catch up with honors due; posthumous honors
Ch'un-feng	春風	Spring breeze; influence of education on life
Chung-chih	終制	To go through the period of mourning
Chung-ching	衷情	Inner emotions; the feelings
Ch'ung-chiu	重九	Double-nine, festival of the 9th day of 9th moon

Chung-ch'ü 衷曲	Inner tune; the mind
Chung-chü 終局	Conclusion
Chung-hsing 中興	Midway rejuvenation; decline arrested and new vigorous progress made
Chung-huai 衷懷	Inner bosom; the heart
Chung-liu 中流	Middle class
Chung-shen 終身	Throughout one's life
Chung-tsai 冢宰	The prime minister
Erh-mu 耳目	Ears and eyes; watchfulness
Fa-chia 法家	Law experts; legalists and political economists
Fa-hsiang 發祥	Source of fortune; birthplace of the founder of a dynasty
Fa-hsien 發現	To burst into view; discover
Fa-piao 發表	To reveal or announce
Fa-ta 發達	Development
Fan-an 翻案	Reversal of original judicial judgment
Fan-ch'ih 繁殖	Prolific growth suggesting increase in prosperity
Fan-lan 氾濫	Flood; deluge
Fan-so 煩瑣	Troubled by petty cares
Fang-chen 方針	Direction-pointing needle; policy
Fang-hsiang 方向	Tending toward
Fang-jen 放任	Noninterference; laissez faire
Fang-k'an-pen 坊刊本	Ordinary or popular edition
Fei-fu 肺腹	Literally "lungs and abdomen," meaning sincerest friendship
Fen-fan 紛繁	Prolific
Fen-fei 分肥	To divide the spoils
Fen-fen 紛紛	Diverse; confused
Fen-jao 紛擾	Disturbed condition
Fen-yun 紛紜	Disturbance
Feng-ch'i 蜂起	Bees swarming; multiple uprisings
Feng-chien 封建	Feudal establishment

Feng-kuang	風光	Breeze and light; scenic **grandeur**
Feng-liu	風流	Carefree floating; romantic
Feng-shan	封禪	Sacrifice to heaven and earth; state sacrifice
Fu-hsin	腹心	Abdomen and heart; trustworthy officials; friends to be counted upon
Fu-mo	覆沒	Sunk; lost
Fu-tzu	付梓	To be sent to press
Fu-yun	浮雲	Floating cloud; a temporary thing
Fu-yung	附庸	Vassal states
Han-chan	酣戰	Bitter fighting
Han-hsüeh	漢學	*Han*-learning; emphasis upon textual criticism
Han-men	寒門	Poor homes
Han-mo	翰墨	Literature
Hao-chao	號招	Calling the masses to follow a slogan
Heng-hsing	橫行	Sidewise walking; to force one's way
Ho-pi	合璧	A good pair
Ho-t'i	劾題	Preliminary inquiry
Ho-tsou	劾奏	To accuse in a memorial
Hsi-wang	希望	Hope
Hsia-fan	下凡	Incarnation
Hsia-kuan	夏官	"Summer" minister; defense minister
Hsia-hsüan	下絃	Last quarter of the moon
Hsiang-ying	響應	Sound-echo; response
Hsiao-jao	削弱	Weakened by territorial losses
Hsiao-t'iao	蕭條	Desolate; poverty stricken
Hsieh-pen	寫本	Edition copied by hand
Hsien-ching	陷阱	A trap
Hsien-ling	憲令	Basic laws
Hsien-shu	憲書	An official calendar
Hsin-shih	信史	Authenticated history
Hsing-chuang	行狀	Obituary; also known as *Hsing-shu* 行述
Hsing-fei	興廢	Rise and fall

Hsing-kung 行宮	Temporary palaces
Hsing-sheng 行省	Territory of political administration; provinces
Hsing-shu 行書	Running-hand style of hand-writing
Hsü-mou 蓄謀	To continue secret plotting
Hsü-nien 蓄念	Thoughts harbored
Hsü-yü 須臾	A single moment
Hsüan hsüeh 玄學	Metaphysical learning, pertaining to Taoism
Hsüan-wo 漩渦	Whirlpool; great turmoil
Hsüeh-p'ai 學派	Schools of thought
Hsüeh-t'ien 學田	Public land for the support of schools
Hsüeh-wen 學問	Learning to make inquiry; knowledge
Hsün-ling 訓令	Order from superior office
Hsün-wei 遜位	Abdication
Hu-i 狐疑	Suspicious; as a fox
Hu-k'ou 糊口	Subsistence
Hu-lo 胡虜	Barbarian from the North
Hua-chi 滑稽	Humorous
Huang-chiao 黃教	Yellow-robe Lamaism
Huang-k'ao 皇考	A deceased father
Huang-pi 皇妣	A deceased mother
Hui-fu 恢復	Restored
Hui-hao 揮毫	Wave the brush; to write or paint
Hui-huo 揮霍	To spend money freely
Hung-pen 紅本	Red-copy; memorials approved and marked with comments written in vermillion ink
Huo-p'iao 火票	Fire warrant; mounted couriers carrying imperial orders to provinces
Huo-tung 活動	Activities
I-chih 異志	A desire to rebel
I-ch'uan 驛傳	To send by couriers
I-feng 遺風	Bequeathed spirit; tradition in the good sense
I-fu 義父	Godfather

I-hsüeh	義學	A free school
I-i	異議	Objections
I-lao	遺老	Elder statesmen
I-nien	異年	Next year
I-shih	逸士	Righteous scholar; giving for a public cause
I-shuo	異說	Heterodox theories
I-tu	義渡	A free ferry
I-tuan	異端	Heterodox
Jan-chih	染指	To dye one's finger; to "chisel in" on a deal
Juan-hua	輭化	To become softened; to be conciliatory
K'ai-hsüan	凱旋	Victorious return
Kai-k'uang	概況	General condition or appearance
Kai-tsu	改組	To change the structure of an organization
Kan-hsüan	斡旋	To mediate; to use good offices
Kan-k'ai	感慨	Inwardly moved; indignant
K'an-pen	刊本	Published editions
Kao-ming	誥命	Imperial decree of honors
Keng-tieh	更迭	Replacements
Ko-ai	割愛	To part with a beloved object
K'o-chi	克己	Victory over oneself; self denial
K'o-chia	客家	Guest families; the *Hakka* tribes
Ko-chü	割據	Political and territorial rivalries among states
Ko-jang	割讓	Cession of territory
K'o-kuan	客觀	Objective view
Kou-hsin	搆釁	To stir up a quarrel
Kou-nan	搆難	To create problems or trouble
Ku-chu	孤注	The last chip
K'u-hai	苦海	The miserable world
Ku-tung	骨董	Antiques
Ku-yü	故雨	Familiar rain; old friends
Kua-fen	瓜分	Melon divided; partition of a country
Kuan-chien	關鍵	Crucial point; turning point

DESCRIPTIVE TERMS 113

Kuan-chin	關津	Gateway and ford; strategic points of land and water
Kuan-chin	關禁	Embargo
Kuan-pan	官版	Published by official bureaus
Kuan-pen	官本	Government printing bureau editions
Kuang-lan	狂瀾	Mad deluge; ravaging disturbance in the country
Kuei-hua	歸化	Surrender to civilization; frontiers brought to submission
Kuei-i	皈依	Converted to a religious faith
K'uei-san	潰散	Dispersed
Kuei-t'ien	歸田	To retire from official life
Kuei-yüeh	規約	Regulations adopted by common consent
K'un-chung	昆仲	Brothers
Kung-ch'en	功臣	Officials of great merit
K'ung-ch'ien	空前	Unprecedented
Kung-t'ien	公田	Public land
Kung-wen	公文	Document on official affairs
Lai-li	來歷	Antecedent; background
Lan-pen	藍本	Primary sources for documents or books
Lan-yü	濫竽	Pretender in an orchestra of *Yü*; lacking sufficient knowledge to hold a position
Lang-pei	狼狽	Wolf and jerboa; evil conspirators
Lei-shih	累世	Successive generations
Lei-shu	類書	Reference books arranged by topics
Lei-ssu	耒耜	Farming implements
Leng-yen	冷眼	To appear indifferent
Leng-yü	冷語	Ironical remarks
Li-chin	例禁	Prohibited by law
Liao-yuan	燎原	Fire in the wilderness; revolt quickly spreading
Ling-hsiu	領袖	Collars and sleeves; leadership
Ling-i	凌夷	To fall into decay
Ling-jo	凌弱	To oppress the weak

Ling-yün 凌雲	Reaching to the clouds; pre-eminent
Liu-yen 流言	Floating words; gossip
Lu-lu 錄錄 or 鹿鹿	The common herd; ordinary
Lung-t'i 隆替	Ascendancy and decline
Lung-tuan 壟斷	To monopolize profit by reason of high position
Mang-ts'ung 盲從	Blind adherence
Mao-ming 冒名	A forged name
Men-hu 門戶	Social status; partisan
Meng-chu 盟主	Chief of a league of kingdoms
Meng-fu 盟府	Oath palace; where a league of states makes pledges of peace
Meng-ya 萌芽	Smallest bud; the beginning
Ming-fu 冥府	Hades
Ming-mai 命脈	Pulse of life; important
Na-chien 納諫	To accept criticism
Nan-mien 南面	Facing south (throne); the ruler
Nei-luan 內亂	Civil wars
Nei-t'ang 內帑	Imperial treasury
Nei-ying 內應	Traitors
Nung-chang 弄璋	Playing with jade; birth of a boy
Nung-wa 弄瓦	Playing with tile; birth of a girl
Pa-hu 跋扈	Tyrannical control
Pa-tao 霸道	Reign by force rather than by law or virtue
Pan-pen 版本	Block edition; impressions from wood blocks
Pao-fu 抱負	Working toward the realization of an ideal
P'ao-ying 泡影	Bubble and shadow; disappearing quickly
Pei-yüeh 背約	To break a treaty or a contract
Pen-chi 本紀	Annals of emperors
Pen-tsou 奔走	Working hard for a good cause
P'eng-chang 澎漲	Swollen river; economic inflation
P'eng-tang 朋黨	Associations for a common cause
P'i-lu 披露	To announce

DESCRIPTIVE TERMS 115

P'i-shih	避世	To retire from the world
P'i-t'ai	胚胎	Embryonic beginning
Pieh-chi	別集	Collected works of one individual
Pieh-chuan	別傳	Supplements to existing biography
Pieh-shu	別墅	A villa
Pien-ch'ien	變遷	Change and move; changes
Pien-t'ung	變通	Accommodating
Pin-jeng	頻仍	Unchanged; repetition
P'ing-tse	平仄	Stressed and unstressed words in poetry
Ping-t'un	并吞	Annexation
P'o-chu	破竹	To split bamboo; easily achieved
Po-hsing	勃興	Sudden rise to power
Po-hsing	百姓	100 surnames; the people
Pu-jih	不日	Before long
Shan-huo	扇惑	To agitate
Shan-nen	山門	Mountain gate; outer gate of a Buddhist temple
She-cheng	攝政	The regency
Shen-yüan	伸冤	To redress a wrong
Sheng-chih	聖旨	Holy edict
Sheng-mo	繩墨	Inked line; to determine a straight line
Shih-chi	世紀	A century
Shih-chia	世家	Kings and feudal lords
Shih-chiao	世交	Friendship for many generations
Shih-ching	石經	Classics engraved on stone
Shih-fa	諡法	Rules for posthumous honors
Shih-hsi	世襲	Hereditary
Shih-hsi	世系	Genealogy
Shih-pen	石本	Editions from stone inscriptions
Shih-pien	事變	Incident; emergency
Shih-shih	矢誓	To take an oath
Shou-shan	首善	Chief good; national capital
Shu-li	署理	To hold an acting appointment

Shu-niu	樞杻	Hinge of door and handle of seal; vital points
Shu-sheng	書生	Book person; scholar
Shu-shu	術數	Magical calculations
Shuang-yüeh	爽約	To fail to keep a promise
So-shih	瑣事	A trifling affair
So-wen	瑣聞	Rumor
Su-p'in	素貧	In a chronic state of poverty
Tang-chin	蕩盡	Exhausted by wastefulness
Tao-hsüan	倒懸	Hanging upside down; great suffering
T'ao-t'ai	淘汰	Natural selection; to weed out
Tao-t'ung	道統	The Way's succession or continuity
Ti-kuan	地官	Minister of the earth; in charge of education
Tiao-lo	凋落	To wither and fall; condition of decline
Tieh-ch'i	迭起	To rise again repeatedly
Tien-fu	顛覆	Having tumbled down; chaotic condition
Tien-hsing	典型	A prototype
Tien-pen	殿本	Palace edition
Tien-shih	典史	A district police officer
Ting-chien	丁艱	In mourning for parents
Ting-li	鼎立	To stand like a tripod; rival kingdoms in a state of balance of power
Ting-pen	定本	Edition after final judgment and publication
Ting-shui	丁稅	Poll tax
Ting-yu	丁憂	In mourning for parents
Ts'ai-ch'e	裁撤	Abolished
Tsai-pan	再版	Second edition
Ts'ai-tzu	才子	Talented persons
Ts'an-chü	慘劇	Tragedy
Ts'an-k'ao	參考	Comparative investigation; references
Ts'an-shih	蠶食	Eaten by silkworms; gradual annexation
Ts'ao-an	草案	Draft; unpromulgated regulations
Ts'ao-tsung	操縱	Ability to control affairs

DESCRIPTIVE TERMS

Ts'ao-yün	漕運	Water transportation of grains
Tse-jen	責任	Responsibilities
Ts'e-shih	策士	Scholar of strategy; state planning politician
Tso-yu	左右	Left and right; assistants
Tsou-i	奏議	Memorials of proposed projects
Tsou-shu	奏書	Memorials; also known as *Tsou-chang* 奏章
Ts'u-chin	促進	Promoting
Ts'u-jan	卒然	All at once
Tsui-chuang	罪狀	Statement of circumstances of a crime
Tsung-chi	踪跡	Footprint; evidence
Tsung-ch'iu	縱囚	Release of prisoners
Tsung-pien	總編	General compilation
T'u-ch'eng	屠城	Sack of a city and murder of its people
Tuan-ch'ang	斷腸	Heartbroken
Tuan-tai	斷代	Separated by periods; dynastically
Tui-shih	對峙	Stalemated rivals
T'un-t'ien	屯田	Garrison troops working on a farm
Tung-chi	動機	Motives
T'ung-keng	同庚	Same age
T'ung-liao	同僚	Fellow worker; colleague
T'ung-shih	通事	Interpreter
T'ung-yin	同寅	Fellow officials
Tzu-ch'eng	咨呈	A communication between equals
Tzu-fu	資斧	Traveling expenses
Tzu-heng	恣橫	Perverse and unrestrained
Tzu-hsü	自序	Author's own preface
Tzu-shou	自首	To surrender voluntarily
Tzu-wang	資望	Highly regarded reputation
Tzu-wen	咨文	Official despatch between equals
Wa-chieh	瓦解	Crumbled tiles; collapsed
Wai-ch'i	外戚	External relations; relatives of an empress
Wang-tao	王道	Way of the Ideal Ruler, by law and moral ideals

Wang-yen 妄言		Careless remarks; ignorant use of words
Wei-chi 危機		Danger and opportunity; crisis
Wei-ching 偽經		Spurious classics
Wei-pen 偽本		Forgery of the original edition
Wei-shu 偽書		Unaccepted interpretation of the classics
Wen-ching 問津		Inquiry for a ferry; asking for guidance
Wen-tsui 問罪		To send a military expedition to a neighboring state to "investigate" a crime; attempt to justify the attacking state
Wen-jang 醞釀		Fomenting trouble
Wu-wei 無爲		Do nothing; doctrine of inaction
Wu-wei 無謂		Nothing said; meaningless
Ya-hang 牙行		Guild of middlemen
Ya-shui 牙稅		Taxes collected from middlemen
Yao-hai 要害		Vital or strategic
Yao-ling 要領		Essential parts; crux of a matter
Yen-ch'uan 眼穿		Piercing eyes; intense expectation
Yen-i 演義		Story
Yen-i 演繹		Deduction
Yen-jen 閹人		Attendants in the palace; eunuchs
Yen-ko 沿革		The old and its change; successive changes
Yen-kuan 言官		The official who speaks; the censor
Yen-shih 厭世		Pessimistic
Yin-mou 陰謀		Secret plotting; conspiracy
Yü-nien 餘年		Remaining years; old age
Yu-shui 遊說		Roving politicians attempting to persuade a ruler
Yü-yen 寓言		Hidden words; fables
Yüan-chi 圓寂		The death of a priest
Yüan-yüan 淵源		Source of great rivers; sources
Yüeh-fa 法約		Provisional law
Yün-han 雲漢		The Milky Way
Yung-yen 庸言		Eternal words; words of great significance

A document concerning the Veritable Records (p. 8)

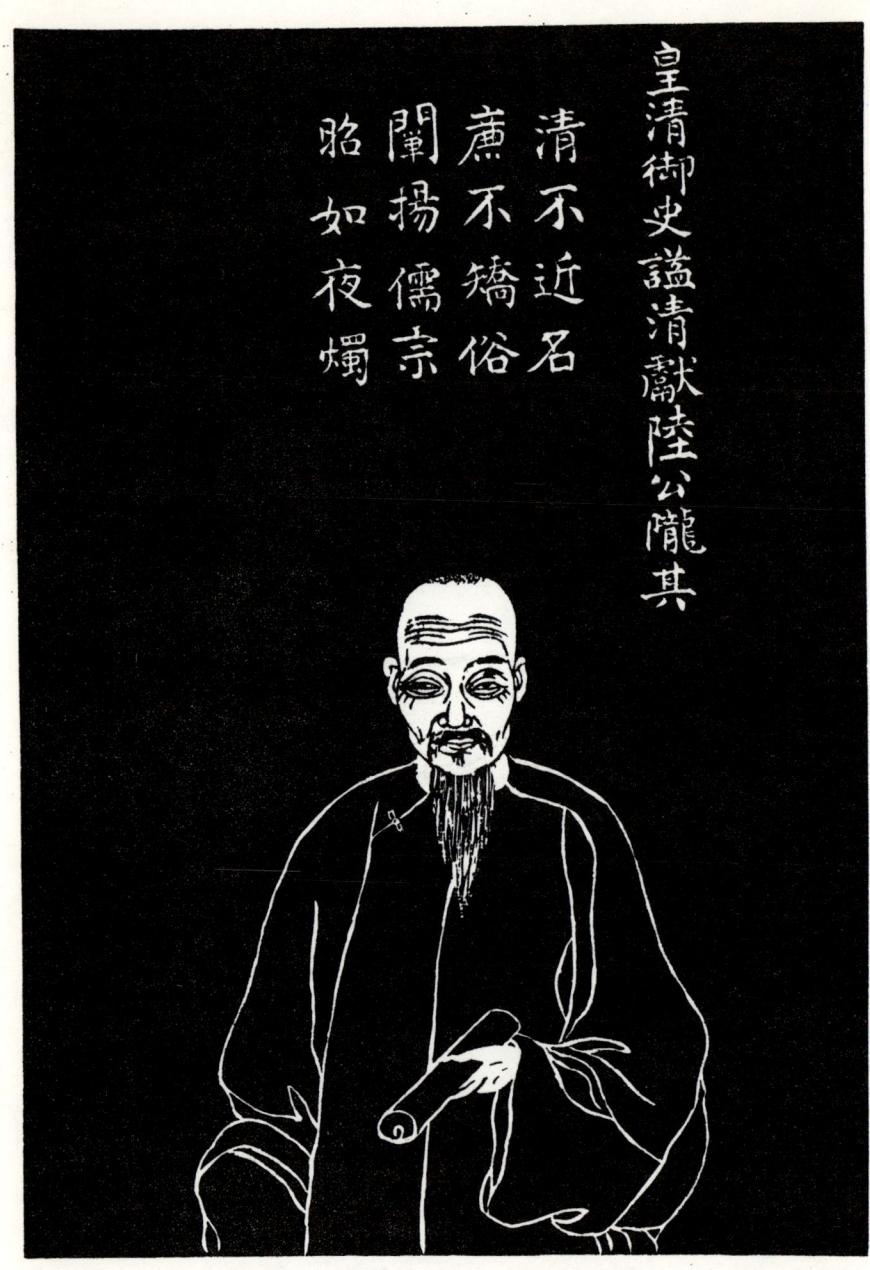

Portrait of *Lu Lung-ch'i* (p. 21)

Chapter VIII

HISTORIANS AND THEIR MAJOR WORKS

In China, between the years 1644 and 1911, comprensive scholarship was required, as specialization is today. The scholar might have his individual interest, but he was expected to exhibit a sound knowledge of all the related liberal arts. Success in civil service examinations required broad knowledge, and a successful scholar might be appointed to serve as geographer, astronomer, historian, hydraulic engineer, political and economic administrator, or military strategist. It was also demanded of a scholar that he be a calligrapher, a poet and an essayist. Records were often preserved because of their calligraphic value. Grace of diction and the art of composition added to the prestige of the historian. Verse making was a universal source of recreation for Chinese scholars, and if they recorded in verse the celebration of some day or time of personal, social or national importance, their verse afforded historical evidence additional to official records.

We have given whenever possible the two highest literary degrees gained by the scholars in the list which follows. These were the degrees of *Chü-jen* 舉人 Promoted Man and *Chin-shih* 進士 Achieved Scholar. Such degrees were awarded to candidates who had successfully passed the triennial provincial and national examinations. In the case of *Liu Wen-ch'i* 劉文淇 the degree of *Hsiu-ts'ai* 秀才 Elegant Talent is given. This was the initial literary degree awarded to successful candidates at the annual county examination. In order to avoid the evil of over-regulation at the expense of talent, two exceptions were made for the recognition of scholars. One was for those who held no degrees prerequisite to participation in the national examinations; it was called *Po-hsüeh hung-tz'u* 博學宏詞 Extensive Learning Amply Versed. The other was for those scholars who also held no degrees but were recognized as men of great personal character; it was called *Hsiao-lien fang-cheng* 孝廉公正 Filial, Incorruptable, Square, Upright.

Two other facts pertaining to the historians are noted in this chapter: (1) the place of birth, to indicate the geographical distribution of intellectual leadership in the country after the seventeenth century, (2) teaching in academies, which were regarded as places for retirement or for future opportunity.

FORTY-SIX REPRESENTATIVE HISTORIANS

Chang Hsüeh-ch'eng 章學誠 1738-1801

Native of *Chekiang;* son of a magistrate at *Ying-ch'eng, Hupeh:* excellent student in history at the Imperial Academy, 1762-1770; *Chü-jen* 舉人, 1777; *Chin-shih* 進士, 1778; director of *Ching-sheng* Academy 敬勝書院, 1782-1783; director of *Lien-ch'ih* Academy 蓮池書院, 1784-1787; director of *Wen-cheng* Academy 文正書院, 1788; compiler, *Hupeh t'ung-chih*, 1790-94.

Chiao-ch'ou t'ung-i 校讐通義
Fundamental principles of historical criticism

Wen-shih t'ung-i 文史通義
Fundamental principles of cultural history

Hsiu-chih shih-i 修志十議
Ten proposals for the writing of gazetteers

T'ien-men hsien-chih 天門縣志
Gazetteer of *T'ien-men, Hupeh*

Ho-chou chih 合州志
Gazetteer of *Ho-chou, Anhui*

Yung-ch'ing hsien-chih 永清縣志
Gazetteer of *Yung-ch'ing, Hopei*

Hu-pei t'ung-chih wei-ch'eng kao 湖北通志末成稿
Incomplete draft of the general gazetteer of *Hupeh*

Shih-chi k'ao 史籍考
A survey of historical works (lost)

Chang Mu 張穆 1805-1849

　　Native of *Shansi;* descendant of men of letters; expelled from the Examination Hall in *Peking* for a display of temper, 1839; intensive research studies in editing historical works, 1844-1848.

Meng-ku yu-mu chi 蒙古游牧記
A topographical study of Mongolia

Ku t'ing-lin nien-p'u 顧亭林年譜
Chronological biography of *Ku Yen-wu* 顧炎武

Yen Ch'ien-ch'iu nien-p'u 閻若璩年譜
Chronological biography of *Yen Jo-chu* 閻若璩

Lien-yün-i ts'ung-shu 連筠簃叢書
Collectanea of twelve works (includes *Yüan-ch'ao pi-shih* 元朝秘史 and publications of his friends, edited by *Chang*

Yen-ch'ang ti-hsing chih 延昌地形志
A topographical study of the *Yen-ch'ang* district

Chang Tsung-t'ai 張宗泰 fl. 1790-1830

　　Native of *Kiangsu;* high honor from a special Court examination, 1790; educational officer, 1791-1811; preferred appointment in educational work rather than official position (requiring administrative duties) in order to continue historical research studies.

Erh-shih-erh shih jih-shih cheng 二十二史日食徵
Evidences of the eclipses of the sun in the 22 dynastic histories

Chiu-T'ang-shu shu-cheng 舊唐書疏證
Annotations to the old *T'ang* history

Hsin-T'ang-shu ho-ch'ao 新唐書合鈔
Notes on the new *T'ang* history

T'ang tung-hsia liang-chih k'ao 唐冬夏兩至考
A study of the two solstices of the *T'ang* period

Chih-i ou-ts'un 質疑偶存
Notes on the inquiry into the doubtful

Chao I 趙翼 1727-1814

 Native of *Kiangan;* son of a teacher in private schools, *Chü-jen,* 1750; *Chin-shih,* 1761; served as examiner in various places, 1762-1766; director of *An-ting* Academy 安定書院, 1784-1792.

Fang-weng nien-p'u 方翁年譜
Chronological biography of *Lu Yu* 陸游

Kung-shih 宮史
History of the palace

Huang-ch'ao wu-kung chi-sheng 皇朝武功紀盛
Record of the military achievements of the *Ch'ing* dynasty

Kai-yü ts'ung-k'ao 陔餘叢考
Miscellaneous notes made while attending his aged mother

Nien-erh shih cha-chi 廿二史扎記
Critical notes on the 22 dynastic histories

Ch'en Chan 陳鱣 1753-1817

 Native of *Chekiang;* received the honorary title *Hsiao-lien kung-cheng* 孝廉公正, 1796; collected rare books; devoted to textual criticism; participated in the *Ching-chi tsuan-ku* 經籍纂詁 *Juan Yüan's* Dictionary of the Classics.

Lun-yü ku-hsün 論語古訓
Original meanings of the Analects

Chien-chuang shu-chi 簡莊疏記
Private notes and comments

Hsü T'ang-shu 續唐書
Supplements to the *T'ang* history: in 70 *chüan*. The 10 *chüan* of treatises constitute an invaluable history of the institutions of the *Wu-tai* 五代, Five Dynasties, 907-960

Ch'en Ching-yün 陳景雲 1670-1747

 Native of *Kiangsu;* received first honors in an examination given by governor *T'ang Pin* 湯斌, 1685; was influenced greatly by *Ho Ch'o* 何焯, a noted bibliophile. Historical research work continued by his son, *Ch'en Huang-chung* 陳黃中.

Tu-shu chi-wen 讀書紀聞
Notes from historical studies

Kang-mu ting-wu 綱目訂誤
Mistakes in the "fundamental elements" of the Comprehensive Mirror of History

Liang Han chü-cheng 兩漢舉正
Corrections of the two *Han* histories

San-kuo-chih chü-cheng 三國志舉正
Corrections to the History of the Three Kingdoms

T'ung-chien Hu-chu chü-cheng 通鑑胡注舉正
Corrections to *Hu's* Annotations to the Comprehensive Mirror

Chi-yüan k'ao-lüeh 紀元考略
A history of the system of marking new eras

Chiang Fan 江藩 1761-1831

Native of *Kiangsu*; traveled in many provinces; director of the *Li-cheng* Academy 麗正書院, 1813; editorial work under *Juan Yüan* 阮元, 1819-1822; disciple of *Hui Tung* 惠棟 and an ardent exponent of the School of *Han* Learning.

Kuang-tung t'ung-chih 廣東通志
General gazetteer of *Kwangtung* province. (One of the best local histories of the period)

Kuo-ch'ao Han-hsüeh shih-ch'eng chi 國朝漢學師承記
Biographies of 56 scholars of the School of *Han* Learning

Kuo-ch'ao Sung-hsüeh yüan-yüan chi 國朝宋學淵源記
Biographies of 40 *Ch'ing* adherents of *Sung* neo-Confucianism

Li Ching-wen 隸經文
Essays on ancient institutions

Yüeh-hsüan k'ao 樂縣考
A study of ancient musical instruments

Ch'ien Ta-hsin 錢大昕 1728-1804

    Native of *Kiangsu*; reared in a family of scholars; *Chin-shih*, 1754; edited works on geography for the government, 1756-1758; officiated in provincial examinations in *Shantung*, 1759; in *Hunan*, 1762; in the Metropolitan area, 1766; director of the *Chung-shan* Academy 鍾山書院, 1778; director of the *Lou-tung* Academy 婁東書院, 1785-1787; director of the *Tzu-yang* Academy, 紫陽書院, 1789-1804.

Nien-erh-shih k'ao-i 廿二史考異
Discrepancies in the 22 dynastic histories

Yüan-shih shih-tsu piao 元史氏族表
Table of the Mongol clan and family names

Yüan-shih i-wen-chih 元史藝文志
Bibliography of the literary productions of the *Yüan* period

Jo-ho chih 熱河志
Gazetteer of *Jehol*, *Hopei*

Yin-hsien chih 鄞縣志
Gazetteer of *Yin-hsien*, *Chekiang*

T'ien-i-ko pei-mu 天一閣碑目
Epigraphical rarities in the library of *Fan Mao-chu* 范懋柱

Chu Kuo-chen 朱國楨 1557-1632

    Native of *Chekiang*; *Chin-shih*, 1589; declined several official appointments and kept clear of partisan rivalries; spent years compiling a general history of the *Ming* dynasty, basis for a glaring literary inquisition of the Manchus.

Huang Ming shih-kai 皇明史概
General history of the *Ming* dynasty

Yung-ch'uang hsiao-p'in 湧幢小品
Collection of miscellaneous notes   Also known as

Hsi-jung hsiao-p'in 希容小品
Notes on miscellaneous events

HISTORIANS AND THEIR MAJOR WORKS

Ch'üan Tsu-wang 全祖望 1705-1755
　　Native of *Chekiang*; descendant of men of letters; *Chü-jen*, 1732; *Chin-shih*, 1736; director of the *T'ien-chang* Academy 天章書院, 1752-1753; died in abject poverty.

Ching-shih ta-wen 經史答問
Questions and answers on the classics and histories

Ch'i-chiao shui-ching chu 七校水經注
The seventh collation of the Classic of Waterways

Kung-chü cheng-shih lu 公車徵士錄
Biographies of candidates for the *Po-hsüeh hung-tz'u* 博學宏詞

Han-shu ti-li chih chi-i 漢書地理志稽疑
The doubtful in the treatise on geography in the *Han* history

Hang Shih-chün 杭世駿 1696-1773
　　Native of *Chekiang*; *Chü-jen*, 1724; *Po-hsüeh hung-tz'u*, 1736; collator of the palace edition of the Thirteen Classics, 1737-43; director of the *Yüeh-hsiu* Academy 粵秀書院, 1752-1755; professor at the *Ting-an* Academy 定安書院, 1756-1770.

San-kuo pu-chu 三國補注
Additional notes on the History of the Three Kingdoms

Chin-shih pu 晉史補
Supplement to the *Chin* history

Liang Han-shu shu-cheng 兩漢書疏證
Analytical comments on the histories of the two *Han* dynasties

Chu-shih jan-i 諸史然疑
The verified and the doubtful in histories

Pei-shih ch'ien-lang 北史搴稂
Capture the undesirable in the Northern History

Hai-t'ang t'ung-chih 海塘通志
A history of the seashore dikes at *Hai-t'ang, Chekiang*

Shih-chi k'ao-i 史記考異
Notes on discrepancies in the *Shih-chi*

Ho Ch'iu-t'ao 何秋濤 1824-1862

    Native of *Fukien*; *Chü-jen*, 1843; *Chin-shih*, 1844; served in the Ministry of Justice, 1845-1853; director of *Lien-ch'ih* Academy 1862; best historical research work done 1853-1860.

Shuo-fang pei-sheng 朔方備乘
Historical source book of the northern regions

Pei-chiao hui-pien 北徼彙編
A compendium of documentary sources with notes, commentaries, tables and maps

P'ing-ting Lo-ch'a fang-lüeh 平定羅刹方案
Account of the campaigns against the Russians to the Treaty of Nerchinsk in 1689

Hsing-lü t'ung-piao 刑律通表
Comprehensive tables of laws and punishments

Wang-hui p'ien chien-shih 王會篇箋釋
Annotations to the chapter on "Assembly of the Princes"

Meng-ku yu-mu chi pu-chu 蒙古游牧記補注
Commentary on topographical study of Mongolia by *Chang Mu*

Hou K'ang 侯康 1798-1837

    Native of *Shantung*; orphaned in a poverty stricken home; literary ability recognized by *Juan Yüan*; *Chü-jen*, 1835; director of the *Hsüeh-hai t'ang* Academy 學海堂書院. He stressed the difference between *chu-shih* 注史, annotations to history, and *hsiu-shih* 修史, compilations of history; the annotations demanding extensive notes, the compilations proper selection of material.

Pu hou Han-shu i-wen-chih 補後漢書藝文志
Supplement to the bibliographical sections of the Later *Han* history

Pu San-kuo-chih 補三國志
Supplements to the bibloigraphical section of the History of Three Kingdoms

Hsü Sung 徐松 1781-1848

Native of *Peking*; *Chü-jen*, 1800; *Chin-shih*, 1805; compiler and revisor of a compilation of history, 1808-1810; made intensive studies of the history and geography of *Sinkiang* while in exile there, 1813-1820.

Hsü-chi Sung-hui-yao kao-pen 徐輯宋會要稿本
Collated edition of rules and regulations of the state during the *Sung* period, 960-1279. The *Sung-hui-yao* was copied into the *Yung-lo ta-tien* 永樂大典 1403. After *Hsü's* death, the manuscript was owned by *Miao Ch'üan-sun* 繆荃孫 1844-1919. *Miao* presented it to the *Kuang-ya shu-chu* in *Canton*, but in 1915 it came into the possession of *Liu Ch'eng-kan* 劉承幹, who had it collated under its present title.

Sung san-ssu t'iao-li k'ao 宋三司條例考
History of the laws governing the three ministries of the *Sung*

T'ang teng-k'o chih-k'ao 唐登科志考
History of the civil service system and its examinations

T'ang liang-ching ch'eng fang k'ao 唐兩京城坊考
A study of the two *T'ang* capitals (*Sian* and *Loyang*)

Hsi-yü shui-tao chi 西域水道記
River systems of *Sinkiang*

Hsin-chiang chih-lüeh 新疆志略
Topography of *Sinkiang*

Hu Wei 胡渭 1633-1714

Native of *Chekiang*; reared in a family of scholars; failed several times in the provincial examinations; one of the compilers for the *Ta-Ch'ing i-t'ung-chih* 大清一統志, 1690-1694; his best work was on historical geography 1694-1706.

Yü-kung chui-chih 禹貢錐指
Notes on the "Tribute of *Yü*", the geographical section of the

Classic of History (*Chui-chih* is translated literally "awl pointing at the earth", meaning a modest approach to a vast subject)

Hung-fan cheng-lun 洪範正論
On the "Great Plan" in the Classic of History

Ts'ung-shu yao-lu 叢書要錄
A catalog of collectaneas

Yü-kung t'u 禹貢圖
47 maps of *Yü-kung*

Yüeh-lü piao-wei 樂律表微
Secrets of music

Huang Tsung-hsi 黃宗羲 1610-1695

Native of *Chekiang*; from a family of scholars; member of *Fu-she* 復社, a politico-literary group, 1630-1641; resisted the Manchu invasion 1645-1649; studied in retirement 1649-1695.

Ming-ju hsüeh-an 明儒學案
History of philosophies during the *Ming* period

Sung-Yüan hsüeh-an 宋元學案
Schools of thought during the *Sung* and *Yüan* dynasties

Ming-shih an 明史案
Draft history of the *Ming* period

Kung-chou shih-shih 贛州失事
An account of the fall of *Kung-chou*

Shao-Wu cheng-li chi 紹武爭立紀
An account of the struggle between *Shao* and *Wu*

Jih-pen ch'i-shih chi 日本乞師紀
Mission to Japan for military assistance

Chou-shan hsing-fei 舟山興廢
The rise and fall of the *Chusan* area

Hung Liang-chi 洪亮吉 1746-1809

Native of *Kiangsu*; orphaned early in a poverty stricken home;

Chin-shih, 1780; served as archivist and compiler, 1780-1799; traveled and studied after return from exile in *Sinkiang,* 1800.

Ch'un-hua hsien-chih 淳化縣志
Gazetteer of *Ch'in-hua* County

Ning-kuo fu-chih 寧國府志
Prefectural gazetteer of *Ning-kuo-fu*

Ch'ien-lung fu, t'ing, chou, hsien, chih 乾隆府廳州縣志
Geography of the empire

Kuei-chou shui-tao k'ao 貴州水道考
Survey of the river system of *Kuei-chou*

Pu San-kuo chiang-yü chih 補三國志疆域志
Supplements to the treatise on geography in the *San-kuo*

Tung Chin chiang-yü chih 東晉疆域志
Treatise on the geography of Eastern *Chin*

Shih-liu-kuo chiang-yü chih 十六國疆域志
Treatise on the geography of the sixteen kingdoms

I-li jih-chi 伊犂日記
A diary of his journey to *I-li*

T'ien-shan k'o-hua 天山客話
Notes on the *T'ien-shan* regions

K'ang Yu-wei 康有爲 1858-1927

Native of *Kuangtung*; reared in a family of scholars; a devout Buddhist and Confucianist; challenged and inspired by observations in his travels in China; pioneered in organizing an intellectual society for political objectives — *Ch'iang-hsüeh hui* 強學會, Society for the Rejuvenation of China; memorialized the throne for reforms, 1888; directed the "100 day Reform", 1898.

Hsin-hsüeh wei-ching k'ao 新學僞經考
A critical study of the authenticity of the Classics

K'ung-tzu kai-chih k'ao 孔子改制考
Study of Confucius as a reformer

Ch'un-ch'iu Kung-yang-chuan chu 春秋公羊傳注
Notes on *Kung-yang's* Commentary on the Spring-Autunm Annals

Ta-t'ung shu 大同書
A program of world unity

K'o Shao-min 柯紹忞 1850-1933

    Native of *Shantung*; orphaned early in childhood; studied with his mother; *Chü-jen,* 1867; *Chin-shih,* 1886; dean of the Department of Classics, Peking University; director of the bureau for the compilation of the history of the *Ch'ing* dynasty.

Hsin Yüan-shih 新元史
New history of the *Yüan* dynasty

Ch'ing-shih t'ien-wen-chih k'ao 清史天文志考
A draft treatise on astronomy in the *Ch'ing* history

Ch'un-ch'iu Ku-liang-chuan chu 春秋穀梁傳註
Annotations to the *Ku-liang* Commentary on the Spring-Autnmn Annals

Shih-hsien-chih k'ao 時憲志考
Draft history of ancient calendars

Ku Tung-kao 顧棟高 1679-1759

    Native of *Kiangsu*; trained under noted scholars; *Chin-shih,* 1721; lived in retirement; spent thirty years completing historical studies of the *Ch'un-ch'iu* period.

Ch'un-ch'iu ta-shih-piao 春秋大事表
Tables of events during the Spring-Autumn period 722-481 B.C.

Ta-ju ts'ui-yü 大儒粹語
An intellectual history of 27 scholars

Huai-an-fu chih 淮安府志
Gazetteer of *Huai-an-fu, Kiangsu*

Shang-shu chih-i 尚書質疑
A study of the doubtful in the Classic of History

HISTORIANS AND THEIR MAJOR WORKS 133

Ku Yen-wu 顧炎武 1613-1682

Native of *Kiangsu*; associated with *Fu-she* 復社 scholars; devoted to travel and studies after the Manchu occupation; fathered the *Han-hsüeh p'ai* 漢學派, School of *Han* Learning.

T'ien-hsia chün-kuo li-ping shu 天下郡國利病書
Strategic military places of the empire

Chao-yü chih 肇域志
A compendium of historical geography

Shan-tung k'ao-ku lu 山東考古錄
A treatise on antiquities of *Shantung*

Ming-chi shih-lu 明季實錄
Verified accounts of the last days of the *Ming*

Erh-shih-i shih nien-piao 二十一史年表
Chronological tables of the 21 dynastic histories

Ku Ying-t'ai 谷應泰 d. after 1689

Native of *Chihli* (*Hopei*); *Chin-shih*, 1647; educational commissioner of *Chekiang*, 1656-1660.

Ming-shih chi-shih pen-mo 明史紀事本末
History of the *Ming* dynasty (this was arbitrarily revised by order of the emperor *Ch'ien-lung* in 1786

Ming ts'ao-yün chih 明漕運志
History of grain transport during the *Ming* period

Ming Wo-k'ou shih-mo 倭明寇始末
History of Japanese raids on the coast during the *Ming* period

Kuo Sung-t'ao 郭嵩濤 1818-1891

Native of *Hunan*; studied at *Yüeh-lu* Academy 嶽廬書院; *Chin-shih*, 1847; author of the *likin* 釐金 tax; grain intendent and salt controller, 1862; acting governor of *Kuangtung*, 1863-66; first Chinese minister to England; 1876-1878; taught at *Ch'eng-nan* Academy, 城南書院 ca. 1880-1890.

Shih-hsi chi-ch'eng 使西紀程
Diary of trip between Shanghai and London

Hsiang-yin t'u-chih 湘陰圖志
Local history of *Hsiang-yin, Hunan,* with maps

Chih-ming kuang-li 誌銘廣例
Styles and patterns of epigraphy

Li Ch'ing 李清 1602-1683

Native of *Kiangsu*; came of a scholarly family; *Chin-shih,* 1631; censor in *Peking* 1638-1640, in *Nanking* 1644-1645.

Chu-shih t'ung-i lu 諸史同異錄 also known as *Erh-shih-i shih t'ung-i* 二十一史同異
Similarities and differences in the 21 dynastic histories

Nan-pei shih ho-chu 南北合注
Comments on Southern and Northern histories 386-589

San-yüan pi-chi 三垣筆記
Historical notes for the years 1637-1645

Liang Ch'i-ch'ao 梁啓超 1873-1929

Native of *Kuangtung*; a precocious child; inaugurated the *Shih-wu Pao* 時務報, "Needs of the Time Periodical" 1896; lecturer at the *Shih-wu hsüeh-t'ang* 時務學堂, School for the Needs of the Time, *Changsha, Hunan,* 1897-98; editor of the *Hsin-min ts'ung-pao* 新民叢報, *Tokio,* 1898-1912; lecturer and writer, 1920-29.

Hsien-ch'in cheng-chih shih 先秦政治史
History of political thought of the pre-*Ch'in* period

Ch'ing-tai hsüeh-shu kai-lun 清代學術概論
Introductory history of learning of the *Ch'ing* period

Chung-kuo li-shih yen-chou fa 中國歷史研究法
Methods of research in Chinese history

Mo-tzu hsüeh-an 墨子學案
A critical study of *Mo-tzu*

Liang Yü-sheng 梁玉繩 1745-1819

   Native of *Chekiang*; reared among scholars; failed in provincial examinations eight times; thorough scholar in historical studies.

Shih-chi chih-i 史記質疑
Critical study of the Historical Record

Jen-piao k'ao 人表考
A history of eminent men

Yüan-hao k'ao 元號考
Table of reign titles (A list of Japanese reign names added, 1800)

Liao P'ing 廖平 1852-1932

   Native of *Szechuan*; *Chin-shih*, 1896?; associate director of the *Tsun-ching* Academy 尊經書院, 1898-1905.

   The revival of the *Kung-yang* school of thought after sixteen centuries began with *Chuang Ts'un-yü* 莊存與 (1719-88), was continued by *Liu Feng-lu* 劉逢祿 (1776-1829), and culminated in *Wang K'ai-yun, Liao P'ing,* and *K'ang Yu-wei*. From their main interest in political evolution there developed a bold spirit of "doubting the ancient" 疑古, a new movement for scientific research in all branches of knowledge.

Ku-chin hsüeh-k'ao 古今學考
On the ancient-script and the modern-script school of thought

Shang-shu hsin-chieh 尚書新解
New interpretation of the Classic of History

Kung-yang san-shih lun 公羊三十論
Thirty essays on the *Kung-yang* Commentary

Chih-sheng p'ien 知聖篇
On the true knowledge of the Sage

Liu Wen-ch'i 劉文淇 1789-1856

   Native of *Kiangsu*; *Hsiu-ts'ai* 秀才 1807; failed in *Kiangnan* provincial examination four times; remained a private teacher and

researcher in the field of historical geography.
Pei-shih Nan-shih 北史南史
Annotations to histories of the Southern and the Northern dynasties
Chiu T'ang-shu chiao-k'an chi 舊唐書校勘記
Textual criticism of the Old *T'ang* history
Tso-chuan chiu-shu k'ao-cheng 左傳舊疏考證
A study of *Tso's* commentary on the Spring and Autumn Annals
Chia-ting Chen-chiang chih 嘉定鎮江志
A critique of the gazetteers of *Chen-chiang*
Ch'u-Han chu-hou chiang-yü k'ao 楚漢諸侯疆域考
A study of the fiefs of the lords under *Hsiang-chi* 項籍
Yang-chou shui-tao chi 揚州水道記
A history of the water courses of the *Yang-chou* region

Lo Chen-yü 羅振玉 1866-1940

Native of *Chekiang*; councillor of the Ministry of Education; archeologist; loyal to the Manchus.
Yin-hsü shu-ch'i lei-pien 殷虛書契類編
Inscriptions found in the ruins of *Yin*
Ssu-ch'ao ch'ao-pi t'u-li 四朝鈔幣圖例
Illustrated history of the paper currency of four dynasties
Shih-ku wen k'ao-shih 石鼓文考釋
Notes on the history of the inscriptions on the stone drums
Li-tai kuan-yin chi-ts'un 歷代官印集存
A history of official seals throughout the dynasties
Li-tai fu-p'ai lu 歷代符牌錄
History of proofs of identity and credentials throughout the ages
Hsi-ch'ui shih-k'o lu 西陲石刻錄
A catalog of inscriptions on stone monuments
Tao-te-ching k'ao-i 道德經考異
Discrepancies in *Tao-te-ching*

HISTORIANS AND THEIR MAJOR WORKS

Ma Su 馬驌 1621-1673

Native of *Shantung*; orphaned early; *Chin-shih,* 1659; served as educational officer, prefectural judge, and magistrate at times.

I-shih 繹史
An encyclopedic history of China from antiquity to 209 B.C.

Tso-chuan shih-wei 左傳事緯
Exegetical clarification of *Tso-chuan*

Shih-san-tai wei-shu 十三代緯術
History of divination during 13 dynasties

P'an Ch'eng-chang 潘檉章 1626-1663

Native of *Kiangsu*; refused to take civil service examinations under the Manchus; murdered by emperor *K'ang-hsi* in 1663 on account of involvement in the case of *Chuang T'ing-lung's Ming-shih chi-lüeh* 明史輯略 for which *Wu Yen* was also killed.

Kuo-shih k'ao-i 國史考異
Discrepancies in the national histories

Chin yüeh-fu 今樂府
A poetical account of the *Ming* dynasty. In addition to this there was a *Ming* history; both were co-authored with *Wu Yen* 吳炎.

Shao Chin-han 邵晉涵 1743-1796

Native of *Chekiang*; descendant of scholars; *Chü-jen,* 1765; *Chin-shih,* 1771; assistant editor for the compilation of the *Ssu-k'u-ch'üan-shu* 四庫全書, 1773; exemplified excellent historiography; recovered the *Chiu Wu-tai shih* 舊五代史, older history of the Five Dynasties by *Hsüeh Chü-cheng* 薛居正 from the *Yung-lo ta-tien* 永樂大典.

Hang-chou fu-chih 杭州府志
Local history of *Hangchow*

Yü-yao hsien-chih 餘姚縣志
Local history of *Yü-yao*

Nan-tu shih-lüeh 南都事略
A history of southern *Sung*

Chiu-kuo chih 九國志
History of nine kingdoms during the Five Dynasties

Wu-tai shih k'ao-i 五代史考異
A study of discrepancies in the History of the Five Dynasties

Huang-ch'ao shih-chi lu 皇朝謚迹錄
A list of posthumous honors bestowed during the *Ch'ing* dynasty

Shen Ping-chen 沈炳震 1679-1738

  Native of *Chekiang*; concentrated on historical studies after several failures at provincial examinations; spent 20 years completing the comparative study of the two *T'ang* histories.

Hsin-chiu T'ang-shu ho-ch'ao 新舊唐書合鈔
A comparative study of the new and old *T'ang* histories

Nien-i shih ssu-p'u 廿一史四譜
Four chronological lists of eminent names in the 21 dynastic histories

Chiu-ching pien-tzu tu-meng 九經辨字瀆蒙
An etymological study of the characters used in the Nine Classics

Sun I-jang 孫詒讓 1848-1908

  Native of *Chekiang*; reared in a family of scholars; *Chü-jen*, 1867; made cooperative studies in epigraphy with noted scholars in *Peking*; devoted to educational work after Sino-Japanese war.

Liu-li chen-wei 六歷甄微
A study of six ancient calendars

Mo-tzu chien-ku 墨子間詁
A study of the texts of *Mo-tzu*

Shang-shu pien-chih 尙書駢枝
Duplications in the Classic of History

Ch'i-wen chü-li 契文舉例
Methods of studying inscriptions on oracle bones

HISTORIANS AND THEIR MAJOR WORKS

Ts'ui Shu 崔述 1740-1816

　　Native of *Chihli*; *Chü-jen*, 1762; editor for the compilation of the *Ta-ming* gazetteer, 1787-1789; magistrate in *Fukien*, 1796-1802; remaining years devoted exclusively to historical studies.

　　Value of *Tsui Shu's* critical scholarship was not fully recognized until the third and fourth decades of the 20th century.

K'ao-hsin lu 考信錄
A record of beliefs investigated

Wu-fu i-t'ung hui-k'ao 五服異同彙考
A comprehensive treatise on mourning rituals

Ta-ming shui-tao k'ao 大名水道考
A history of the river courses at *Ta-ming*

Chiu-huang ts'e 救荒策
A project for famine relief

T'u Chi 屠寄 fl. 1885-1912

　　Native of *Kiangsu*; *Chin-shih*, 1892; traveled through Manchuria and Mongolia, 1886-1890; chief professor at the *I-tung hsüeh t'ang* 儀董學堂, formerly the *An-ting* Academy, 1896-98; studied in retirement, 1899-1912.

Meng-wu-erh shih-chi 蒙兀兒史記
Historical memoirs of the Mongols

Ch'ang-chou pien-t'i-wen lu 常州駢體文錄
Anthology of poetic prose of writers of *Changchow*

Wan Ssu-t'ung 萬斯同 1638-1702

　　Native of *Chekiang*; delayed formal education and marriage on account of family and national misfortunes; studied under *Huang Tsung-hsi* 黃宗羲 and in a monastery 海會寺, 1659-67; taught and studied at a private scholar-official home, 1669-1678; declined offers from the Manchu court but worked privately under directors of the Historiographical Board, 1679-1694. *Wan* held that private historical work is always objective and superior to official work.

Li-tai shih-piao 歷代事表
Important events arranged topically in tabular form

Sung-chi chung-i lu 宋季忠義錄
Biographies of the loyalists at the close of the *Sung* dynasty

Ju-lin tsung-p'ai 儒林宗派
Philosophers of the Confucian school

Ming Yüeh-fu 明樂府
Collection of ballads relating to incidents of the *Ming* court

Wang Hsien-ch'ien 王先謙 1842-1918

Native of *Hunan*; *Chin-shih*, 1865; educational commissioner of *Kiangsu*, 1884-1888; the *Nan-ching* Academy 南菁書院, established by *Huang T'i-fang* 黃體芳, further enriched by noted scholars under *Wang's* commissionership; director of the *Nan-ch'eng* Academy 南城書院, 1889-1906; sub-chancellor of the Grand Secretariat 內閣學士, 1906-1909.

Han-shu pu-chu 漢書補注
Supplementary comments on the *Han-shu*

Huang-ch'ao ching-chieh hsü-pien 皇朝經解續編
Supplement to treatises on the classics during the *Ch'ing* period

Hsün-tzu chi-chieh 荀子集解
A critical analysis of works on *Hsün-tzu*

T'ien-ming i-lai shih-ch'ao tung-hua lu 天命以十朝來東華錄
Records from the palace History Office 1616-1861

Wang Hui-tsu 汪輝祖 1731-1807

Native of *Chekiang*; struggled against poverty; *Chü-jen*, 1768; *Chin-shih*, 1775; secretary under 16 magistrates, 1752-1785; magistrate, 1788-1792; as a practical historian, he stressed the imporance of research tools such as indices and ready references.

Shih-hsing yün-pien 史姓韻編
Index of proper names in dynastic histories

Chiu-shih t'ung hsing-ming lüeh 九史同姓名略
Identical names borne by different persons in the nine histories

Liao Chin Yüan san-shih t'ung hsing-ming lu 遼金元三史同姓錄
Identical names borne by different persons in the *Liao*, *Chin*, and *Yüan* dynastic histories

Yüan-shih pen-cheng 元史本證
A critique of the *Yüan* history

Ping-t'a meng-hen lu 病榻夢痕錄
Traces of dreams from a sick bed — an autobiography

Wang K'ai-yün 王闓運 1833-1916

    Native of *Hunan*; known as *sheng-t'ung* 神童, a precocious child; taught at the *Nan-ch'eng* Academy at the age of 19; director of the *Tsun-ching*, the *Ch'uan-shan* 船山, and the *Liang-hu* 兩湖 Academies at various times; director-general of the Bureau of National Historiography, 1913.

Heng-yang hsien-chih 衡陽縣志
Gazetteer of *Heng-yang*, *Hunan*

Hsiang-t'an hsien-chih 湘潭縣志
Gazetteer of *Hsiang-t'an*, *Hunan*

Kuei-yang chou-chih 桂陽州志
Gazetteer of *Kuei-yang*, *Hunan*

Hsiang-chün chih 湘軍志
History of the *Hunan* Army

Shang-shu chan 尚書箋
Interpretations of the Classic of History

Ch'un-ch'iu Kung-yang-chuan chan 春秋公羊傳箋
Interpretations of *Kung-yang's* Commentary on the Spring-Autumn **Annals**

Wang Kuo-wei 王國維 1877-1927

Native of *Chekiang*; after two failures in the provincial examinations he determined to pursue modern learning; substituted as a private secretary and studied meanwhile at the *Tung-wen hsüeh-she* 東文學社, 1897-1900; studied in Japan, 1901-1902; professor of philosophy at the *Kiangsu* Normal School, 1904-07; at *Tsing-hua* College 清華學校, 1915-1927.

Ku-shih hsin-cheng 古史新證
New evidences for ancient history

Sung Yüan hsi-ch'ü shih 宋元戲曲史
Dramatic literature of the *Sung* and *Yüan* dynasties

Wu-tai liang-Sung chien-pen k'ao 五代兩宋監本考
History of the official editions during the Five dynasties and the two *Sung* dynasties

Ta-Yüan kuan-chih tsa-chi 大元官制雜記
Notes on the governmental organization of the *Yüan* dynasty

Yüan-tai ts'ang-k'u chi 元代倉庫記
On the official granaries of the *Yüan* period

Ta-Yüan chan-chi kung-wu chi 大元氈罽工物記
On the imperial weaving factories

Yüan Kao-li chi-shih 元高麗紀事
History of the Mongol conquest of Korea

Wei Yüan 魏源 1794-1856

Native of *Hunan*; devoted to historical studies during early years though poverty stricken; *Chü-jen,* 1822; *Chin-shih,* 1847; served under the financial commissioner of *Kiangsu* and made improvements on salt-revenue administration, 1826-1841; magistrate and prefect, 1847-1852.

Yüan-shih hsin-pien 元史新編
Newly revised history of the *Yüan* dynasty

HISTORIANS AND THEIR MAJOR WORKS 143

Sheng-wu chi 聖武記
A history of military operations of early *Ch'ing* rulers
Hai-kuo t'u-chih 海國圖志
A geography of oceanic countries

Wu Jen-ch'en 吳任臣 1628-1689?

    Native of *Chekiang*; passed the *Po-hsüeh hung-tz'u* examination, 1679; corrector of the *Han-lin* Academy, 1679-1686.
Shih-kuo ch'un-ch'iu 十國春秋
History of the ten kingdoms
Shan-hai-ching kuang-chu 山海經廣註
Amplification of the *Shan-hai ching* commentary of *Kuo P'u* 郭璞
Nan-Pei-shih ho-chu 北南史合注
Annotations to histories of the Northern and Southern dynasties
Tzu-hui pu 字彙補
Supplement to the dictionary *Tzu-hui* which was the first to arrange the characters under 214 radicals

Wu Jung-kuang 吳榮光 1773-1843

    Native of *Kuangtung*; son of a wealthy family; *Chin-shih*, 1799; served in various literary capacities, 1801-1804; censor, 1805-1808; high official position in the capital, 1810-1818, and in the provinces, 1818-1839.
Li-tai ming-jen nien-p'u 歷代名人年譜
Dates of births and deaths of famous people in Chinese history, including chronological tables of historical events
Wu hsüeh lu 吾學錄
Notes on laws and regulations
Yün-ch'ing kuan chin-wen 筠清館金文
Inscriptions on bronzes
Hsin-ch'ou hsiao-hsia chi 辛丑銷夏記
Summer recreation of 1841 (comments on paintings, calligraphy)

Wu Ta-cheng 吳大澂 1835-1902

Native of *Kiangsu*; *Chü-jen*, 1864; *Chin-shih*, 1868; one of the editors at the *Kiangsu* Provincial Printing Office, 1868-1870; educational commissioner of *Shensi* and *Kansu*, 1873-1876; national defense work at *Kirin* 吉林, 1880-1884; governor of *Kuangtung*, 1887-1888, and of *Hunan*, 1892-1896; director of the *Lungmen* Academy 龍門書院, 1898-1899.

Chi-lin k'an-chieh chi 吉林勘界記
Records of mission establishing boundary lines in *Kirin*

Huang-hua chi-ch'eng 皇華紀程
Memoirs of the envoy

Heng-hsüan so-chien so-ts'ang chi-chin lu 恒軒所見所藏吉金錄
Critical notes on bronze and copper objects

Ch'üan-heng tu-liang shih-yen k'ao 權衡度量實驗考
A history of weights and measures

Shuo-wen ku-chou pu 說文古籀補
An analysis of 5,700 ancient characters

Yen Yen 嚴衍 1574-1645

Native of *Kiangsu*; devoted entire life to the study of history; spent 30 years writing notes and additions to the Comprehensive Mirror. He stressed the importance of social, intellectual, and economic histories.

Tzu-chih t'ung-chien pu 資治通鑑補
Notes and additions to the Comprehensive Mirror

Sung-Yüan hsü-pien 宋元續編
Continuation of the Comprehensive Mirror, covering the period from 960 to 1368

春秋經傳集解襄六第十九

杜氏　盡卅一年

經廿有九年春王正月公
在楚夏五月公至自楚庚
午衛侯衎卒閽弒吳子餘

Rubbing from the Stone Classics cut in the *T'ang* Dynasty

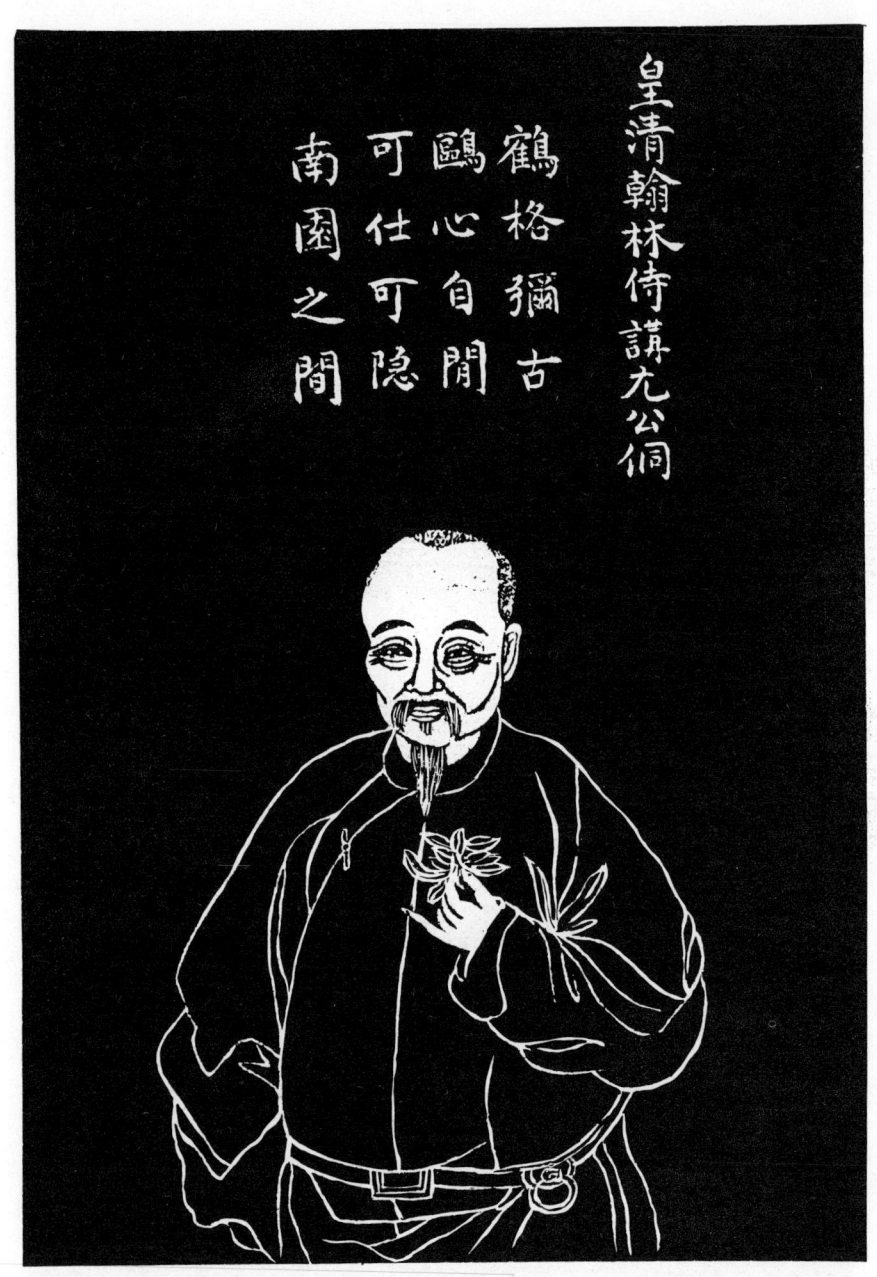

Yu T'ung 尤侗 (1618-1704) A compiler of the *Ming* History

Chapter IX

TRADITIONAL TYPES OF HISTORICAL RESEARCH

In the chapter on the classification of histories, we observe the variations in scope, in approach, in emphasis, in content, and in importance. In the list of terms used in the titles of historical publications (chapter VI) we see similar variations. These terms exhibit the desire of the historians to employ new names for their work, though the shades of difference are very pale and at times, nothing. The works of the forty-six historians in the previous chapter indicate at once the diversity and the recurrent types of historical research.

The main types of historical research done by Chinese historians, especially during the period of the *Ch'ing* dynasty, are in this chapter represented by selected historical writings listed under eight classifications. The name of the work in romanization, in Chinese, and in English translation is followed by a number in parentheses representing the number of *chüan* 卷, Chinese volumes. Dates are given with the historian's name, if available.

CH'UANG-TSO 創作 THE CREATIVE

The word "creative" is used in the sense of both pioneering and uniqueness. In this sense, few Chinese historical writings can be called creative, and yet every innovation in style, in approach, and in synthesis is in some measure creative. For example, *Ssu-ma Chien's* Historical Memoirs represents such creative work. *Wang Ch'eng's* 王稱 *Tung-tu shih-lüeh* 東都事略 Events of the Eastern Capital is also a piece of creative work in that Wang had no precedent in writing this history and in it he laid the pattern for later histories of the *Sung* and set high standards of historical scholarship.

Chu-shih 注釋 Annotations

Chu 注 means to annotate; *shih* 釋 means to explain. Literally, *chu* means soaking, soaking in the meaning of words and sentences, especially those of the ancient classics. *Shih* 釋 means liberation, freeing meanings not evident. The first three versions of annotations to the Historical Memoirs are the best examples of this type of research: *Shih-chi chi-chieh* 史記集解 Comprehensive Annotations to the Historical Memoirs by *P'ei Yin* 裴駰, of the fifth century; *Shih-chi cheng-i* 史記正義 Correct meaning of the Historical Memoirs by *Chang Shou-chieh* 張守節; and *Shih-chi so-yin* 史記索隱 To Search into the Hidden Meanings in the Historical Memoirs by *Ssu-ma Chen* 司馬貞, of the eighth century.

Annotations have been made in several ways: 釋詞, by exegetical analysis; *shih-yin* 釋音, by phonological studies; *hsün-shih* 訓釋, by textual interpretation; *chüeh-i* 決疑, by judgment upon the doubtful; and *k'an k'an-wu* 勘刊誤, by correction of mistakes in printing.

Shih-chi yin-i 史記音義 Pronunciations and meanings in the *Shih-chi*
    Hsü Yeh-min 徐野民 6th century

Shih-chi-yin 史記音 Pronunciations in the *Shih-chi* (3)
    Tsou Tan-sheng 鄒誕生 6th century

Han-kuan-i 漢官儀 Officers and rites of *Han* (2)
    Ying Shao 應劭 d. 195 A.D.

Ch'un-ch'iu tso-shih-chuan chieh 春秋左氏傳解 Explanations of *Tso's* commentary on the Spring-Autumn Annals
    Fu Ch'ien 服虔 2nd century

Kuan-chih-hsün 官職訓 Expositions of functions of officers
    Wei Chao 韋昭 3rd century

Han-shu yin-i 漢書音義 Pronunciations and meanings in the *Han-shu*
    Chin Shuo 晉灼 4th century

Han-chiu-i 漢舊儀 Ancient rites of *Han* (2)
    Wei Hung 衛宏 1st century
Han-shu-chu 漢書注 Annotations to the *Han-shu*
    Yen Shih-ku 顏師古 579-645
Liang-Han-shu k'an-wu 兩漢書刊誤 Mistakes in the *Han-shu* corrected
    Liu Pin 劉邠 1022-1088, *Liu Ch'ang* 劉敞 1019-1068, and his son *Liu Chang-shih* 劉章世
Han-shu pien-i 漢書辨疑 Clarifying the doubtful in the *Han-shu*
Hou-Han-shu pien-i 後漢書辨疑 Same on *Hou-Han-shu* (11)
Hsü hou-Han-shu pien-i 續後漢書辨疑 Supplement to above (9)
    Ch'ien Ta-chao 錢大昭 1744-1813
Liang-Han k'an-wu pu-i 兩漢刊誤補遺 Supplement to the corrected mistakes in the two *Han-shu* (10)
    Wu Jen-chieh 吳仁傑 fl. 1174-1204
Han-shu shu-cheng 漢書疏證 Annotations to the *Han-shu* (36)
Hou-Han-shu shu-cheng 後漢書正疏 Annotations to *Hou-Han-shu*
    Shen Ch'in-han 沈欽韓 1775-1832
Hou-Han-shu pu-chu 後漢書補注 Supplementary annotations to the *Hou-Han-shu* (24)
    Hui Tung 惠棟 1697-1758
Han-shu ti-li-chih chi-i 漢書地理志稽疑 Investigation of the doubt- in the treatise on geography in the *Han-shu* (6)
    Ch'üan Tsu-wang 全祖望 1705-1755
San-kuo-chih chu 三國志注 Annotations to the History of the Three Kingdoms
    P'ei Sung-chih 裴松之 fl. 400-430
Chin-shu-yin-i 晉書音義 Pronunciations and meanings in the *Chin-shu*
    Ho Ch'ao 何超 *T'ang* period
Sui-shu ching-chi-chih k'ao-cheng 隋書經籍志考證 Evidence for the treatise on literature in the *Sui-shu* (52)
    Yao Chen-tsung 姚振宗 late 19th century

Hsin-T'ang-shu pu-chu 新唐書補注 Supplementary annotations to the New *T'ang-shu* (225)
    Li Hui 李繪 12th century

Hsin-T'ang-shu t'ien-wen-chih shu-cheng 新唐書天文志疏證 (100) Evidence for the treatise on astronomy in the New *T'ang-shu*
    Chang Tsung-t'ai 張宗泰 fl. 1790-1830

Hsin-Wu-tai-shih chu 新五代史注 Annotations to the New Five Dynasties History
    Hsü Wu-tang 徐無黨 10th century

Pu-ch'üeh 補闕 Supplements

Pu-ch'üeh 補缺 means to make up what is incomplete or to supply omissions. The earliest and best example of this type of research is the supplement to the treatises in the *Hou Han-shu* by *Liu Chao* 劉昭. *Fan Yeh* 范曄 had failed to complete the *Hou Han-shu*. Also in this work there were no chronological tables. *Hsiung Fang* 熊方, of the *Sung* dynasty, therefore, made such supplements. It is interesting to note that most work of this kind consists of supplements to treatises in the dynastic histories.

Pu Han ping-chih 補漢兵志 Supplement to the military treatise of the *Han-shu* (1)
    Ch'ien Wen-tzu 錢文子 *Sung* period

Pu hou-Han-shu nien-piao 補後漢書年表 Supplement to the chronological table of the Later *Han* (10)
    Hsiung Fang 熊方 *Sung* period

Hou-Han-shu pu-piao 後漢書補表 Supplementary table to the Later *Han* (8)
    Ch'ien Ta-chao 錢大昭 1744-1813

Pu hou-Han-shu i-wen-chih 補後漢書藝文志 Supplement to the treatise on literature of the Later *Han* (4)
    Hou K'ang 侯康 1798-1837

Pu hou-Han-shu i-wen-chih 補後漢書藝文志 Supplement to the treatise on literature of the Later *Han* (10)
    Ku Huai-san 顧懷三 middle 19th century

Pu hou-Han-shu i-wen-chih 補後漢書藝文志 Supplement to the treatise on literature of the Later *Han* (1)
    Tseng P'u 曾樸 d. 1935

San-kuo-chih kuan-piao 三國志官表 List of offices in the *San-kuo* (3)
    Hung I-sun 洪詒孫 1773-1816

Pu San-kuo chiang-yü-chih 補三國疆域志 Supplement to the treatise on geography in the *San-kuo* (2)
    Hung Liang-chi 洪亮吉 1746-1809

Pu San-kuo i-wen-chih 補三國藝文志 Supplement to the treatise on literature in the *San-kuo* (4)
    Hou K'ang 侯康 1798-1837

San-kuo i-wen-chih 三國藝文志 Treatise on literature in the *San-kuo*
    Yao Chen-tsung 姚振宗 late 19th century

Hsin-chiao Chin-shu ti-li-chih 新校晉書地理志 Newly corrected treatise on geography in the *Chin-shu* (1)
    Fang K'ai 方楷 (愷) middle 19th century

Chin ti-li-chih pu-cheng 晉地理志補正 Supplementary corrections of the treatise on geography of *Chin*
    Pi Yüan 畢沅 1730-1797

Tung-Chin chiang-yü-chih 東晉疆域志 Treatise on geography of Later *Chin* (4)
    Hung Liang-chi 洪亮吉 1746-1809

Pu Chin-ping-chih 補晉兵志 Supplement to the military treatise of *Chin* (1)
    Ch'ien I-chi 錢儀吉 1783-1850

Pu Chin-shu i-wen-chih 補晉書藝文志 Supplement to the treatise on literature in the *Chin-shu*
    Wen T'ing-shih 文廷式 1856-1904

Shih-liu-kuo chiang-yü-chih 十六國疆域志 Treatise on geography of the Sixteen Kingdoms (16)
    Hung Liang-chi 洪亮吉 1746-1809
Pu Sung-shu hsing-fa-chih 補宋書刑法志 Supplement to the treatise on punishments in the *Sung-shu* (1)
Pu Sung-shu shih-huo-chih 補宋書食貨志 Supplement to the treatise on food and commodities in the *Sung-shu* (1)
    Hao I-hsing 郝懿行 1757-1825
Pu Sung-shu i-wen-chih 補宋書藝文志 Supplement to the treatise on literature in the *Sung-shu* (1)
    Nieh Ch'ung-ch'i 聶崇岐 1940's
Pu Ch'en chiang-yü-chih 補陳疆域志 Supplement to the treatise on geography in the *Ch'en-shu* (4)
    Tsang Li-ho 臧勵龢 1930's
Nan-pei-shih pu-chih 南北史補志 Supplementary treatises to the *Nan-pei-shih* (14)
    Wang Shih-to 汪士鐸 1802-1889
Pu Nan-pei-shih i-wen-chih 補南北史藝文志 Supplement to the treatise on literature in the *Nan-pei-shih* (3)
    Hsü Ch'ung 徐崇 late 19th century
Pu Wu-tai-shih i-wen-chih 補五代史藝文志 Supplement to the treatise on literature in the *Wu-tai-shih* (1)
    Ku Huai-san 顧懷三 middle 19th century
Sung-shih i-wen-chih-pu 宋史藝文志補 Supplement to the treatise on the literature in the *Sung-shih* (1)
    Lu Wen-ch'ao 盧文弨 1717-1796, Ni-Ts'an 倪燦 1627-1688
Hsi-hsia i-wen-chih 西夏藝文志 Treatise on literature of *Hsi-hsia* (1)
    Wang Jen-tsun 王仁俊 late 19th century
Liao i-wen-chih 遼藝文志 Treatise the literature of *Liao* (1)
    Miao Ch'üan-sun 繆荃孫 1844-1919

Pu Liao-shih ching-chi-chih 補遼史經籍志 Supplement to the treatise on literature in the *Liao-shih* (1)
    Huang Jen-heng 黃仁恒 1920's
Chin-shih shih-tsu-chih 金史氏族志 Treatise on the kinship in the *Chin-shih* (2)
    Ch'en Shu 述陳 1930's
Pu Yüan-shih shih-tsu-chih 補元史氏族志 Supplement to the treatise on the kinship in the *Yüan-shih* (3)
    Ch'ien Ta-hsin 錢大昕 1728-1804
Pu Yüan-shih i-wen-chih 補元史藝文志 Supplement to the treatise on literature in the *Yüan-shih* (4) 元史 by *Ch'ien Ta-hsin*

HSIU-TING 修訂 REVISION OF GENERAL WORKS

    Hsiu-ting 修訂 means repair and edit. Another term for revision is *kai-hsiu* 改修 correct-repair. If an existing work is unsatisfactory to a Chinese historian he may write a new one on the same subject by revising the old. *Ou-yang Hsiu* regarded the *Wu-tai shih* 五代史 of *Hsüeh Chü-cheng* 薛居正 as unsatisfactory and compiled his *Wu-tai shih-chi* 五代史記 Historical Memoirs of the Five Dynasties. *K'o Shao-min* 柯劭忞 wrote his *Hsin Yüan-shih* 新元史 New History of the *Yüan* Dynasty when he saw the weakness of the *Yüan-shih* 元史 compiled by official historians of the *Ming* dynasty.

Hsü Hou-Han-shu 續後漢書 Supplement to the Later *Han* history
    Hao Ching 郝經 1223-1275
Chi Han-shu 季漢書 Later *Han* history (56)
    Hsieh Pi 謝陛 early 17 century
Chi Han-shu 季漢書 Later *Han* history (90)
    Chang T'ao 章陶 fl. 1725-1750
Chin-chi 晉紀 Annals of *Chin* (68)
    Kuo Lun 郭倫 *Ch'ing* period
Chin-lüeh 晉略 Essentials of *Chin* History (66)
    Chou Chi 周濟 fl. 1805-1810

154   ELEMENTS OF CHINESE HISTORIOGRAPHY

Ch'ung-hsiu Nan-Pei-shih 重修南北史 Revised version of the Southern and Northern History (110)
    Fang Yüeh 方岳 fl. 1228-1255
Wu-tai shih-chi 五代史記 Historical memoirs of the Five Dynasties.
    Ou-yang Hsiu 歐陽修 1007-1072
Hsü T'ang-shu 續唐書 Supplement to the *T'ang* history (70)
    Ch'en Chan 陳鱣 1753-1817
Sung-shih-chih 宋史質 Substance of the *Sung* history (100)
    Wang Chu 王洙 fl. 1500-1540
Sung-shih hsin-pien 宋史新編 New edition of the *Sung* history (200)
    K'o Wei-ch'i 柯維騏 1497-1574
Sung-shih-chi 宋史記 Historical memoirs of the *Sung* (250)
    Wang Wei-chien 王維儉 chin-shih 1595
Yüan-shih-lei-pien 元史類編 *Yüan* history topically arranged (42)
    Shao Yüan-p'ing 邵遠平 fl. 1664-1700
Yüan-shih-hsin-pien 元史新編 New edition of the *Yüan* history (95)
    Wei Yüan 魏源 1794-1856
Men-wu-er shih-chi 蒙兀兒史記 History of the Mongols (160)
    T'u Chi 屠寄 fl. 1885-1912
Hsin-Yüan-shih 新元史 New *Yüan* history (257)
    K'o Shao-min 柯劭忞 1850-1933

TSUNG-CHI 總輯 COMPHEHENSIVE COMPILATIONS

Tsung-chi, comprehensive compilation, is the reverse of *fen-chuan*, separate compilation. The former is one compilation produced out of several works; the latter is one of many possible compilations taken from one work. The first general history, *T'ung-shih* 通史, written during the sixth century, may be regarded as a comprehensive compilation. More accurately, three later works may be classed as comprehensive compilations: *T'ung-tien* 通典 Comprehensive Institutes by *Tu Yu* 杜佑, of the eighth century; the *T'ung-chih* 通志 Comprehensive

Treatises by *Cheng Ch'iao* 鄭樵, of the twelfth century; and *T'ung-k'ao* 通考 Comprehensive History of Civilization by *Ma Tuan-lin* 馬端臨 of the thirteenth century. These works contain materials from many earlier works. The comprehensive types of specialized histories in Chapter V may be classed as comprehensive compilations.

Ho-ch'ao 合鈔 Comparative Compilations

Comparative compilation requires a study of the similarities and differences between two or more works, especially the differences in words, sentences, chapters, quotations, biographies, and description of events. The best example of this work of the Manchu period is the *Hsin-chiu T'ang-shu ho-ch'ao* 新舊唐書合鈔. A comparative study of the new and old dynastic histories of the *T'ang* dynasty by *Shen Ping-chen* 沈炳震.

Pan-ma i-t'ung 班馬異同 Differences and similarities between the *Han-shu* and the *Shih-chi* (35)
  Ni Ssu 倪思 1147-1220

Nan-Pei-shih ho-chu 南北史合注 Combined annotations to the Southern and the Northern Histories (191)
  Li Ch'ing 李清 1602-1683

Nan-T'ang-shu ho-ting 南唐書合訂 Combined edition of the *Nan-T'ang-shu* (25)
  Li Ch'ing 李清

Hsin-chiu-T'ang-shu ho-ch'ao 新舊唐書合鈔 Comparative study of the new *T'ang-shu* and the old *T'ang-shu* (260)
  Shen Ping-chen 沈炳震 1679-1738

Wu-tai-shih-chi pu-chu 五代史記補注 Supplementary annotations to the *Wu-tai-shih-chi* (74)
  P'eng Yüan-jui 彭元瑞 1731-1803
  Liu Feng-kao 劉鳳誥 1761-1830

Fen-chuan 分撰 Separate Compilations

Fen-chuan 分撰 is used in the sense of a partial compilation "culled out" of a larger work of history. *Hsi Wei-shu* 西魏書 History of Western *Wei* by *Hsieh Ch'i-k'un* 謝啓昆, 1737-1802, is a separate compilation taken from the *Wei-shu* 魏書. *Li Hsiu-ch'eng Kung-chuang* 李秀成供狀 Confessions of *Li Hsiu-ch'eng* relates just one aspect of the *T'ai-p'ing* revolution, from the history of the *T'ai-p'ing t'ien-kuo* 太平天國.

Nan-T'ang-shu 南唐書 Southern *T'ang* history (18)
    Lu Yu 陸游 1125-1210

Chiu-kuo-chih 九國志 History of nine kingdoms (12)
    Lu Chen 路振 10th century

Shih-kuo ch'un-ch'iu 十國春秋 Annals of ten kingdoms (114)
    Wu Jen-ch'en 吳任臣 1628-1689

Nan-Han-shu 南漢書 Southern *Han* history (18)
    Liang T'ing-nan 梁廷枏 1796-1861

Nan-Han-chi 南漢紀 Southern *Han* annals (5)
    Wu Lan-hsiu 吳蘭修 *chü-jen* 1808

Po-hai-kuo chih 渤海國志 History of *Po-hai* kingdom (4)
    T'ang Yen 唐晏 fl. 1890-1919

Nan-Sung-shu 南宋書 History of Southern *Sung* (60)
    Ch'ien Shih-sheng 錢士升 fl. 1600-1650

Hsi-hsia shu-shih 西夏書事 History of *Hsi-Hsia* (the Tanguts) (42)
    Wu Kuang-ch'eng 吳廣成 fl. 1830-1855

Hsi-hsia-chi 西夏記 History of *Hsi-hsia* (28)
    Tai Hsi-chang 戴錫章 fl. 1910-1940

Nan-chiang i-shih 南疆逸史 Lost history of the southern domain (44)
    Wen Jui-lin 溫睿臨 *chü-jen* 1705

Hsiao-tien-chi-nien fu-k'ao 小腆紀年附考 Studies on the annals of petty kingdoms (20)
    Hsü Nai 徐鼒 d. 1858

Hsiao-tien chi-chuan 小腆紀傳 Annals of petty kingdoms (70)
    Hsü Nai 徐鼒

Nan-Ming-shu 南明書 History of Southern *Ming* (36)
    Ch'ien Ch'i 錢綺 fl. 1823-1853

Ch'ing chien-kuo pieh-chi 清建國別記 Separate account of the founding of the *Ch'ing* kingdom (1)
    Chang Ping-lin 章炳麟 1869-1936

Ch'ing ch'ao ch'ien-chi 清朝前紀 Early annals of the *Ch'ing* dynasty
    Meng Sen 孟森 fl. 1910-1920

Tsui-ch'ing hui-chuan 賊情彙纂 Comprehensive accounts of the rebels (*T'ai-p'ing*) (12)
    Chang Te-chien 張德堅 fl. 1830-1855

T'ai-p'ing-t'ien-kuo shih-liao 太平天國史料 Source materials for the history of the *T'ai-p'ing* kingdom
    Ch'eng Yen-sheng 程演生 fl. 1915-1930

T'ai-p'ing-t'ien-kuo chan-chi 太平天國戰紀 Military operations of the *T'ai-p'ings*
    Lo Tun-jung 羅惇曧 fl. 1880-1910

CHI-I 輯逸 RESTORATION OF THE LOST

Chi 輯 means to collect and arrange; *I* 逸 means to get away or to become lost. The loss of a published work may be a complete loss or a partial loss, a temporary loss or a permanent loss. The lost may also be restored in numerous ways: by discovery and recognition of the lost work in larger works, by collecting and piecing together of the scattered parts of a work into a reasonably authentic restoration. Certain *pu-ch'üeh*, supplements, may be regarded as *chi-i*, and the method of *ho-ch'ao*, comparative study, may serve the cause of *chi-i*.

    Wang Wen-t'ai 汪文臺, 1796-1844, excelled in restoring lost works. His best work is the *Ch'i-chia hou-Han-shu* 七家後漢書 History of Later *Han* by Seven Historians. T'ang Ch'iu 湯球, 1804-1881, was another historian noted for this type of historical research.

His best work is the *Chiu-chia chiu-Chin-shu* 九家舊晉書 old dynastic history of the *Chin* dynasty by nine historians.

From the treatise on literature in the *Ch'ing* History Draft, we learn that works restored by private historians during the eighteenth century amounted to only a hundred or so *chüan*, whereas ten times as many were written under government patronage. The restoration done under sponsorship was a cooperative enterprise of several noted historians who had not only rich libraries but also excellent reward in honor, in position, and in emolument. From the work of private historians the following titles have been selected.

Hsieh-ch'eng hou-Han-shu chi-pen 謝承後漢書輯本 A restored edition of *Hsieh Ch'eng's* Later *Han* history
    Sun Chih-tsu 孫志祖 1737-1801
Han-hsüeh-t'ang chi-i-shu 漢學堂輯佚書 Collected Works on restored editions of *Han* Learning Hall
    Huang Shih 黃奭 18th century
Sui-shu ching-chi-chih k'ao-cheng 隋書經籍志考證 Verification of the treatise on literature in the *Sui-shu*
    Chang Tsung-yüan 章宗源 1752-1800
Chiao-chi shih-pen 校輯世本 Revised edition of *Shih-pen* (2)
    Lei Hsüeh-ch'i 雷學淇 *chin-shih* 1814
Sung-chung shih-pen-chu 宋衷世本注 Annotations to the *Shih-pen* by Sung Chung (5)
    Chang Shu 張澍 fl. 1794-1825

A document concerning the Annals of *Wen-tsung*

皇清江蘇巡撫梁公章鉅

三吳士庶
被德獨久
滄浪水清
共茲不朽

楊文蓀題

Portrait of *Liang Chang-chü* (p. 90)

Chapter X

CONTINUITY OF HISTORICAL CRITICISM

There are reasons for the seemingly limited development of criticism in Chinese historiography, particularly prior to the *T'ang* dynasty. Major sources for historical studies lay in official documents, and the historian's goal was the objective narration of events based upon documentary sources. Books were scarce and scholars few. Annotations, commentaries, and supplements were in greater demand than were works of criticism. The domination of one school of thought in any age usually brought imperial patronage; thus open criticism could be construed as political opposition. There was, then, the tendency to limit criticism, especially in the field of historical works being compiled under imperial decree. Generally speaking, the Chinese people were skeptical of any eccentric scholar who seemed to wish to draw attention to himself by voicing opposition to works of long standing. They believed there was room for a new approach and for new discovery without creating intellectual strife.

It is equally true that independent thinking and courageous skepticism have always been characteristic of the best periods of Chinese thought. This great tradition of reasonable skepticism has made possible literary, philosophical, and historical criticism. Reconstruction of the old was regarded as valid criticism, provided it was achieved in an acceptable manner. Though it might be at the cost of great personal sacrifice, scholars did not withhold criticism from highly venerated texts or ideas.

A history of historical criticism in China, in the true sense of the word, has yet to be written. Suffice it here to indicate the continuity of interest in historical criticism from the beginning of the *Han* dynasty to the present time.

Liu Chih-chi to Chang Hsüeh-ch'eng

The first real challenge to scholars to devise a technique for historical criticism arose in the restoration of the classics at the beginning of the *Han* period. At this time problems of textual criticism and phonology were predominant and necessitated a technique of criticism. In this atmosphere congenial to the critical spirit, the first standard history, the Historical Memoirs, was written by *Ssu-ma Ch'ien*. His critical approach to history is evidenced by his discriminating selection of source material, his arrangement of history in five major sections, and his clear formulation of the ultimate goal of history.

In the second standard history of China, the *Han-shu* 漢書, Pan Ku 班固 wrote a critical biography of *Ssu-ma Ch'ien*. Regarding the Historical Memoirs, *Pan* says: "*Ssu-ma Ch'ien* made an excellent selection from earlier historical works, but oversimplification, the prominence given *Lao-tzu's* philosophy, and emphasis on economic affairs lent evil results. However, great scholars had high regard for his historical talent."

The *Han-shu* was itself subjected to the penetrating scrutiny characteristic of the time. *Hsün Yüeh* 荀悅, 148-209, in his *Han-chi* 漢紀 Annals of the *Han* Dynasty, criticized *Pan* by modifying the *Han-shu*. Similarly, at a later date, *Yüan Hung* 袁宏, 328-376, corrected the *Hou-Han-shu* 後漢書 of *Fan Yeh* 范曄 in writing his *Hou-Han-chi* 後漢紀 Annals of the Eastern *Han*. *Yüan* says in his preface: "In reading the *Hou-Han-shu* I always find it tedious and unsystematic... Mistakes and discrepancies must be corrected. This task is not completed after eight years of hard work...."

From such beginnings, historical criticism before long achieved a central place in Chinese historiography. In one form or another historical criticism engaged the attention of historians over a period of eight centuries before *Liu Chih-chi* 劉知幾 wrote his epochal work on historical criticism, *Shih-t'ung* 史通 Historical Perspectives, published about 710. In writing this work, *Liu*, 661-721, was influenced by the works of critical historians from *Yang Hsiung* 楊雄, 35 B.C.-18 A.D. to *Liu Hsieh* 劉勰 fl. 500-525.

Believing that he could not exercise his own judgment in writing history under government control, *Liu* retired in order to write his historical critique for future generations.

His moral concept of history was a continuation of the view of Confucius, but he was revolutionary in spirit and in technique. Some of *Liu's* statements are still relevant. He stressed loyalty to truth as opposed to tradition and authority, the necessity of distinguishing source materials of history from history itself, and the advantage of writing simply and clearly without neglecting contributing factors or established evidence.

He further held that historians wishing to demonstrate critical scholarship must observe the following fundamentals:

I-KU 疑古 THE SPIRIT OF DOUBT

Ancient records should not be regarded as absolute; doubtful events and records should be investigated but not accepted.

TSA-PO 雜駁 THE SPIRIT OF ARGUMENT

Historians as individuals could be prejudicial in their narration of events and in their judgment of right and wrong, but argument supported by wider evidence and fairer deliberations must be the ideal to be followed.

WU-SHIH 忤時 THE SPIRIT OF INDEPENDENCE

Independence on the part of the historian must be maintained in spite of the deference traditionally accorded the older scholars and the pressure of official restrictions and dictations.

TIEN-FAN 點煩 SELECTION FROM EXTENSIVE STUDIES

Simplicity must be achieved by careful collection of extensive source materials and rational discrimination to resolve their complexity and attain a well defined classification. Extensive knowledge is the initial step in discriminative selection.

Ho-ts'ai 覈才 Critical Judgment

The separation of literary arts and history is advisable because the objective of the two disciplines is essentially different. The literary word may color the fact beyond recognition, unless critical judgment is used. The separation becomes dangerous, however, if the historical writer neglects to cultivate literary ability and fails to describe the historical processes clearly and artistically: for then history becomes clumsy accounts.

Liu Chih-chi's useful work on historical criticism was not brought to the foreground until 200 years after his time by *Liu Ts'an* 柳燦 in his *Shih-t'ung hsi-wei* 史通析微 Analysis of the Subtle in the Historical Perspectives. This work was greatly cherished by historians for a while, but their energy and attention were soon directed to writing new types of histories. These histories may be regarded as works of indirect historical criticism. The interest in creative history continued for four hundred years, between 1060, when *Ou-yang Hsiu* 歐陽修 published his *Hsin T'ang-shih* 新唐史, and c. 1515, when *Lu Shen* 陸深 completed his *Shih-t'ung hui-yao* 史通會要 Essentials of the Historical Perspectives.

With the emergence of the *Han-hsüeh p'ai*, or the school of *Han* learning, during the early *Ch'ing* period, historical criticism again attracted the attention of historians. *Huang Shu-lin* 黃叔琳, 1672-1756, published his *Shih-t'ung hsün-ku pu* 史通訓詁補 Annotations to the Historical Perspectives; *P'u Ch'i-lung* 浦起龍, 1679-1761, his *Shih-t'ung t'ung-shih* 史通通釋 Comprehensive Explanations of the Historical Perspectives; and *Chi Yün* 紀昀, 1724-1805, his *Shih-t'ung hsiao-fan* 史通削繁 Historical Perspectives Condensed.

Chang Hsüeh-ch'eng 章學誠, 1738-1801, was determined to blaze a new trail, and this he did by his intensive interest in a genetic view of history and a new method of study. Even though his *Wen-shih t'ung-i* 文史通義 Fundamental Principles of Cultural History and his *Chiao-ch'ou t'ung-i* 校讎通義 Fundamental Principles of Historical Criticism demonstrated his position, he himself did not write a general history as he conceived it.

Chang agreed with *Liu Chih-chi* in holding that there is a great difference between creative writing of history 撰述 and compilation of history 記注. He regarded the two as supplementary. *Chang* looked upon *Cheng Ch'iao* 鄭樵 as a great historian with keen historical insight but without thorough historical learning, *Tseng Kung* 曾鞏 as a great historian with deep historical learning but without historical method, and *Liu Chih-chi* as a great historian with historical method but without understanding of historical meaning.

"I wrote the Fundamental Principles of Cultural History," writes *Chang*, "so as to articulate the meaning of history." This work is made up of a number of essays dealing chiefly with the meaning of history and its relation to other types of literature. According to *Chang*, history is not only genetic but synoptic, as historical sources are also sources of the classics and other types of literature.

As a companion volume to his Fundamental Principles of Cultural History, *Chang* wrote *Chiao-ch'ou t'ung-i* 校讐通義. This work is a treatment of the points *Chang* believed it essential to observe in textual criticism: discrepancies in texts, the significance of various editions, the restrictions and styles of the time, the authentic objectives of a publication, the terminology, and the selection of evidence.

Chang used the following five phrases to elucidate further five aspects of historical criticism: *shih-k'ao* 史考 historical investigation, stressing extensive examination of all possible records; *shih-hsüan* 史選 historical selection, giving preference to those works of excellent literary qualities; *shih-tsuan* 史纂 historical compilation, articulating the stream of events; *shih-p'ing* 史評 historical criticism, passing judgment upon persons, events, and records; *shih-li* 史例 historical precedents, involving style and method of approach.

In his views on history, *Chang* exemplified the belief that history is normative in that it provides fundamental principles governing humanity and is not merely a collection of records or reports of events.

In the century following *Chang's* death two schools of thought predominated in intellectual circles in China, the school of *Han* learning and the *Kung-yang* school. Not until the twentieth century did Chinese and Japanese scholars give special attention to *Chang's* work.

The School of Han Learning

The school of *Han* learning had emerged in the seventeenth century and by the nineteenth century had attained a place of leadership. Though it took the name of *Han*, this school did not necessarily follow the ideas of the *Han* scholars or treat the subjects that occupied their attention. Members of this school did follow the methods of textual criticism and the principle of annotation employed by the *Han* scholars in their later works. Writings of the school of *Han* learning were further characterized by etymological criticism and comparative studies.

Because scholars of the *Han* school insisted on making a search for evidence, they are also known as the *K'ao-cheng p'ai* 考證派, or *K'ao-chü p'ai* 考據派. They looked for both the *pen-cheng* 本證 internal evidence, and the *p'ang-cheng* 傍證, external evidence. Their motto, a great pronouncement of *Tai Chen* 戴震, 1724-1777, was *k'ung-so i-p'ang* 空所依傍 "Lean on nothing but the facts."

The term *Cheng-hsüeh* 鄭學, learning of *Cheng Hsüan* 鄭玄, was sometimes used in place of *Han-hsüeh* because of *Cheng's* emphasis upon evidence to support annotations.

The *Han* school is also at times identified as the *K'ao-chü* school 考據派, or the *K'ao-cheng* school 考證派. *K'ao-chü* or *K'ao-cheng* means inductive method of research in historical and textual criticism, phonetics, and etymology.

Several works on the school of *Han* learning and biographies of its leaders have been published. *Chiang Fan* 江藩, 1761-1831, wrote the initial publication, *Han-hsüeh shih-ch'eng chi* 漢學師承記 Biographies of fifty-six scholars of the School of *Han* Learning. Two works by *Liu Shih-p'ei* 劉師培, 1884-1919, are his *Chin-ju hsüeh-shu t'ung-hsi lun* 近儒學術統系論 Schools of Learning of Modern Confucian Scholars and *Chin-tai Han-hsüeh pien-ch'ien lun* 近代漢學變遷論 Development of the *Han* Learning in Modern Times. Another of the biographies of members of the school is *Ch'ing-tai p'u-hsüeh ta-shih lieh-chuan* 清代樸學大師列傳 Biographies of the Great Masters of the Unadorned Learning (Shanghai, 1925) by *Chih W'ei-Ch'eng* 支偉成 *P'u-hsüeh* 樸學 "the unadorned learning" is another name for the *Han-hsüeh* 漢學, *Han* learning signifying research methods and results rather than literary elegance.

From the interest in the inductive method employed by the *Han* school, the method that originated the name *K'ao-cheng* 考證 or *K'ao-chü* 考據 "searching for evidence," came minor schools that applied the inductive method to special fields of research: the *Hsün-ku p'ai* 訓詁派 school of textual criticism, the *Yin-yün p'ai* 音韻派 school of the phonetics, the *Chin-shih p'ai* 金石派 school of inscriptions on metal and stone, the *Chiao-k'an p'ai* 校勘派 school of collation of texts, and the *Chi-i p'ai* 輯逸派 school of restoration of the lost.

The popularity of the school of *Han* learning was not without challenge from its opponent, the *Sung-hsüeh p'ai* 宋學派 school of *Sung* learning. The noted work voicing this challenge is the *Han-hsüeh shang-tui* 漢學商兌 Deliberations on the School of *Han* Learning by *Fang Tung-shu* 方東樹, 1772-1851. *Fang* revived the philosophical approach of the *Sung* scholars as well as their literary styles. Most important of all was his emphasis upon ethics rather than methods. *Fang* gained many followers who in turn produced works of value. But the call of the time and the need of Chinese scholarship for a sound methodology continued to give support to the school of *Han* learning, for the methods of this school seemed to concur with the modern, scientific goals in the writing of true history.

It is also of interest that within the school of *Han* learning itself there was some self-criticism. The best example of this is in the *Han-ju t'ung-i* 漢儒通義 Fragments of Writings of *Han* Scholars by *Ch'en Li* 陳澧, 1810-1882. In this work, *Ch'en Li* tried to prove that a number of the *Han* scholars gave attention to philosophical studies, contrary to the general practice of the school of *Han* learning. Also *Ch'en*, though an ardent follower of the *Han-hsüeh*, did not wish to leave the impression that the school of *Sung* learning, *Sung-hsüeh*, was making no contribution.

THE KUNG-YANG SCHOOL

The beginnings of the *Kung-yang* school can be identified in the eighteenth century. By the next century a sufficient number of scholars had become interested in the *Kung-yang* interpretation of Confucius to form a school of thought. *Kung-yang*, fifth century B.C., after whom the school is named, wrote one of the three commentaries on the Spring-Autumn Annals. He wrote in the modern script.

Ho Hsiu 何休, 129-182, made annotations to the *Kung-yang* Commentary, interpreting it as having discovered "the true meaning and great principles of the Annals." He saw in the Commentary a theory of social and political evolution in three stages: world confusion 亂世, limited peace 小康, and universal brotherhood 大同. Such a theory would incite dissatisfaction and encourage the desire for change. Consequently, the Commentary of *Kung-yang* did not receive so much patronage as did the Commentary of *Tso Ch'iu-ming*, which was rendered politically acceptable by the conservative interpretation of *Liu Hsin* 劉歆. The *Kung-yang* Commentary, therefore, was long eclipsed by the Commentary of *Tso*.

Not until the late eighteenth century or early nineteenth century did the *Kung-yang* interpretation of Confucius become prominent. It was revived by the *Kung-yang* school under the leadership of *Chuang Ts'un-yü* 莊存與 and *Liu Feng-lu* 劉逢祿.

Chuang Ts'un-yü is regarded as the founder of the *Kung-yang* school because he was the first to stress the importance of the modern-text school of historical criticism. *Liu Feng-lu* favored the *Kung-yang* Commentary because it embodied certain recondite concepts that could be elaborated into a social and political philosophy consonant with the needs of a changing order. "Finding in antiquity the sanction for present-day changes," *t'o-ku kai-chih* 託古改制, was a technique fully employed by *Liu* and the *Kung-yang* school. In addition to *Ho Hsiu's* interpretations of the *Kung-yang* Commentary, *Liu Feng-lu* found valuable support for his theories in an ancient history by *Tung Chung-shu* 董仲舒, written a century and a half before the Christian era, and entitled *Ch'un-ch'iu fan-lu* 春秋繁露.

Although every member of the *Kung-yang* school cherished the objective study of ancient texts and held modern texts to be superior, any examination of the *Kung-yang* school will reveal two groups of followers. The chief interest of one group was in textual and historical criticism designed to obtain better histories and truer classics. Members of the other group were deeply concerned with signs of political decay and the imperative need for reforms.

Prominent in this second group were four nineteenth century scholars. *Kung Tzu-chen* 龔自珍, 1792-1841, regarded the *Kung-yang* learning as encouraging scholars to be politically minded and to advocate reforms. *Wei Yüan* 魏源, 1794-1856, championed the *Kung-yang* school because he keenly felt the twofold problem of the time, the inadequacy of the official histories, especially that of the *Yüan* dynasty, and the rapid decay of government coupled with the seriousness of foreign relations. *K'ang Yu-wei* 康有爲, 1858-1927, whose famous reforms and publications were highlights of the last decade of the nineteenth century, was the most important exponent of political reforms. *T'an Ssu-t'ung* 譚嗣同, 1865-1898, was at once a thinker, a reformer, and a martyr.

Criticism in the Twentieth Century

The achievements of both the school of *Han* learning and the *Kung-yang* school, coupled with the impact on Chinese scholars of the studies of Western Sinologists, afforded a sure base for a further development in the twentieth century of the critical method. With the discovery of the oracle bones, the findings at *Tun-huang* caves, the dissemination of old archives, and the establishment of research institutions, materials and means for historical criticism were at hand. A new historiography was required, and this requirement provided a challenge to the critical method. Old patterns and traditional requirements as well as taboos had to be overthrown and new forms as well as new principles had to be ushered in. The first call of the intellectual revolution at the beginning of the twentieth century was one for a new historiography employing more adequate critical techniques.

After the failure of the 1898 reform movement, *Liang Ch'i-ch'ao* 梁啓超, 1873-1929, devoted his attention to a critical review of Chinese learning for practical objectives and to the introduction of Western learning for the rejuvenation of China. He aroused the scholar class through his coinage of new terms for new intellectual, social, and political ideas.

In 1902 *Liang* published an article entitled *"Hsin shih-hsüeh"* 新史學 "New Historiography." He outlined a general history of three sections: political, cultural and socio-economic. Each section was to contain special treatises on related subjects. For example, under cultural history there were to be eight subdivisions: language, religion, philosophy, literature, art, music and drama, painting, and education. This outline reveals a departure from the traditional mechanics of historical writing.

Liang insists that one of the chief shortcomings of traditional history must be eliminated; namely, the writing of history for and about the privileged class. To achieve a new history he held that scholars must revolutionize not only the scope and purpose of their work, but also their approach.

Although *Liang's* publications on method, Research Method of Chinese History, received a good deal of criticism by reason of the mistakes and illogical arrangements in this hurried collection of notes, as he had anticipated, these two little volumes succeeded in inspiring young scholars to accept reforms, new knowledge, and new methods of study.

Another scholar of the old school who attempted to introduce a new historiography in China is *Chang Ping-lin* 章炳麟, 1868-1936. Like *Liang Ch'i-ch'ao, Chang* also was interested in general history. In discussing the problem of general history he made the observation that although many histories of China may be regarded as objective and concrete they have lost sight of the causal relations and the trend of events. To capture the details at the expense of the essentials destroys the very meaning of history. The new historiography, he held, depends upon a new definition of the scope of history, the function of the historian, the scrutiny of primary and secondary sources, and the ability to analyze and synthesize historical materials.

Ho Ping-sung 何炳松, 1890-, trained in both the classical school of old China and Western universities, tried to redefine the meaning of history as a mirror for the future and to adopt a new historical methodology involving synoptic, sociological, and scientific approaches. More specifically, he believed that the rapid changes of our own times and the complexity of modern life demand a topical treatment of history and that in this specialized history the principle of genetic history can be realized since human activities are interrelated. Critical methodology *Ho* thought to be necessary to the new historiography because the new histories require that the findings of the social sciences be harmonized and that the general history of any period be reflected in these specialized histories.

Wang Kuo-wei 王國維, 1877-1927, is regarded as one of the architects of the new histories. Even though his untimely death cut short his work in the several branches of history and philology in which he excelled, he did complete his critical research into the sources of dramatic literature, one of the neglected fields in Chinese historical writings. In the preface to his *Sung Yüan hsi-ch'ü shih* 宋元戲曲史 A History of Drama of the *Sung* and *Yüan* Dynasties, *Wang* says, "For the collection of source materials, I am responsible. The critical interpretations are also mine. I am also responsible for the initiation of the critical study of this field."

His work attracted many young scholars, who pursued historical research in the entire field of folk literature.

Ts'ui Shu 崔述 1740-1816, reached back through nineteen centuries and took from the Historical Memoirs of *Ssu-ma Ch'ien* the phrase *K'ao-hsin,* "beliefs to be investigated," to make it the title of his book *K'ao-hsin lu* 考信錄 A Record of Beliefs Investigated. This work represented thirty years of the most exacting and laborious research on the unwarranted accretions in spurious books and the fallacies in popular theories.

A hundred years after *Tsui's* death, in the second decade of the twentieth century, "beliefs to be investigated," became the inspiration of *Ku Chieh-kang* 顧頡剛, 1893-, at a time when China was going through a radical cultural transformation and the skeptical approach to the past was so vehement. One of *Ku's* contributions to the new historiography of the twentieth century was in historical criticism. He set himself the task of bringing together and annotating earlier publications relating to the detection of forgeries. In this we find a continuation of one of the objectives of the school of *Han* learning. *Ku's* interest in criticism also found expression in his effort to enhance the intelligibility of old texts through emendation, punctuation, and indices. Many aspects of historical criticism were scrutinized in *Ku's Ku-shih pien* 古史辨 A Symposium on Ancient Chinese History. His critical hypotheses and methods were themselves the subject of attack.

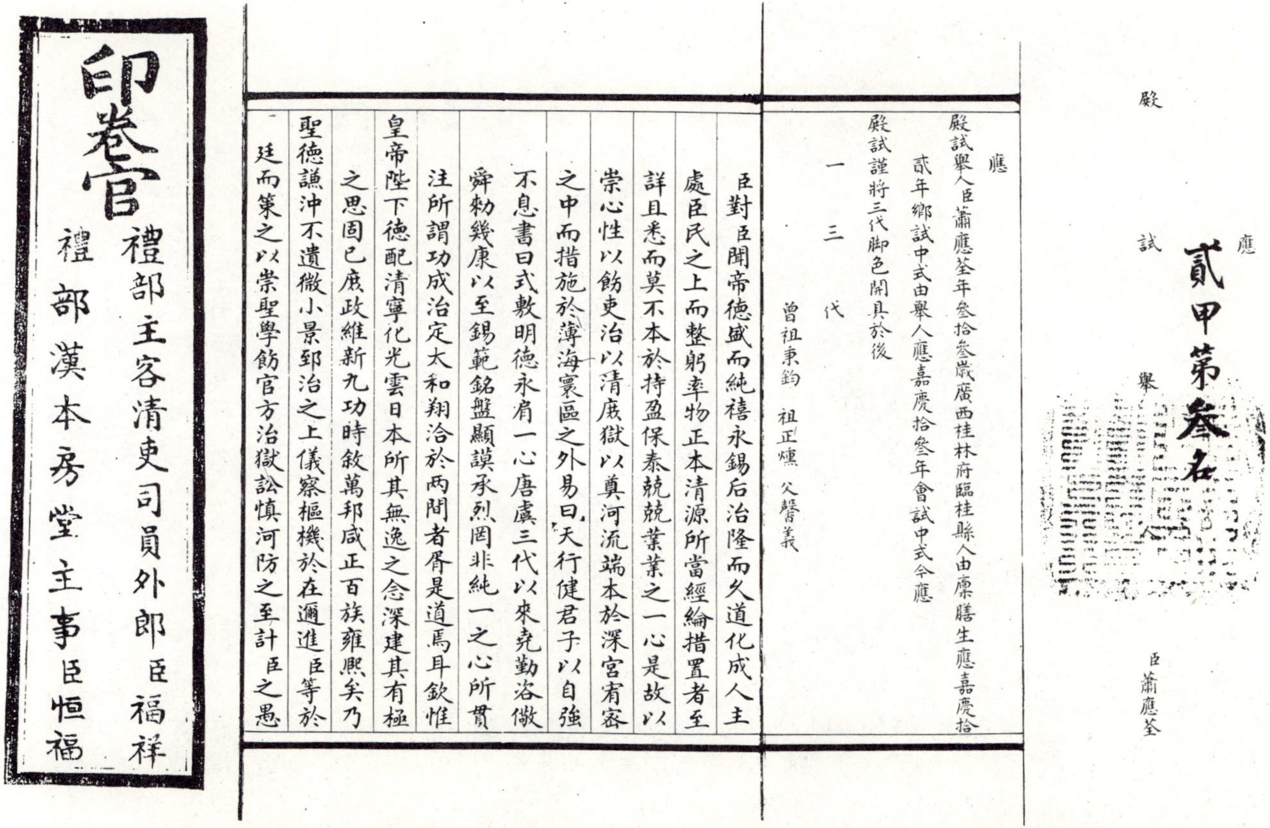
殿試 應舉
貳甲第叁名
臣蕭應荃

應
殿試舉人臣蕭應荃年叁拾叁歲廣西桂林府臨桂縣人由廩膳生應嘉慶拾
貳年鄉試中式由舉人應嘉慶拾叁年會試中式今應
殿試謹將三代脚色開具於後
一 三 代
曾祖秉鈞 祖正燻 父馨義

臣對臣聞帝德盛而純禧永錫后治隆而久道化成人主
處臣民之上而整躬率物正本清源所當經綸措置者至
詳且悉而莫不本於持盈保泰兢兢業業之一心是故以
崇心性以飭吏治以清庶獄以奠河流端本於深宮宥密
之中而措施於薄海寰區之外易曰天行健君子以自強
不息書曰式敷明德永肩一心唐虞三代以來堯勤洛儆
舜勑幾康以至錫範銘盤顯謨承烈罔非純一之心所貫
注所謂功成治定太和翔洽於兩間者胥是道焉耳欽惟
皇帝陛下德配清寧化光雲日本所其無逸之念深建其有極
之思固已庶政維新九功時敘萬邦咸正百族雍熙矣乃
聖德謙沖不遺微小景郅治之上儀察樞機於在邇進臣等於
廷而策之以崇聖學飭官方治獄訟慎河防之至計臣之愚

印卷官
禮部主客清吏司員外郎臣福祥
禮部漢本房堂主事臣恒福

Civil Service examination paper of *Hsiao Ying-ch'üan* for *Chin-shih* in 1808

Portrait of *Chen Hung-mo* (p. 178)

Chapter XI

HISTORICAL GEOGRAPHY

The term *fang-chih* 方志, meaning geographic record, is taken from the phrase denoting the duties of the office of the outer historian 外史 in charge of the records of the four directions. This office is under the Ministry of the Spring. *Fang-chih* implies at once history and geography. Offices in charge of national and local geographic records began with Chinese political life. National geography from great antiquity has been highly regarded as essential to economic administration and national defense. Historical and geographical records, especially the latter, were always securely guarded by the government because they contained information of vital importance. They usually contained topographic maps of strategic centers for national defense and of areas for irrigation and river conservancy.

Among Chinese historians the interest in writing local history was deep-seated because it afforded them both intellectual and practical gratification. They were free to select and organize materials and to write without restrictions. The soundness of national records depended upon the value of the local gazetteers.

The geographic divisions of China were closely related to efficient administration and to dynastic security. An incoming dynasty would make new geographical divisions of the country. Annexation of frontier territories or the loss of territories to invaders brought inevitable changes in the boundary lines of provinces, as might also the shifting of a river course, especially that of the Yellow River, or change in population arising from human or natural catastrophies. New geographic names often reflect historic events. So it is to be expected that every standard history of China has a treatise on geography, and most of them have treatises on rivers and canals, economic geography, and national defense.

HISTORICAL GEOGRAPHY: NATIONAL AND LOCAL

The writing of national geography required governmental patronage for the best work because of the secrecy surrounding national geography, the difficulty of travel, and the restrictions placed on the use of archives. Patronage was not withheld, because every ruler wished to exhibit his achievements by decreeing a compilation of national geography and by enlisting scholars in so important a work.

Similarly, patronage supported the writing of local history. The magistrate, the prefect, and even the governor were usually men appointed because of their literary achievements exhibited in civil service examinations. Whether their intellectual interest persisted or not, it was a tradition that they should initiate revision and compilation of local histories. This compilation served at once to demonstrate the officer's good work and to place scholars in need of work. To give patronage to the worthy but unfortunate scholars was a traditional practice, and such patronage made possible many of the local histories.

The following selection of outstanding works on national and local historical geography, many from the *Ch'ing* period, reveals a good balance of intellectual and practical achievements. The general gazetteers of the provinces were in the main written under patronage of the viceroy or governor; the national geographical works, historical or contemporary, were compilations made under imperial decrees. With regard to the gazetteers of the prefectures, the greater number are official and semiofficial compilations. Gazetteers of counties, twelve of which are listed in chapter VIII are mainly endeavors of private historians. The numbers in parenthesis represent *chüan*.

Huang-yü piao 皇輿表 Tables of imperial geography (16) decreed by *K'ang-hsi* in 1704

Man-chou yüan-liu k'ao 滿洲源流考 An historical and geographical study of Manchuria (20) decreed by *Ch'ien-lung* in 1777

 Tung Kao 董誥 1740-1818, director for the compilation

HISTORICAL GEOGRAPHY

Jih-hsia chiu-wen k'ao 日下舊聞 History of Peking and its environs
    Chu I-tsun 朱彝尊 1629-1709

Ch'ü-yü t'u-chih 區宇圖志 Historical geography illustrated with maps
    Ts'ui K'uo 崔廓 fl. 560-610

Ti-li chih 地理志 Historical geography
    Hsiao Te-yen 蕭德言 558-654, and others

T'ai-p'ing huan-yü chi 太平寰宇記 Geographical records of the empire (200)
    Yüeh Shih 樂史 930-1007

Yüan-feng chiu-yü chih 元豐九域志 History of the nine regions during the *Yüan-feng* period 1078-1086 (10)
    Wang Ts'un 王存 fl. 1060-1085

Ta i-t'ung-chih 大一統志 Great official gazetteer of the *Yüan* dynasty
    Cha-ma-la-ting (Jamal-ud-Din) 札馬拉丁 and *Yü Ying-lung* 虞應龍 late thirteenth century

Ta-Yüan ta-i-t'ung-chih 大元大一統志 Comprehensive geography of the *Yüan* empire (1300)
    Po Lan-hsi 孛蘭盼 1298-1342, Yüeh Hsüan 岳鉉 fl. 1300-50

Huan-yü t'ung-chih 寰宇通志 General gazetteer of the empire
    Shang Lo 商輅 1414-1486

Kuang-yü t'u 廣宇圖 Terrestial maps based on the *Yü-t'u* 宇圖 of Chu Ssu-pen 朱思本 1273-1335 ?; foundation for Norvus Atlas Sinesis of Martin Martini
    Lo Hung-hsien 羅洪先 1504-1564

Ta-Ming i-t'ung-chih 大明一統志 Comprehensive geography of the *Ming* dynasty
    Li Hsien 李賢 1408-1466

Ta-Ch'ing i-t'ung-chih 大清一統志 Comprehensive geography of the *Ch'ing* dynasty (342)
    Hsü Ch'ien-hsüeh 徐乾學 1631-1694

178   ELEMENTS OF CHINESE HISTORIOGRAPHY

Li-tai ti-li yen-ko-piao 歷代地理沿革表 Tables showing changes in geographical names (47)
  Ch'en Fang-chi 陳芳績 1630-1670
Li-tai ti-li-chih yün-pien chin-shih 地理志韻編今釋 A dictionary of geographical names with modern notes (20)
  Li Chao-lo 李兆洛 1769-1841
Ku kuo-tu chin-chün-hsien ho-k'ao 古國都今郡縣合考 A comparative study of ancient capitals and modern areas
  Min Lin-ssu 閔麟嗣 18th century

PROVINCIAL AND PREFECTURAL GAZETTEERS

An-hui t'ung-chih 安徽通志 General gazetteer of *Anhui* (250)
  Liu K'un-i 劉坤一 1830-1902
Che-chiang t'ung-chih 浙江通志 General gazetteer of *Chekiang* (280)
  Chi Tseng-yün 稽曾筠 1671-1739
Chi-fu t'ung-chih 畿輔通志 General gazetteer of *Chihli* (300)
  Li Hung-chang 李鴻章 1823-1902
Chiang-hsi t'ung-chih 江西通志 General gazetteer of *Kiangsi* (206)
  Pai Huang 白潢 fl. 1700-1725
Chiang-nan t'ung-chih 江南通志 General gazetteer of *Chiangnan*
  Chao Hung-en 趙宏恩 fl. 1720-1740   (200)
Fu-chien t'ung-chih 福建通志 General gazetteer of *Fukien* (120)
  Mai Chu 邁柱 fl. 1715-1740
Ho-nan t'ung-chih 河南通志 General gazetteer of *Honan* (80)
  Wang Shih-tsen 王士俊 d. 1756
Hsin-chiang t'ung-chih 新疆通志 General gazetter of *Sinkiang*
  Wang T'ing-chen 汪廷珍 1757-1827   (13)
Hu-nan t'ung-chih 湖南通志 General gazetteer of *Hunan* (170)
  Ch'en Hung-mou 陳宏謀 1696-1771
Hu-pei t'ung-chih 湖北通志 General gazetteer of *Hupeh* (100)
  Wu Hsiung-kuang 吳熊光 1750-1833

HISTORICAL GEOGRAPHY

Kan-su t'ung-chih 甘肅通志 General gazetteer of *Kansu* (50)
    Hsü Jung 許容 1686-1751
Kuang-hsi t'ung-chih 廣西通志 General gazetteer of *Kuangsi* (280)
    Chi Ch'ing 吉慶 d. 1802
Kuang-tung t'ung-chih 廣東通志 General gazetteer of *Kuangtung*
    Juan Yüan 阮元 1764-1849 [(334)]
Kuei-chou t'ung-chih 貴州通志 General gazetteer of *Kueichou* (46)
    O Erh-t'ai 阿爾泰 d. 1745
Shan-hsi t'ung-chih 山西通志 General gazetteer of *Shansi* (184)
    Chang Hsü 張煦 *chin-shih*, 1863
Shan-tung t'ung-chih 山東通志 General gazetteer of *Shantung* (36)
    Yüeh Chün 岳濬 1704-1753
Shen-hsi t'ung-chih 陝西通志 General gazetteer of *Shensi* (100)
    Liu Yü-i 劉於義 fl. 1703-1740
Sheng-ching t'ung-chih 盛京通志 General gazetteer of *Shengking*
    A Kuei 阿桂 1717-1797 [(48)]
Ssu-ch'uan t'ung-chih 四川通志 General gazetteer of *Szechuan* (47)
    Huang T'ing-kuei 黃庭桂 1691-1759
Yün-nan t'ung-chih 雲南通志 General gazetteer of *Yünnan* (30)
    A Erh-t'ai 阿爾泰 d. 1745

Ch'ang-sha-fu chih 長沙府志 Gazetteer of *Changshafu* (50)
    Lü Su-kao 呂肅高
Chi-nan-fu chih 濟南府志 Gazetteer of *Tsinanfu* (72)
    Wang Tseng-fang 王贈芳 *chin-shih* 進士 1811
Chiang-ning-fu chih 江寧府志 Gazetteer of *Chiangningfu*
    Yao Nai 姚鼐 1732-1815
Fu-chou-fu chih 福州府志 Gazetteer of *Fuchowfu* (76)
    Kao Ching-sung 高景崧
Hang-chou-fu chih 杭州府志 Gazetteer of *Hangchowfu*
    Shao Chin-han 邵晉涵 1743-1796

180   ELEMENTS OF CHINESE HISTORIOGRAPHY

Hsi-an-fu chih 西安府志   Gazetteer of *Sianfu* (80)
 Yen Ch'ang-ming 嚴長明 1731-1787
K'ai-feng-fu chih 開封府志   Gazetteer of *Kaifengfu* (40)
 Kuan Chieh-chung 管竭忠
Kuang-chou-fu chih 廣州府志   Gazetteer of *Kuangchowfu* (60)
 Shen T'ing-fang 沈廷芳 1702-1772
Kuei-yang-fu chih 貴陽府志   Gazetteer of *Kueiyangfu*
 Tsou Han-hsün 鄒漢勛 1805-1854
Lan-chou-fu chih 蘭州府志   Gazetteer of *Lanchowfu* (4)
 Ch'en Ju-chi 陳如稷
Nan-ch'ang-fu chih 南昌府志   Gazetteer of *Nanchangfu*
 Huang Liang-tung 黃良棟 *chin-shih*, 1754
Pao-ting-fu chih 保定府志   Gazetteer of *Paotingfu* (80)
 Li Chen-hu 李振祜 fl. 1810-1830
Shun-t'ien-fu chih 順天府志   Gazetteer of *Shuntienfu*
 Li Hung-chang 李鴻章 1823-1902
T'ai-yüan-fu chih 太原府志   Gazetteer of *Taiyüanfu* (60)
 Shen Shu-sheng 沈樹聲
T'ien-chin-fu chih 天津府志   Gazetteer of *Tientsin* prefecture
 Li Mei-shih 李梅實 *chin-shih*, 1721
Wu-ch'ang-fu chih 武昌府志   Gazetteer of *Wuchangfu* (12)
 P'ei T'ien-hsi 裴天錫
Yün-nan-fu chih 雲南府志   Gazetteer of *Yünnanfu* (30)
 Chang Yü 張毓

GEOGRAPHICAL DIVISIONS OF THIRTY CENTURIES

Many American geographical names have common prefixes or suffixes, such as New Jersey, New York, Newport, Charlestown, Youngstown, Hartville, Greenville. Chinese names reveal a similar pattern: *Hunan,* south of the Lake; *Hupeh,* north of the lake; *Shantung,* east of the mountain; *Shansi,* west of the mountain; *Peking,* northern capital; *Nanking,* southern capital; *T'ai-an,* great peace; *Si-an,* western peace.

American geographical names may indicate the founder, settlers, or the ideals of these settlers, whereas most Chinese geographical names indicate the four directions, mountains, rivers, plains, and such life ideals as happiness, dignity, peace. Some names record historical events such as pacification and annexation and such topographic features as the confluence of two rivers and strategic locations.

The persistence of the basic terms is notable both in the names of the geographic divisions and in the names of capitals. The old names continue to be used instead of or parallel to the modern names of provinces and cities in both official and unofficial writings and in the speech of educated persons. The terms *Chi, Chin, Ch'in, Ch'u, Lu, Shu, Yü,* and *Wu* parallel, respectively, *Hopei, Shansi, Shensi, Hupeh, Shantung, Szechuan, Honan,* and *Kiangsu.* Names of old capitals and cities remain in the names of cities today: *Loyang, Tsingchow, Sian, Hsüchow, Yangchow,* and *Chengtu.*

The historical geography of China reveals a continuity almost identical with that of China's history. Geographic names serve as carriers of historical experience. Valley Forge to the American is no longer just a village northwest of Philadelphia, and so it is that *Wu-chiang* 烏江 is not just a stream in *Anhui* province. *Hsiang Chi* 233-202 B.C., defeated in battle, committed suicide at *Wu-chiang.* When "wagon road" is mentioned in the United States, the history of westward movement presents itself; likewise, *"Hakkas"* 客家 "guest families" suggests to the Chinese the rugged migration from the north across the *Tsingling* mountains caused by the Tatar invasions during the fourth and ninth centuries. The *Hakkas* migrated to *Fukien* and *Kwangtung* from *Honan* and *Shantung.*

The geographic divisions listed in this section show not only the persistence of the basic terms in the names of these divisions but also the small number of changes in names from dynasty to dynasty. Brief

182   ELEMENTS OF CHINESE HISTORIOGRAPHY

notes on the addition, omission, or combination of provinces indicate why and how changes were made by a new dynasty.

GEOGRAPHIC DIVISIONS ACCORDING TO YU-KUNG AND ERH-YA

Yü-kung 禹貢 is the name given to the geographical section in the Classic of History. *Kung* means tribute. The nine provinces described in the *Yü-kung* sent tribute to the central authorities. The author of the *Yü-kung,* or "Tribute of *Yü,*" according to Chinese tradition, is *Yü,* reportedly a great engineer who brought the deluge under control. His record of the observations he made in these nine provinces became the first geography of China.

The names of the nine provinces described in the *Yü-kung* are given here with the names of the equivalent modern geographic areas. *Chi* 冀 hopeful, *Shansi; Ching* 荆 thorny, *Hupeh; Ch'ing* 青 blue or east, *Shantung; Hsü* 徐 gentle, *Kiangsu; Liang* 梁 bridge, *Szechuan; Yang* 揚 praise, *Kiangsu; Yen* 兗 faithful, *Shantung; Yü* 豫 happy, *Honan; Yung* 雍 harmonious, *Shensi.*

Another work of antiquity, the *Erh-ya* 爾雅, an ancient lexicon, also gives nine geographical divisions of China. Authorship of this work is attributed to Confucius, to his disciples, and to a number of other ancients. It was probably compiled during the second century before the Christian era. The nine geographical divisions named in the *Erh-ya* probably represented the end of *Yin,* 1301-1051 B.C., and the beginning of *Chou.*

Two of the nine provinces in the *Erh-ya* are not named in the "Tribute of *Yü.*" *Yu-chou* is a new province extending eastward from *Chi-chou.* The other new province, *Ying-chou,* covers the same area in eastern *Shantung* as *Ch'ing-chou* of the earlier period. *Yu* 幽 means "hidden;" *Ying* 營 means "camps".

GEOGRAPHIC DIVISIONS OF THE CHOU PERIOD 1050-256 B.C.

During the early *Chou* period, from the founding to the removal of the capital in 770, China was unified under one rule. It is therefore

HISTORICAL GEOGRAPHY 183

possible to accept the record of geographic divisions in this period. One section of the *Chou-li* 周禮 Rites of *Chou,* known as *Chih-fang* 職方, describes the names of eight of the nine provinces of *Erh-ya.* *Hsü-chou* is not named. The ninth province in the *Chih-fang* is *Ping-chou* 并州 united province.

The small variation in the names of the nine provinces described in the *Yü-kung,* the *Erh-ya,* and the *Chih-fang* suggests a common tradition.

From the time of removal of *Chou* capital to *Loyang* 洛陽 to the death of Confucius is approximately the traditional demarcation of the *Ch'un-ch'iu* period, 722-480. During this period some one hundred seventy kingdoms were reduced to twelve powerful states. Geographic divisions, like the map of Europe for the last century, went through repeated changes. Suffice it here to enumerate the leading states and to give their corresponding territories in modern China: *Ch'i* 齊, *Shantung; Chin* 晉, *Shansi; Ch'in* 秦, *Shensi; Ch'u* 楚, *Hupeh; Lu* 魯, *Shantung; Sung* 宋, *Honan; Wu* 吳, *Kiangsu; Yen* 燕, *Hopei; Yüeh* 越, *Chekiang.*

The third traditional divsion of the *Chou* period, 478-256, is well characterized by the name Chinese historians give to the shorter period between 403 and 221, *Chan-kuo* 戰國 contending states. Two of the states, *Ch'in* in the north and *Ch'u* in the south, became increasingly strong. *Ch'in* annexed her neighbors on the east and west. *Ch'u* absorbed the entire lower *Yangtze* valley to the sea. *Chin* was divided into three kingdoms: *Han* 韓, *Chao* 趙, and *Wei* 魏. *Shu* 蜀 and *Pa* 巴 were for a brief period states in west China. *Yen* extended herself to southern Manchuria.

GEOGRAPHICAL DIVISIONS OF THE CH'IN DYNASTY, 221-207 B.C.

Ch'in Shih-huang-ti 秦始皇帝 First Great Ruler of *Ch'in,* after having brought the country under a unified and centralized administration, divided the country into 36 *chün* 郡. Etymologically the word *chün* is made up of king 君 and city 阝. Here *chün* is used instead of *chou* to mean province. The names of the thirty-six provinces bear meanings which may be grouped as relating to rivers, valleys, ranges, mountains, sand, forests, animals, numerals, and directions.

Ch'ang-sha 長沙 long sand, *Hunan*
Ch'i 齊 even, *Shantung*
Chiu-kiang 九江 nine rivers, *Hunan*
Chiu-yüan 九原 nine plains, *Sui-yüan*
Chü-lu 鉅鹿 giant deer, *Hopei*
Han-chung 漢中 *Han* river center, *Shensi*
Han-tan 邯鄲 mountain terminus, *Hopei*
Ho-tung 河東 east of the river, *Shansi*
Hsiang 象 elephant, *Kuangtung-Kuangsi-Anam*
Hsüeh 薛 marsh grass, *Shantung*
K'uai-chi 會稽 collective inquiry, *Chekiang*
Kuei-lin 桂林 laurel forest, *Kuangsi*
Lang-ya 琅琊 jade-like mountain, *Shantung*
Liao-hsi 遼西 west of *Liao* river, *Jehol*
Liao-tung 遼東 east of *Liao* river, south Manchuria
Lung-hsi 隴西 dike west, *Kansu*
Nan 南 south, *Hupeh*
Nan-hai 南海 south sea, *Kuangtung*
Nan-yang 南陽 sunny south, *Honan*
Pa 巴 serpent, *Szechuan*
Pei-ti 北地 northern territory, *Kansu*
San-ch'uan 三川 three rivers, *Honan*
Shang 上 upper, *Shensi*
Shang-ku 尚谷 upper valley, *Hopei*
Shang-tang 上黨 upper clan, *Shansi*
Shu 蜀 *Shu*-tribe, *Szechuan*
Ssu-shui 四水 four streams, *Kiangsu*
Tai 代 generations, *Shansi*
T'ai-yüan 太原 great plain, *Shansi*

Tang 碭 rock, *Honan*
Tung 東 east, *Hopei*
Yen-men 燕門 swallow gate, *Shansi*
Ying-ch'uan 郢川 clear river, *Honan*
Yu-pei-p'ing 右北平 right north peace, *Jehol*
Yün-chung 中雲 cloud center, *Sui-yüan*
Yü-yang 漁陽 fishing in the sun, *Hopei*

THIRTEEN PROVINCES OF HAN 206 B.C.-220 A.D.

In the treatise on geography in the *Han-shu*, the term *pu* 部, department, is used. The term *Chou* 州 is used for province during the Later *Han*. It is interesting to note that only four of the thirteen provinces bear new names: *Liang* 涼 cold, *Kansu-Ninghsia-Sinkiang*; *I* 益 benefit, *Szechuan-Yünnan*; *Chiao-chih* 趾交 cross toes, *Annam*; and *Ssu-li hsiao-wei* 司隷校尉 peace administrator, *Shensi-Shansi-Honan*. The other nine names are those of antiquity. They are *Chi* 冀, *Ching* 荊, *Ch'ing* 青, *Hsü* 徐, *Liang* 梁, *Yang* 揚, *Yen* 兗, *Yü* 豫, *Yung* 雍.

NINETEEN PROVINCES OF THE CHIN 265-418 A.D.

Under the *Chin*, China was divided for a century and a half into nineteen provinces, thirteen of which had old names. Four names are new and two are adaptations. The new ones are as follows: *Ch'in* 秦, *Shensi*; *Ning* 寧, *Yünnan*; *P'ing* 平, south Manchuria; *Kuang* 廣, *Kuangtung*. *Ssu-li hsiao-wei* was simplified into *Ssu* 司 and *Chiao-chih* into *Chiao* 交, and they correspond in territories also.

NINE PROVINCES OF THE SUI DYNASTY 590-618

After the collapse of China, Southern *Sung*, 420-479, instituted twenty-two provinces; Southern *Ch'i*, 479-502, twenty-three provinces; and Northern *Wei*, 386-535, one hundred and thirteen *chou*. When the *Sui* reunited China, the geographical division of the country reverted back to the nine provinces of *Yü-kung*.

TEN PROVINCES OF THE T'ANG DYNASTY 618-960

Instead of *chou* 州, *chün* 郡, *pu* 部, the new term for province in the *T'ang* period is *Tao* 道 circuit or regions. In the names of these ten regions, two main characteristics are evident: directions and geographic features. These names furnish a pattern for names of modern provinces. The ten regions are as follows:

Chiang-nan 江南 river south, bounded north by the *Yangtze,* south by the mountain ranges, west by *Szechuan,* and east to the sea

Chien-nan 劍南 dagger south, bounded by barbarians in the south, north to the *Chien-shan,* dagger mountain, west to *Turfan* 土番, and east to the sea

Ho-nan 河南 river south, bounded south by the *Huai* river, north by the Yellow river, west to *Han-ku-kuan* 函谷關, enveloping valley gateway, and east to the sea

Ho-pei 河北 river north, bounded south by the Yellow river, north by *Yü-kuan* 楡關 elm gateway, or *Shan-hai-kuan* 山海關 and *Chi-men* 薊門 thistle gate, *Chü-yung-kuan* 居庸關 west to the *T'ai-hang* 太行 and *Heng* 恒 mountains, and east to the sea

Ho-tung 河東 river east, bounded south by the *Shou-yang* 陽首 and *T'ai-hang* mountains, north to the *T'u-ch'üeh* 突厥 or eastern Turks, west by the Yellow river, and east to the *Heng-shan*

Huai-nan 淮南 *Huai* river south, bounded south by the *Yangtze,* north by the *Huai* river, west by the *Han* river 漢水, and east to the sea

Kuan-nei 關內 inside the gateway, bounded south by the *Chung-nan* 終南 mountains, north by the Tatars, west by *Lung-pan* 隴坂, and east by the Yellow river

Ling-nan 嶺南 range south, bounded south by barbarian lands, north by the Dagger mountains, west by *Turfan,* and east to the sea

HISTORICAL GEOGRAPHY 187

Lung-yu 隴右 south of *Lung* mountain, bounded south by the *Yangtze*, north by the *Huai* river, west by the *Han* river, and east to *Ch'in-chou* 秦州

Shan-nan 山南 mountain south, bounded south by the *Yangtze*, north by the *Shang* 商 and *Hua* 華 mountains, west to *Lung-chou* 隴州, and east to *Ching-chou* 荊州

GEOGRAPHICAL DIVISIONS OF THE SUNG DYNASTY 960-1276

The geographical divisions of the *Sung* went through two changes: first expansion from fifteen *Lu* 路 routes, to nineteen, to twenty-three, to twenty-six; second, contraction to seventeen, limited to the *Yangtze* valley and south.

Sixteen of the twenty-six were divided or designated with reference to the national capital, to the Yellow, the *Huai*, and *Yangtze* Rivers, to the *Tung-t'ing* 洞庭 lake, and to the "extended areas." As these names had little meaning to the dynasties listed below we give here just two examples: *Ching-chi lu* 京畿路 capital area route, *Ching-tung tung-lu* 京東東路 east route of capital east, *Ching-tung hsi-lu* 京東西路 west route of capital east, *Ching-hsi pei-lu* 京西北路 north route of capital west, *Ching-hsi nan-lu* 京西南路 south route of capital west, *Huai-nan tung-lu* 淮南東路 east route of *Huai* river south, *Hui-nan hsi-lu* 淮南西路 west route of *Huai* river south

TEN PROVINCES OF THE YUAN DYNASTY 1277-1368

The *Sung* period marked one of the highlights of Chinese cultural history, but the geographical division into *Lu* 路 bears military connotation. The Mongols were not highly regarded by the Chinese on account of their lack of culture in the Chinese sense; curiously enough, the names of their geographical divisions have lasted nearly seven hundred years. The Mongols used the term *Sheng* 省, inspection, to designate a province; they divided the country into ten provinces. Areas of these ten provinces were larger than today, though the same names appear. Under the Mongols, they expanded an old Chinese office of the central government, *chung-shu-sheng* 中書省 central record inspection, into *hsing chung-shu-sheng* 行中書省 enforcing central record inspection for provincial administration. The shortened form has been in use ever since, *hsing-sheng* 行省, meaning province.

  Chung-shu 中書 Hopei and *Shansi*
  Chiang-che 江浙 Kiangsu and *Chekiang*
  Chiang-hsi 江西 Kiangsi
  Ho-nan 河南 Honan
  Hu-kuang 湖廣 Hunan, Hupeh, Kuangsi and *Kuangtung*
  Kan-su 甘肅 Kansu
  Liao-yang 遼陽 southern Manchuria
  Shen-hsi 陝西 Shensi
  Ssu-ch'uan 四川 Szechuan
  Yün-nan 雲南 Yunnan

FIFTEEN PROVINCES OF THE MING DYNASTY 1368-1644

  Generally speaking, there were fifteen provinces during the *Ming* dynasty. Like every other period, there were always changes. Prior to the transfer of the capital from *Nanking* to *Peking* there were thirteen provinces as political divisions and seven important frontiers ruled by seven military governors. Finally, these became fifteen provinces and nine frontier garrison centers. A unique characteristic lies in the two capital provinces: *Nanking* 南京 province, or *Nan Chihli* 南直隸, direct imperial administration in the south, comprising two modern provinces, *Kiangsu* and *Anhui*; *Ching-shih* 京師, *Peking* province, or *Pei Chihli* 北直隸, direct imperial administration in the north.

  Instead of listing the names of the other provinces, we shall give the nine garrison centers: *Liao-tung* 遼東, *Chi-chou* 薊州, *Hsüan-hua* 宣化, *T'ai-yüan* 太原, *Ta-t'ung* 大同, *Yü-lin* 榆林, *Ning-hsia* 寧夏, *Ku-yüan* 固原, and *Kan-su* 甘肅. These names continue to appear in Chinese history during the following three or four centuries because of their strategic importance.

HISTORICAL GEOGRAPHY

GEOGRAPHICAL DIVISIONS UNDER THE CH'ING DYNASTY 1644-1911

Between 1644 and 1875, there were eighteen provinces. The *Nan Chihli* of *Ming* became *Kiangsu* and *Anhui*, and *Hu-kuang* became *Hunan* and *Hupeh*. *Kansu* was restored as a province. The fifteen *Ming* provinces were thus converted into eighteen provinces.

Hsin-chiang 新疆 new boundry, formerly known as Chinese Turkestan, a territory lying east of the Pamirs, west of *Kansu*, north of the *Kunlun* Mountains, became a regular province in 1882. In 1886, *T'ai-wan* 臺灣, known as Formosa, became a new province (ceded to Japan 1895-1945). In 1903 Manchuria was made into three provinces; hence the popular name, *Tung-san-sheng* 東三省 eastern three provinces. They are *Hei-lung-chiang* 黑龍江 black dragon river, *Chi-lin* 吉林 lucky forest, and *Sheng-ching* 盛京 prosperous capital.

GEOGRAPHICAL DIVISION UNDER NATIONALIST CHINA, 1928-1950

Six provinces were added to the existing twenty-two of the *Manchu* period: *Jehol* 熱河, hot river, and *Chahar* 察哈爾, transliteration of a tribal name, parts of *Chihli* province and of Inner Mongolia; *Sui-yüan* 綏遠 tranquil frontier, part of old *Chahar* and a portion of Inner Mongolia; *Ning-hsia* 寧夏 peaceful China, *Ning-hsia* district and territories of Inner Mongolia; *Ch'ing-hai* 青海, blue sea, *Koko Nor*, so named because of a salt lake which the Tibetans called *Tsong-nong-pu*; *Hsi-k'ang* 西康, western peace, formerly known as *Ch'uan-pien* 川邊 part of *Szechuan* borderland, *Szechuan* and part of Tibet. *Sheng-ching* 盛京 was renamed *Feng-t'ien* 奉天, and *Liao-ning* 遼寧 in 1912 and in 1928 respectively. *Chihli* 直隸 was renamed *Hopei* 河北 in 1928.

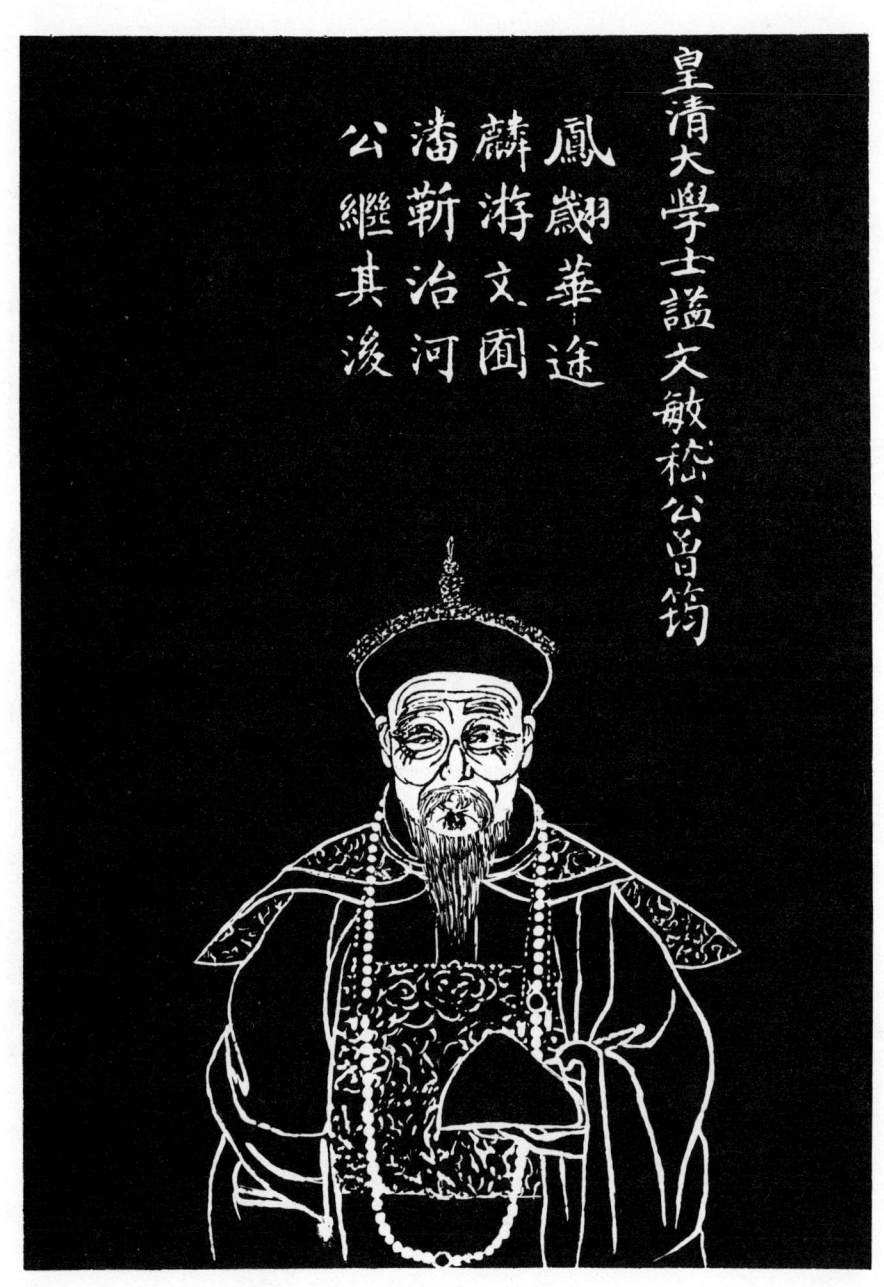

Portrait of *Chi Tseng-yün* (p. 178)

Chapter XII

THE TWENTY-SIX DYNASTIC HISTORIES

SUCCESSIVE GROUPINGS

Even though the twenty-six dynastic histories cover successive periods of Chinese history, they were not produced one by one as each dynasty became "happenings of the past." The compilation of a dynastic history might be undertaken centuries after the last year of the dynasty. So it was with the *Chin-shu*, History of the *Chin* Dynasty, which was not decreed until more than two-hundred and thirty years after the close of the dynasty. By that time, eighteen versions of *Chin* history had been written.

Many studies of dynastic histories relate to groups of these histories: three histories, ten histories, thirteen, seventeen, eighteen,, nineteen, twenty-one, twenty-two. Since the twenty-second dynastic history, three works, by decree or executive order, have been recognized as dynastic histories. Another, the twenty-sixth, remains a draft history, once forbidden to be circulated.

Here we identify the dynastic histories in each of the several groups mentioned above and cite historical studies relating to each.

For a long time, the "three histories" had reference to the *Shih-chi*, Historical Memoirs, the *Han-shu*, History of the Former *Han*, and the *Tung-kuan Han-chi*, Later *Han* Record, by *Liu Chen*, decreed in 109. When *Chang Wen* 張溫, of the third century, wrote his *San-shih lüeh* 三史略 Essentials of the Three Histories, he had reference to the *Shih-chi*, the *Han-shu*, and the *Tung-kuan Han-chi*. By the time *Ch'üeh Yin* 闕駰, of the seventh century, wrote his *San-shih ch'ün-yen* 三史群言 Social Pronouncements of the Three Histories, he dealt with the *Shih-chi*, the *Han-shu*, and *Fan Yeh's Hou-Han-shu*. This Later *Han* history did not appear until two hundred years after the end of the dynasty.

Li An 李安, of the early seventh century, wrote *Shih-shih lei-yao* 十史類要 Classified Essentials of Ten Histories. The "ten" refers to *San-kuo-chih* 三國志 History of the Three Kingdoms, now recognized as the fourth dynastic history, and to nine later ones: *Chin-shu, Sung-shu, Pei-Ch'i-shu, Liang-shu, Ch'en-shu, Wei-shu, Nan-Ch'i-shu, Chou-shu,* and *Sui-shu.*

In another two hundred years or so studies of "thirteen histories" were being made. By the latter half of the eleventh century, the "thirteen histories" were in wide circulation. Of the thirteen, three are those named in the work of *Ch'üeh Yin,* and ten are those included in *Li An's* Classified Essentials of Ten Histories. The treatise on literature in the *Sung-shih* makes reference to works on the "thirteen histories." One of these works is *Shih-san-tai shih po-i* 十三代史駁義 A Critique of the Thirteen Histories, 12 *chüan,* by *Wu Wu-ling* 吳武陵 fl. 800-830. Another is *Shih-san-tai shih-mu* 十三代史目 Classifications of History in the Thirteen Histories, 10 *chüan,* by *Tsung Chien* 宗諫.

By the end of the eleventh century, the term *shih-ch'i-shih,* "seventeen histories," was in wide use. The former thirteen had been increased to seventeen by the addition of the following four works: *Nan-shih, Pei-shih, Hsin T'ang-shu* and *Wu-tai shih-chi.* From comprehensive studies of these seventeen dynastic histories came *Shih-ch'i-shih tsan* 十七史贊 Aids to the Seventeen Histories by *Chou Hu* 周護; *Shih-ch'i-shih ch'üeh-lun* 十七史榷論 Reliable Discussions of the Seventeen Histories, 104 *chüan,* by an unknown author; *Shih-ch'i-shih meng-ch'iu* 十七史蒙求 Introductory Search into the Seventeen Histories, 16 *chüan,* by a Mr. *Wang,* 王某 and *Shih-ch'i-shih shang-ch'üeh* 十七史商榷 A Critical Study of the Seventeen Dynastic Histories, 100 *chüan,* by *Wang Ming-sheng* (p. 93).

Tseng Hsien-chih 曾先之 late in the *Yüan* period, wrote *Shih-pa-shih lüeh* 十八史略 Outlines of the Eighteen Histories. The works he included are in doubt because the *Liao-shih* and the *Chin-shih* were not finished until 1344, and the *Sung-shih* not until 1345.

THE TWENTY-SIX DYNASTIC HISTORIES

The *Yüan-shih* brought the number of dynastic histories to nineteen. *Liang Meng-yin* 梁孟因, of the late fourteenth century, wrote the *Shih-chiu-shih lüeh* 十九史畧 Outline of the Nineteen Histories.

After another century of publication, the term "twenty-one histories" became an accepted name for the ten current dynastic histories. *Liao-shih* and *Chin-shih* had brought the number of dynastic histories to twenty-one. One work on this group of histories is *Erh-shih-i-shih t'ung-i* 二十一史同異. Similarities and Differences in the Twenty-one Dynastic Histories by *Li Ch'ing* (p. 134).

In 1739 an imperial decree was issued to print and circulate the "twenty-two" histories. The *Ming-shih* had brought the number to twenty-two. Two famous works were written on the "twenty-two histories," namely, *Nien-erh-shih k'ao-i* 廿二史考異 Discrepancies in the Twenty-two Dynastic Histories by *Ch'ien Ta-hsin* (p. 126) and *Nien-erh-shih cha-chi* 廿二史箚記 Critical Notes on the Twenty-two Dynastic Histories by *Chao I* (p. 124).

Before long it was decreed that *Chiu T'ang-shu* and *Wu-tai shih-chi*, later known as *Hsin Wu-tai-shih*, be recognized as dynastic histories. These two brought the total number to twenty-four.

Two more dynastic histories were added under more or less unusual circumstances. *Hsin Yüan-shih*, by *K'o Shao-min* (p. 132), was made a dynastic history by executive order of the president of the Chinese Republic in 1921. *Ch'ing-shih-kao* 清史稿, *Ch'ing* History Draft, completed in 1927 but forbidden to be circulated by the Nationalist government, continues to be known as a draft dynastic history. Many scholars refuse to recognize the *Ch'ing-shih-kao* as the twenty-sixth dynastic history. However, since this work is in harmony with the traditional dynastic histories, some include it with the twenty-five and refer to *nien-liu-shih* 廿六史, or the twenty-six dynastic histories.

The twenty-six dynastic histories are given below in chronological order with respect to the dynasties, as evidenced by the date of the dynastic rule following the name of the history. "Bureau" means the

Bureau of Historiography. The name given with compilations made by the Bureau is that of the director of the Bureau who was chiefly responsible for the work.

1. Historical Memoirs, *Shih-chi* 史記 to 122 B.C.
   Compiled 104-87 B.C. by official decree
   Ssu-ma Ch'ien 司馬遷 145-86 B.C.
2. History of the Former *Han, Han-shu,* 漢書 206 B.C.-24 A.D.
   Compiled 58-76 by official decree. *Pan Ku* 班固 32-92
3. History of the Later *Han, Hou-Han-shu* 後漢書 25-220
   Compiled privately by *Fan Yeh* 范曄 398-445
4. History of the Three Kingdoms, *San-kuo-chih* 三國志 220-280
   Compiled privately, 285-297, by *Ch'en Shou* 陳壽 233-297
5. History of the *Chin* Dynasty, *Chin-shu* 晉書 265-419
   Compiled by the Bureau. Decreed 644
   Fang Hsüan-ling 房玄齡 578-648
6. History of the *Sung* Dynasty, *Sung-shu* 宋書 420-478
   Compiled 492-493 by official decree. *Shen Yüeh* 沈約 441-513
7. History of the Southern *Ch'i* Dynasty, *Nan-Ch'i-shu* 南齊書 479-501
   Compiled privately by *Hsiao Tzu-hsien* 蕭子顯 489-537
8. History of the *Liang* Dynasty, *Liang-shu* 梁書 502-556
   Compiled 628-635 by official decree. *Yao Ssu-lien* 姚思廉 d. 637
9. History of the *Ch'en* Dynasty, *Ch'en-shu* 陳書 556-580
   Compiled 622-629 by official decree. *Yao Ssu-lien* 姚思廉 d. 637
10. History of the *Wei* Dynasty, *Wei-shu* 魏書 386-535
    Compiled 551-554 by official decree. *Wei Shou* 魏收 506-572
11. History of the Northern *Ch'i* Dynasty, *Pei-Ch'i-shu* 北齊書 550-577
    Compiled 627-636 by official decree. *Li Po-yao* 李百藥 565-648
12. History of the *Chou* Dynasty, *Chou-shu* 周書 557-581
    Compiled by official decree. *Ling-hu Te-fen* 令狐德棻 583-666
13. History of the Southern Dynasties, *Nan-shih* 南史 420-589
    Compiled privately, 630-650, by *Li Yen-shou* 李延壽 612?-678?

THE TWENTY-SIX DYNASTIC HISTORIES

14 History of the Northern Dynasties, *Pei-shih* 北史 386-581
    Compiled privately, 630-650 by *Li Yen-shou* 李延壽 612?-678?

15 History of the *Sui* Dynasty, *Sui-shu* 隋書 581-617
    Compiled by the Bureau, 629-636. *Wei Cheng* 魏徵 580-643

16 Old History of the *T'ang* Dynasty, *Chiu T'ang-shu* 舊唐書 618-906
    Compiled by the Bureau, 940-945. *Liu Hsü* 劉昫 887-946

17 New History of *T'ang* Dynasty, *Hsin T'ang-shu* 新唐書 618-906
    Compiled 1043-1060 by public officials under supervision of
    O-yang Hsiu 歐陽修, 1007-1072, and *Sung Ch'i* 宋祁, 998-1061

18 Old History of the Five Dynasties, *Chiu Wu-tai-shih* 舊五代史
    907-959. Compiled by the Bureau, 973-974.
    Hsüeh Chü-cheng 薛居正 912-981

19 New History of the Five Dynasties, *Hsin Wu-tai-shih* 新五代史
    907-959. Compiled privately, 1044-1060
    O-yang Hsiu 歐陽修 1007-1072

20 History of the *Sung* Dynasty, *Sung-shih* 宋史 960-1279
    Compiled by the Bureau, 1343-1345. *T'o T'o* 脫脫 1313-1355

21 History of the *Liao* Dynasty, *Liao-shih* 遼史 916-1125
    Compiled by the Bureau, 1343-1344. *T'o T'o* 脫脫 1313-1355

22 History of the *Chin* Dynasty, *Chin-shih* 金史 1115-1234
    Compiled by the Bureau, 1343-1344. *T'o T'o* 脫脫 1313-1355

23 History of the *Yüan* Dynasty, *Yüan-shih* 元史 1206-1367
    Compiled by the Bureau in 370 days. *Sung Lien* 宋廉 1310-1381

24 New History of the *Yüan* Dynasty, *Hsin Yüan-shih* 新元史
    1206-1367. Compiled privately, 1890-1920
    K'o Shao-min 柯紹忞 1850-1933

25 History of the *Ming* Dynasty, *Ming-shih* 明史 1368-1644
    Compiled by the Bureau, 1678-1739
    Chang T'ing-yü 張廷玉 1672-1755

26 *Ch'ing* History Draft, *Ch'ing-shih-kao* 清史稿 1644-1911
    Compiled by the Bureau, 1914-1927. *K'o Shao-min* 1850-1933

THE FIVE MAJOR DIVISIONS

All dynastic histories contain two or more of the five divisions: annals of emperors, noble families, chronological tables, treatises, and biographies. The length of the divisions varies greatly. In the Chinese tradition, the number of *chüan* rather than the number of pages is the unit of measure. The *chüan* may contain from four to seven pages. The twenty-six dynastic histories contain 4,052 *chüan*. The smallest history has 36 and the largest 536. Of the 4,052 *chüan,* approximately 62 per cent is used for biographies, 21 per cent for treatises, 11 per cent for the annals of emperors, 4 per cent for chronological tables, and 2 per cent for the noble families. The number of *chüan* in each division of each history is given in the accompanying table.

It is fitting that the first division of a dynastic history, especially if written under imperial rule, be assigned for the annals of emperors. This division is found in every dynastic history. Biographies also are in every history. Although the division we have called "noble families" appears in only three histories, information on noble families is found in the chronological tables and biographies. Every history written after the tenth century contains chronological tables; but 15 of the 18 earlier ones are without this important division.

Seven of the dynastic histories have no special division for the treatises. For five of these histories, treatises are provided in two other dynastic histories. *Sui-shu* contains treatises for the *Liang, Ch'en,* Northern *Ch'i,* and *Chou* dynasties. *San-kuo-chih* has no treatises, but *Sung-shu* includes treatises covering the period of the Three Kingdoms. The other two histories without treatises are *Nan-shih* and *Pei-shih.* Treatises for the several dynasties included in these works may be found in the individual histories of these dynasties.

In the table on the next page, A, B, C, D, E denote respectively the five divisions of the dynastic histories: annals of emperors, noble families, chronological tables, treatises, and biographies.

THE TWENTY-SIX DYNASTIC HISTORIES

Five Divisions of the Twenty-six Dynastic Histories

A. Annals, B. Noble families, C. Tables, D. Treatises, E. Biographies

Dynastic histories	A	B	C	D	E	TOTAL CHÜAN
1 Hist. Memoirs	12	30	10	8	70	130
2 Former Han	13		10	18	79	120
3 Later Han	12			30	88	130
4 Three Kingdoms	4				61	65
5 Chin	10	30		20	70	130
6 Former Sung	10			30	60	100
7 Southern Ch'i	8			11	40	59
8 Liang	6				50	56
9 Ch'en	6				30	36
10 Wei	14			20	96	130
11 Northern Ch'i	8				42	50
12 Chou	8				42	50
13 So. Dynasties	10				70	80
14 No. Dynasties	12				88	100
15 Sui	5			30	50	85
16 T'ang - Old hist.	20			30	150	200
17 T'ang - New Hist.	10		15	50	150	225
18 5 Dynasties - Old	61			12	77	150
19 5 Dynasties - New	12	10	1	3	48	74
20 Sung	47		32	162	255	496
21 Liao	30		8	32	46	116
22 Chin	19		4	39	73	135
23 Yüan	47		8	58	97	210
24 Yüan - New	26		7	70	154	257
25 Ming	24		13	75	220	332
26 Ch'ing	25		53	142	316	536
Totals	459	70	161	840	2522	4052
Percentages	11.3	1.7	3.7	20.7	62.3	100

ANNALS OF EMPERORS

Though several interpretations have been given to the term denoting the first division of dynastic histories, *pen-chi* 本紀, annals of emperors, all point to three essentials. The annals are chronological, emperor-centric, and concerned with important affairs of state. A few unusual cases are found in the annals. *Ssu-ma Ch'ien* did not write an annal for *I-ti* 義帝, a puppet ruler installed by *Hsiang,* but he wrote one for *Hsiang Chi* 項籍 because *Hsiang Chi* made feudatory appointments after he had established himself in real power as prime minister behind the puppet ruler, *I-ti.* In *Han-shu, Hsiang Chi* found a less favored place in the division of biographies.

The first dynastic history had annals for Empress *Lü* and the second for Empress *Kao* because they occupied the throne. *Han-shu,* the second dynastic history, made improvement upon the first in that *Pan Ku* separated the affairs of state from the ordinary affairs of Empress *Kao* by placing the former in the annals and the latter under *wai-ch'i* 外紀, imperial relatives of the maternal side, in the biographies. *Fan Yeh* in his *Hou-Han-shu* created annals of empresses without any political qualifications, and these annals follow those of the emperors.

A new departure is found in *Wei-shu* 魏書, where *hsü-chi* 序紀, annals of ancestors, is placed before the annals of emperors. This practice was followed in *Chin-shih* and *Hsin Yüan-shih.*

NOBLE FAMILIES

Another division of the dynastic histories is *Shih-chia* 世家. *Shih* 世, literally, means generations; *chia* 家, families. We have here translated the name of this division "noble families," to express the central idea of a genealogical register of noble families. The term has been translated in numerous ways: *maison héréditaire,* genealogical register, genealogical history, feudal families, honorable families, hereditary nobles.

That *Shih-chia* is contained in only three of the dynastic histories

THE TWENTY-SIX DYNASTIC HISTORIES

may perhaps be accounted for by the fact that feudalism prevailed for only a short period in China and data on noble families can generally be found in the chronological tables and biographies.

CHRONOLOGICAL TABLES

In the dynastic histories the term *piao* 表, literally, to make manifest, is generally used to refer to the chronological tables. The function of a table of historical data is to make manifest the essentials, to present a synoptic view of a whole subject. Hence a table is designated by the word *piao*.

The years may appear in either the horizontal or vertical position in the table and in the other position are the items about which the information is given.

TREATISES

Treatises alone among the five divisions of the dynastic histories give accounts of different aspects of human affairs, such as the development of political, economic, judicial, military, and educational institutions. They furnish, therefore, rich deposits for the reconstruction of Chinese histories. Many historians of note have made emphatic statements concerning the great importance of the treatises.

The accompanying table shows which of the twenty-two topics covered in treatises can be found in each of twenty of the dynastic histories. A treatise on astronomy appears in nineteen and a treatise on geography is found in all except the *Shih-chi*. Other topics covered in most of the histories are rites, music, offices in government, food and commodities, and law and punishments. Eight dynastic histories from the *T'ang* dynasty to the *C'hing* dynasty include the treatises on civil service examinations.

It is quite understandable that the two treatises "communications" and "foreign relations" should be found only in *Ch'ing-shih-kao*, but that the treatise on Buddhism and Taoism is found only in the *Wei-shu*, is a surprise to Western and modern Chinese scholars. An unusual treatise is that in *Nan-Ch'i-shu* on auspicious influences. This subject is usually dealt with in the treatise on the five elements. Furthermore, the author of this treatise on auspicious influences in *Ch'i-shu* went to all lengths to trace the origin and development of auspicious influences from antiquity to his time, with detailed description of auspicious influences in the previous dynasties, *Wei* and *Chin*. He has been censured by later historians.

TREATISES AND THE DYNASTIC HISTORIES IN WHICH THEY APPEAR

1. *Li* 禮, Rites
2. *Yüeh* 樂, Music
3. *Lü* 律, Harmony, (measurements of musical tubes)
4. *Li* 歷, The calendar
5. *T'ien-wen* 天文, Astronomy
6. *Chiao-ssu* 郊祀, Sacrifices
7. *Kou-hsu* 溝洫, Rivers and canals
8. *Shih-huo* 食貨, Food and commodities
9. *Hsing-fa* 刑法, Law and punishments
10. *Wu-hsing* 五行, Five elements
11. *Ti-li* 地理, Geography
12. *I-wen* 藝文, Literature
13. *Po-kuan* 百官, Offices
14. *Yü-fu* 輿服, Chariots and costumes
15. *Fu-jui* 符瑞, Auspicious influences
16. *Shih-lao* 釋老, Buddhism and Taoism
17. *I-wei* 儀衛, Imperial guards
18. *Hsüan-chu* 選舉, Civil service
19. *Ping-wei* 兵衛, The army
20. *Ying-wei* 營衛, Militia and colonization
21. *Chiao-t'ung* 交通, Communications
22. *Pang-chiao* 邦交, Foreign relations

Treatises

Dynastic Histories	1	2	3	4	5	6	7	8	9	10	11	12	13	14	15	16	17	18	19	20	21	22
Hist. Memoirs	x	s	x	x	x	x	x	E														
Former Han	x	x	x		x	x	x	x	x	x	x	x										
Later Han	x		x	x	x	x	x			x	x	x										
Chin	x	x	x	x	x			x	x	x	x	x										
Former Sung	x	x	x	x	x					x	x	x		x								
Southern Ch'i	x	x								x	x	x		x								
Wei	x	x	x					x		x		x		x	x							
Sui	x	x		x	x			x	x	x	x	x										
T'ang - Old hist.	x	x	x	x	x			x	x	x	x	x										
T'ang - New Hist.	x	s	x	x	x		x	x	x	x	x	x					x	x				
5 Dynasties - Old	x	x	x	x	x		x	x	x	x	x	x										
5 Dynasties - New					x					x												
Sung	x	x	x		x		x	x	x	x	x	x					x	x				
Liao	x	x		x				x	x	x	x	x					x	x	x			
Chin	x	x		x	x		x	x	x	x	x	x					x	x				
Yüan	x	s		x	x	x	x	x	x	x	x	x										
Yüan - New	x	x		x	x		x	x	x	x	x	x					x	x				
Ming	x	x	x	x			x	x	x	x	x	x					x	x				
Ch'ing	x	x		x			x	x	x	x	x	x				x	x	x			x	x

X indicates treatise is present; S - subject is in the treatise on rites; E - economic affairs.

BIOGRAPHIES

Biographies in the dynastic histories occupy 62 per cent of the total number of *chüan*. This emphasis reveals that the worth of individuals and human achievements is considered crucial in the making of histories. Because people occupy different levels of importance in the histories and because space must be conserved, biographies are written in three major forms: *chuan-chuan* 專傳 single biography; *ho-chuan* 合傳 parallel or combined biographies of two persons; *fu-chuan* 附傳 attached biography, in which less important persons are described under the principal figure.

The individual biographies appear under a class name, such as scholars, officials, philosophers, artists, eminent women, technicians, aborigines, frontier territories, and vassal states. Some classifications are seldom found. *Hua-chi* 滑稽, humorists, is in only *Shih-chi*. Adopted children, mathematicians, frontier territories, and vassal states are class names used only once. *Huo-ch'ih* 貨殖, meaning increase of wealth, the self-made rich person, appears in *Shih-chi* and *Han-shu*. *Tang-ku* 黨錮, partisans, or party politicians, occupy a section only in *Hou-Han-shu*. *Kuan-ling* 官伶, official actors, is a section in *Sung-shih* and *Chin-shih*. The table below shows distribution of 17 selected classes.

The biographies are a summary of the main achievements of the individuals concerned. The date for the highest literary degree usually is the first date given, or perhaps the only date. Unless the individual is a national character, few dates are given for his other achievements, which are likely to be covered only briefly. Inadequate information in the dynastic histories may be supplemented by the gazetteers of the localities where the men and women were born or where they served. Also *Nien-p'u* 年譜, chronological biographies, give a strict year to year account of the individual's career. Many of those whose names appear in the dynastic histories have written autobiographies or have biographers in their admirers, disciples, sons, or grandsons. These fuller, more personal accounts are valuable sources additional to the biographies in the dynastic histories.

Classes of Biographies and the Histories in Which They Appear

	Dynastic Histories	Dutiful Officials	Confucian Scholars	Harsh Officials	Fawning Favorites	Empresses	Medicine Men	Hermits	Eunuchs	Literary Persons	Independent Minded	Eminent Women	The Filial	The Loyal	Imperial Relatives	Traitors	Revolutionists	Rebels
1		X	X	X	X		X											
2		X	X	X	X	X												
3		X	X	X			X	X	X	X	X	X						
4						X	X											
5		X	X			X	X	X		X			X	X	X	X		
6		X		X	X		X						X					
7		X		X	X		X			X			X					
8		X	X		X		X			X			X					
9			X		X					X			X					
10		X		X	X	X	X	X	X	X		X	X	X	X			
11		X	X	X	X	X	X			X					X			
12			X		X	X							X					
13		X	X		X	X		X		X			X					
14		X	X	X	X	X	X	X		X		X	X	X	X			
15		X	X	X		X	X	X		X		X	X	X	X			
16		X	X	X		X	X	X	X	X		X	X	X	X			
17		X	X	X		X	X	X	X	X	X	X	X	X	X	X	X	X
18					X													
19										X		X			X			
20		X	X		X	X	X	X	X	X	X	X	X	X	X	X	X	X
21		X			X	X		X	X	X	X				X			X
22		X		X	X	X	X		X	X		X	X	X	X		X	X
23		X	X			X	X			X		X	X	X		X	X	X
24		X	X			X	X	X	X	X	X	X		X				
25		X	X			X	X	X	X	X	X		X	X	X	X	X	X
26		X	X			X	X	X		X	X	X						

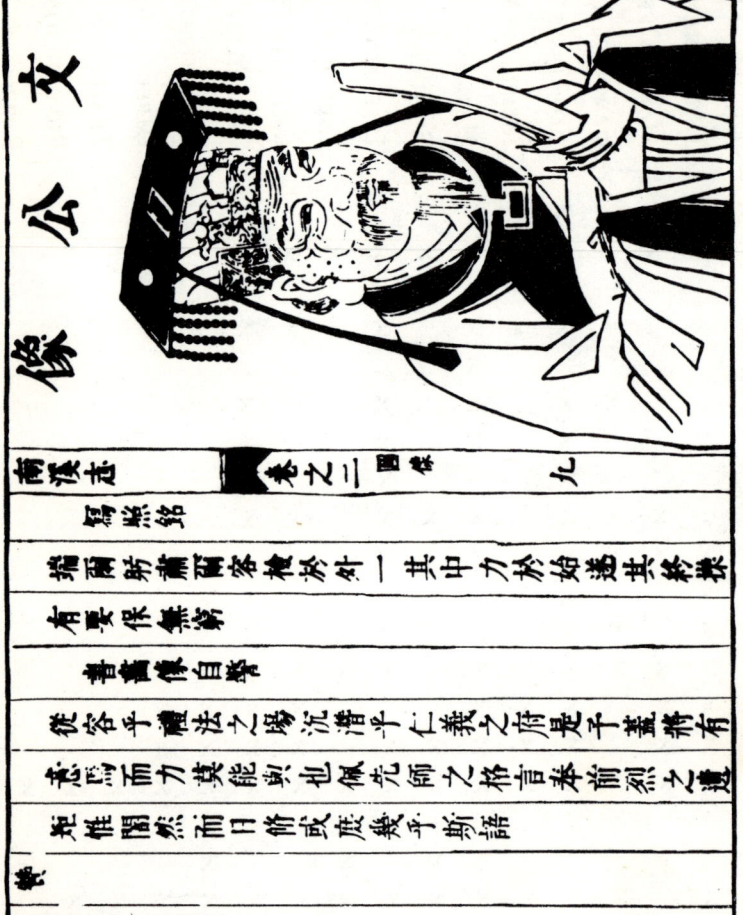

Portrait of *Chu Hsi* in the *Nan-hsi* Gazetteer (p. 53)

Appendix I

Office of Historian: Titles and Duties

CH'IN 256-207 B.C.

T'ai-shih-ling 太史令 Office of Grand Historian. *T'ai-shih-ling* 太史令 grand historian: making calendar, attending sacrificial affairs, recording unusual natural phenomena.

FORMER HAN 206 B.C.-7 A.D.

T'ai-shih-ling, Office of Grand Historian. *T'ai-shih-ling,* grand historian: determining the four seasons, making planetary calendar, compiling history.

LATER HAN 25-220

Lan-t'ai-ling 蘭臺令 Imperial Office of Historians. *Lan-t'ai ling-shih* 蘭臺令史 Orchid Terrace history officer and *Tung-kuan chu-tso* 東觀箸作 Eastern Palace compilers: compiling annals and biographies and editing *Han* records.

THREE KINGDOMS 220-265

Wei 魏 220-265. *Chung-shu-ling* 中書令 Office of Central Records. *Chu-tso-lang* 箸作郎 editor and compiler of official records.

Shu 蜀 221-264. *Tung-kuan-ling* 東觀令 Eastern Palace historian: compiling national histories.

Wu 吳 220-280. *Tung-kuan-ling,* Eastern Palace Historian. *Tso Kuo-shih* 左國史 senior national historiographer, *Yu Kuo-shih* 右國史 junior national historiographer, and *Tung-kuan-ling,* Eastern Palace historian: compiling national histories.

CHIN 265-419

Pi shu-ling 秘書令 Office of Secret Records. *Ta-chu-tso* 大箸作 great compiler, *Tso chu-tso-lang* 佐箸作郎 associate compiler: compiling national histories.

EARLY CHAO 304-329

Tso kuo-shih chu-tso 左國史箸作 senior historian for national history: compiling national records.

LATER CHAO 319-352

Chu-tso 箸作 compiler of national history.

SOUTHERN LIANG 397-415

Kuo-chi chi-chiu 國紀祭酒 national history official: compiling national annals. Here the term *chi-chiu* 祭酒, "sacrificial wine," is used for the first time.

FORMER SUNG 420-479

Chu-tso-lang 箸作郎, official compiler, and *Chu-tso tso-lang* 箸作佐郎 associate compiler: compiling national history and recording the daily life of the court.

SOUTHERN CH'I 429-502

Chu-tso-lang, Shu-tso tso-lang, and *Hsiu-shih hsüeh-shih* 修史學士 compiling-history scholar: compiling and editing national histories. *Hsiu-shih hsüeh-shih* is used for the first time.

LIANG 502-557

Chu-tso-lang, Chu-tso tso-lang, and *Chuan-shih hsüeh-shih* 撰史學士 compiling history scholar. *Chuan-shih* is used instead of *hsiu-shih* with the same meaning.

CH'EN 557-589

Pi-shu-ling 秘書令 Office of Secret Records. *Chu-tso-lang, Chu-tso tso-lang, Chuan-shih hsüeh-shih,* and *Chuan-shih chu-shih* 撰史箸士 compiling-history writer: compiling national histories. *Chu-shih,* "writer," is used for the first time.

LATER WEI 534-550

Hsiu-shih-chü 修史局 Bureau of History Compilation. *Chu-tso lang, Chu-tso tso-lang*: compiling national histories. *Ch'i-chü-chu ling-shih* 起居注令史 imperial-diary historian: recording the daily activities and repose of the emperor.

APPENDIX I

NORTHERN CH'I 550-577

Shih-kuan 史舘 Bureau of National Historiography. *Chu-tso-lang,* and *Chu-tso tso-lang*: compiling national histories. *Shih-kuan,* Bureau of Historiography, was introduced for the first time.

NORTHERN CHOU 557-581

Shih-Kuan, Bureau of Historiography. *Chien-hsiu kuo-shih* 監修國史 director of national history, *Chu-tso shang-shih* 箸作上士 senior compiler, and *Chu-tso chung-shih* 箸作中士 junior compiler: compiling national histories. *Chu-tso shang-shih,* senior compiler, and *Chu-tso chung-shih,* junior compiler, were used for the first time.

SUI 589-617

Nei-shih-ling 內史令 Office of Inner Historian. *Chien-hsiu kuo-shih* and *Chu-tso ts'ao* 箸作曹 sectional compiler: compiling national histories. *Ch'i-chü sheh-jen,* imperial diary attendant: recording activities and repose of the emperor. The term *ts'ao* 曹 is used for the first time.

T'ANG 618-960

Shih-kuan, Bureau of Historiography, *Chu-tso-chü* 箸作局 Bureau of Compilers, *Ch'i-chü-chu,* Office of Imperial Diary, and *Shih-cheng-chi* 時政記 Current Affairs of the State. The duties of these offices were, respectively, having charge of national history, drafting and composing state documents, keeping the diaries of the court, and recording current affairs. The last duty was performed by the prime minister.

SUNG 960-1279

Shih-kuan, Bureau of Historiography, with two divisions: *Kuo-shih-kuan* 國史舘 Office of National History and *Shih-lu-yüan* 實錄院 Office of the Veritable Records.

The Office of National History was manned with *T'i-chü* 提舉 a chancellor, *Chien-hsiu* 監修 a director, *Hsiu-kuo-shih* 修國史 compilers, and *T'ung-hsiu-kuo-shih* 同修國史 associate compilers. The Office of Veritable Records was manned with a chancellor, compilers, and associate compilers.

Under the Bureau of Historiography there were numerous compilers, associate compilers, *Chien-yüeh* 檢閱 proofreaders, *Chiao-cheng* 校正 correctors, and *Pien-chiao* 編校 production managers.

Ch'i-chü-chu, Office for Recording the Activities and Repose of the Court. Manned by *Ch'i-chü-lang,* senior recorders, and *Ch'i-chü sheh-jen* 起居舍人 junior recorders.

Shih-cheng-chi 時政記 Office of Current Affairs of the State. The prime minister himself made the compilations.

Jih-li 日歷 Office for Keeping Daily Summary Reports. Manned by *Chu-tso-lang,* writers, and *Chu-tso tso-lang,* associate writers.

LIAO 907-1124

Kuo-shih-yüan 國史院 Bureau of National Historiography. Manned by *Chien-hsiu kuo-shih,* director of national history, *shih-kuan hsüeh-shih,* scholars of the Bureau of Historiography, *shih-kuan hsiu-chuan* 史舘修撰 senior compilers, and *hsiu-kuo-shih,* compilers.

Ch'i-chü-chu, Office of Imperial Diary. Senior and junior recorders.

CHIN 1115-1234

Kuo-shih-yüan, Bureau of National Historiography. Manned by a director, associate directors, assistant directors, compilers, collators, and proofreaders.

Ch'i-chü-yüan Office of Imperial Diary. Senior and junior recorders.

YÜAN 1260-1368

Han-lin chien kuo-shih yüan 翰林監國史院 Hanlin Academy, in charge of the Bureau of National Historiography. Manned by *hsüeh-shih* Hanlin scholars, senior and junior compilers, and readers.

Ch'i-chü-chu, Office of Imperial Diary. Senior and junior recorders.

MING 1368-1644

Han-lin-yüan, Hanlin Academy, in charge of national history. Manned by *hsiu-chuan* 修撰 senior compilers, *pien-hsiu* 編修 junior compilers, and *Chien-t'ao* 檢討 third class *Hanlin* scholars.

Ch'i-chü-chu, Office of Imperial Diary (for a short time only).

APPENDIX I

CH'ING 1644-1911

Han-lin-yüan chang kuo-shih-kuan, Hanlin Academy, in charge of the Bureau of National Historiography.

Chang-yüan hsüeh-shih 掌舘學士 chancellor of the *Hanlin* and director of the Bureau of National Historiography, *Shih-tu hsüeh-shih* 侍讀學士 reader of the *Hanlin,* compiler and editor; *Shih-chiang hsüeh-shih* 侍講學士 expositor of the *Hanlin; Shih-tu* 侍讀 sub-reader; *shih-chiang* 侍講 subexpositor; *Hsiu-chuan, Hanlin* compiler; *Pien-hsiu, Hanlin* compiler of the second class; *Chien-t'ao, Hanlin* graduate of the third class.

Kuo-shih-kuan, Bureau of National Historiography. *Tsung-ts'ai* 總裁 director-general, *T'i-tiao* 提調 proctor, *Tsung-tsuan* 總纂 historiographer, *Tsuan-hsiu* 纂修 compiler.

Ch'i-chü-chu, Office of Imperial Diary, in charge of imperial daily activities and repose.

Shih-lu-kuan, Office of the Veritable Records.

According to *Ta-Ch'ing-hui-tien* 大清會典 Institutes of the *Ch'ing* Dynasty (1818 edition), the Office of National Historiographer during the Manchu period was for the compilation of national history. Its functions were carried out as a department of the *Hanlin* Academy.

The director-general could be either Chinese or Manchu, but there were to be two Manchu and two Chinese proctors, four Manchu and six Chinese historiographers, twelve Manchu and twenty-two Chinese compilers, and eight Manchu and eight Chinese proofreaders. The office having special charge of the activities and repose of the court had ten Manchu and twelve Chinese historians.

The *Hanlin* Academy had one Manchu and one Chinese chancellor, who were to be in charge of composing and editing official documents under five categories: *Ts'o-pao-wen* 册寶文 inscription for the bestowed seals, *Ts'o-kao-wen* 册誥文 essay for the conferring of titles, *Pei-wen* 碑文 inscriptions for monuments, *Chi-wen* 祭文 essay for offering sacrifices.

Appendix II

NIEN-HAO 年號 YEAR TITLES

Nien-hao is a further development of *Chi-yüan* 紀元, which means recording or marking the beginning. Every ruler marked each "new beginning", the first, second, third and so on until the end of his reign. His successor began again. The first authentic "beginning" was in 841 B.C. though the tradition goes back to the legendary beginning. Prior to the introduction of the *nien-hao* under *Wu-ti* (140-74 B.C.), a proto-type *nien-hao* was used by *Wen-ti* (179-157 B.C.), who had two beginnings, *Yüan* 元, first beginning, in 179 and *Hou-yüan* 後元, later beginning, in 163, and by *Ching-ti* (156-141 B.C.) who had three beginnings: *Yüan* 元, first beginning, in 156 B.C., *Chung-yüan* 中元, middle beginning, in 149, and *Hou-yüan* 後元, later beginning, in 143.

The newly established *nien-hao* had a two-fold character: (1) it resembled the *Chi-yüan* in that it could be changed at any time for any occasion during the reign of any ruler; (2) it inaugurated a new system in which a name or phrase of two characters was generally employed to commemorate special events or good wishes. (p. 15).

The first ruler who adopted this *nien-hao* had eleven year-titles. The system was in use for more than two thousand years, 140 B.C. to 1912 A.D. However, after a period of fifteen hundred years, the practice was simplified to one *nien-hao* for each reign, beginning with the *Ming* dynasty. Japan, since the middle of the 7th century, has been using this system.

Nien-hao or *Nengo* (Japanese) had more significance than merely the year-title of the reign; it represented sovereign power. Out of deference to her powerful neighbor, Korea adopted the Chinese calendar in the middle of the 7th century and prior to the Sino-Japanese war,

APPENDIX II

1894-5, for two centuries and a half Korean official documents carried the contemporary *nien-hao* of China. This practise was also followed by the *Liu-ch'iu* islands (*Ryukyu,* Japanese) until the last quarter of the 19th century. Japan adopted the Gregorian calendar in 1873 but she has never abandoned the *nengo* because of its great significance to her imperial power.

This use of the *nien-hao* in countries other than China adds to the confusion inherent in the Chinese system, in which two difficulties are predominant. In using the *nien-hao* to identify a period of time, a ruler may use a series of them during his reign, or may even take a *nien-hao* used by a former ruler.

To point out the first difficulty, we list nine rulers, each of whom had seven or more *nien-hao* during his reign. The figure in parenthesis indicates the number of *nien-hao* during the reign of each of these rulers.

T'ang Kao-tsung 650-683 (14)   *Han Hsüan-ti* 73-49 B.C. (7)
Han Wu-ti 140-87 B.C. (11)   *Han Huan-ti* 147-167 (7)
T'ang Empress *Wu* 690-705 (11)   *Liang Wu-ti* 502-549 (7)
Sung Jen-tsung 1023-1063 (9)   *T'ang Chao-tsung* 889-906 (7)
Sung Li-tsung 1225-1264 (8)

The second difficulty arises in part because frontier rulers, regional rulers, and usurpers liked to take the *nien-hao* of great rulers. The *nien-hao* that have been used most often are given in the list below with the names of all the rulers who used them, together with the year in which the *nien-hao* was adopted, (A.D. unless indicated).

Chien-p'ing 建平 Establishing peace
    Ai-ti 哀帝 of *Han* 6 B.C.; *Shih-lei* 石勒 of Later *Chao* 330; *Mu-jung Yao* 慕容瑤 of W. *Yen* 386; *Mu-jung Sheng* 慕容盛 of Later *Yen* 398; *Mu-jung Te* 慕容德 S. *Yen* 400; *Pai-ya-li-ssu* 白亞栗斯 of N. *Wei* 415; *I-hsüan* 義宣 of S. Dynasties 454; *Yü* 瑜 of N. *Wei* 508

Chien-wu 建武 Establishing strength
    Kuang-wu 光武 of E. *Han* 25; *Hui-ti* 惠帝 of *Chin* 304; *Yüan-ti* 元帝 of *Chin* 317; *Shih-hu* 石虎 of Later *Chao* 335; *Mu-jung-chung* 慕容忠 of W. *Yen* 386; *Ming-ti* 明帝 of S. *Ch'i* 494

Yung-hsing 永興 Perpetual prosperity
    Huan-ti 桓帝 of E. *Han* 153; *Hui-ti* 惠帝 of *Chin* 304; *Jan-min* 冉閔 of *Wei* 350; *Fu-chien* 苻堅 of Former *Ch'in* 357; *Ming-yüan-ti* 明元帝 of N. *Wei* 409; *Hsiao-wu-ti* 孝武帝 of Northern *Wei* 532

Chien-yüan 建元 Establishing the beginning
    Wu-ti 武帝 of *Han* 140 B.C.; *Liu Ts'ung* 劉聰 of N. *Han* 315; *K'ang-ti* 康帝 of E. *Chin* 343; *Fu-chien* 苻堅 of Former *Chin* 365; *Kao-ti* 高帝 of *Ch'i*, Southern Dynasties 479

Yung-ho 永和 Perpetual peace
    Shun-ti 順帝 of E. *Han* 136; *Mu-ti* 穆帝 of E. *Chin* 345; *Yao-hung* 姚泓 of Later *Ch'in* 416; *Tsu-ch'ü-mu-chien* 沮渠牧犍 of N. *Liang* 433; *Yen-chün* 延鈞 of *Min*, 5 Dynasties 935

Yung-k'ang 永康 Perpetual peace
    Huan-ti 桓帝 of E. *Han* 167; *Hui-ti* 惠帝 of *Chin* 300; *Mu-jung-pao* 慕容寶 of Later *Yen* 396; *Ch'i-fu-chih-p'an* 乞伏熾盤 of Western *Ch'in* 412

Yung-lo 永樂 Perpetual joy
    Chang Chung-hua 張重華 of Former *Liang* 346; *Chang Yü-hsien* 張遇賢 of *Chin* 943; *Fang La* 方臘 of *Sung* 1120; *Ch'eng-tsu* 成祖 of *Ming* 1403

Yung-an 永安 Perpetual peace
    Ching-ti 景帝 of *Wu*, 3 Kingdoms 258; *Tsu-ch'u-meng-hsun* 沮渠蒙遜 of N. *Liang* 401; *Hsiao-chuang-ti* 孝莊帝 of No. *Wei* 528; *Ch'ung-tsung* 崇宗 of *Hsi-hsia* 1099

Appendix III

A LIST OF NEW HISTORIES

The term "new histories" is used here to indicate that the publication is recent (since 1925) and that the approach is modern, that is, not traditional. The list is designed to show the general trend of historical studies in China during the last twenty-five years.

Shih-liao yü shih-hsüeh 史料與史學 Historical Data and History
    Historical and Linguistic Research Institute of the Academia Sinica
    國立中央研究院歷史語言研究所 *Chungking*, 1945

Ch'ing-tai k'ao-shih chih-tu 清代考試制度 The Institution of Civil Service Examinations during the *Ch'ing* Dynasty
    Chang Chung-ju 章中如
    Li-ming Book Company, 1931

    In two parts: (1) types of civil service examinations and certain regulations; (2) types of tests for examinations such as essays, poems, classical explanations, and political strategies.

T'ai-wan t'ung-shih 台灣通史 A General History of Formosa
    Ch'en Heng 陳橫
    Commercial Press, 1946

Chung-kuo fa-chih-shih 中國法制史 History of Chinese Organic Laws and Statutes
    Ch'en Ku-yüan 陳顧遠 1894-
    Commercial Press, 1934

    Begins with a valuable discussion of the problems of writing a history of Chinese institutions by statutes and laws; describes the changes in legal concepts, domination of schools of legal philosophy, and the development of the science of law; finally, the author divides the treatment under four topics: political institutions, educational institutions including civil service examinations, judicial and economic institutions, each supplied with primary sources of documentation.

Chung-kuo chin-tai shih 中國近代史 History of Modern China
Commercial Press, 1935.   *Ch'en Kung-lu* 陳恭祿

First published in one volume, but after the war, in two. Contains 19 chapters. First chapter is a general introduction to pre-Opium-war China. Chapter 18 is a conclusion regarding China's domestic problems and directions of reconstruction. Last chapter deals with a critical review of historical materials.

T'ang-tai cheng-chih-shih hsü-lun-kao 唐代政治史述論稿
Tentative Studies in the Political History of the *T'ang* Dynasty
The Commercial Press, 1947.   *Ch'en Yin-k'o* 陳寅恪

Three chapters: (1) the ruling class, its rise and fall; (2) political revolutionary movements and their distinctive features and programs; (3) the alien influence on *T'ang* politics. A learned and suggestive piece of work.

Ch'ing-shih t'an-wei 清史探微 Researches on the History of the *Ch'ing* Dynasty   The *Tu-li* Press, *Chungking*, 1946
Cheng T'ein-t'ing 鄭天挺

T'ai-p'ing-t'ien-kuo shih-liao 太平天國史料 Historical Sources of the *T'ai-p'ing* Heavenly Kingdom   *Peking* University Press, 1926
Ch'eng Yen-sheng 程演生

Three *ts'e* 册 or Chinese volumes, containing ten groups of documents copied from the Library of Oriental Languages, Paris.

Chung-hua-min-kuo cheng-chih shih 中華民國政治史 Political History of the Chinese Republic   Peiping Cultural Association, 1929
Chia I-chün 買逸君

These two volumes cover the period of the Chinese Republic from the Revolution and inauguration of the Republic to the People's National Convention of 1931. Numerous proclamations of war-lords during the civil wars of China are quoted. Gives references of recent publications and short biographies of leading personalities. As a whole the author's point of view is objective.

Chung-kuo chin-san-pai-nien hsüeh-shu-shih 中國近三百年學術史
A History of Chinese Culture during the Last 300 Years, 2 vols.
The Commercial Press, 1945. *Ch'ien Mu* 錢穆 1895-

Chung-kuo shih-hsüeh-shih 中國史學史 A History of Chinese
Historiography, Commercial Press, 1946. *Chin Yü-fu* 金毓黻
First published in *Chungking* in 1944. One of the best on the subject. Ten chapters with documentation.

Erh-tz'u shih-chieh ta-chan shih-liao 二次世界大戰史料 Materials
for the History of the Second World War, 4 vols.
Ta Shih Tai Book Store, 1946. *Chou K'ang-ching* 周康靖
and others
One of the most complete compilations; 4 vols.

Chang Chü-cheng ta-chuan 張居正大傳 Biography of *Chang Chü-cheng*, *K'ai-ming* Book Co., 1945, *Chu Tung-jun* 朱東潤
Chang received his *chin-shih* in 1547; became Grand Secretary, 1567; introduced national economic recovery, 1579-1582; d. 1582

Chung-kuo t'ung-shih chien-pien 中國通史簡編 A General History
of China Simplified, *Hsin-hua* Book Store, 1950.
Fan Wen-lan 范文瀾 and others
First published in *Yenan* (the Chinese Communist headquarters) in 1941. For the revised edition, eight members participated:
Fan Wen-la, *Wang Nan* 王南, *Wang K'o-feng* 王可風, *Kao Shan* 高山, *Jung Meng-yuan* 榮孟源, *Mou An-shih* 牟安世, *Liu Kuei-wu* 劉桂五, *Chi Chih-ch'iao* 紀志翹.

Chung-kuo chin-tai-shih 中國近代史 History of Modern China
Hsin-hua Book Co., 1949. *Fan Wen-lan* 范文瀾
The author is completing this work in two parts: 1, on traditional democratic revolution; 2, on new democratic revolution.

Tseng Kuo-fan p'ing-chuan 曾國藩評傳 A Critical Biography of
Tseng Kuo-fan, *Chung-cheng* Book Co., 1947.
Ho I-k'un 何貽焜

Chung-kuo chin-tai ching-chi fa-chan-shih 中國近代經濟發展
History of Economic Development of Modern China
Ta-tung Book Company, 1932.   Hou Hou-p'ei 侯厚培

Eight chapters discussing population, agriculture, industry, currency, modern banks, international trade, communications, and labor movement. A sketchy survey without documentary support. The student should find the topics and terms helpful.

Ch'ing-tai t'ung-shih 清代通史 General History of the *Ch'ing* Dynasty
Commercial Press   Vol. I, 1927; Vol. II, 1928.
Hsiao I-shan 蕭一山 1902-

The first two volumes constitute the most thorough treatment of the *Ch'ing* history to date; unfortunately the last volume was never published.

Volume I has 7 sections: (1) Later *Chin* Kingdom's establishment and development; (2) Replacement of the *Ming* by the *Ch'ing* and the new institutions; (3) Policies of unification and the Three Frontier Rebellions; (4) Social organization of the Early *Ch'ing* period; (5) China-foreign relations and negotiations; (6) Political administration and military achievements of Emperors *K'ang-hsi* and *Yung-cheng;* (7) Tendencies of thought and intellectual pursuits of Early *Ch'ing*.

Volume II has 4 sections: (1) The glorious period of *Ch'ien-lung* and the decline of *Chia-ch'ing;* (2) Economic conditions of the first half of the *Ch'ing* period; (3) The Glorious period of Classical Learning; (4) The situation of the world and China during the 19th century.

Chung-kuo cheng-chih-ssu-hsiang shih 中國政治思想史   History
of Chinese Political Thought,   Commercial Press, 1945
Hsiao Kung-ch'üan 蕭公權 1897-

Covers the history of Chinese political thought in five volumes: (1) The Creative Period, (2) The Imitative Period, (3) The Revolutionary Period, (4) Continuation of volume III in modern period, (5) Fruition period. Prolific documentation.

Nien-wu shih lung-kang 廿五史論綱　On the Fundamentals of the Twenty-five Dynastic Histories,　World Book Company, 1947. *Hsü Hao* 徐浩

Three parts: Part I deals chiefly with forms of Chinese histories; Part II, gives analyses of 25 standard histories, including the *Ch'ing* History Draft; Part III, concluding remarks, tables, charts, objectives, and schools of historians.

Tang-tai Chung-kuo shih-hsüeh 當代中國史學　Chinese Historiography of the Recent Past　*Tu-li* Publishing Company, 1947 *Ku Chieh-kang* 顧頡剛 1893-

A general survey of Chinese historiography of the last century; somewhat biased in character.

Chung-kuo tsai-hsiang chih-tu 中國宰相制度　A History of the System of Prime Ministers in China,　Commercial Press, 1947 *Li Chün* 李俊

Cheng Ch'eng-kung 鄭成功　Biography of *Cheng Ch'eng-kung* Youth Publishing Co., 1945.　*Li Hsü* 李旭

Cheng Ch'eng-kung is better known in the West as Koxinga, a Portuguese corruption of *Kuo-hsing-yeh* 國姓爺, which means "the Imperial Surnamed One". *Cheng* supported the *Ming* when the Manchus invaded China, and as a reward for his loyalty was given the imperial surname, *Chu* 朱.

Chung-kuo chin-tai shih 中國近代史　History of Modern China *Kuang-ming* Book Company, 1948.　*Li Ting-sheng* 李鼎聲

One of the several post-war publications on history of modern China. A good treatment of the period covered within 310 pages.

Chung-kuo wen-hua-shih 中國文化史　Cultural History of China *Chung-shan* Book Company, 1932.　*Liu I-cheng* 柳貽徵

The Cultural History of China has a sketchy outline form, but is supported by sources of long standing. The designation of the chapters is well chosen.

Shih-chi shih-erh-chu-hou nien-piao k'ao-cheng 史記十二諸侯年表考證 Verification of the Chronology of the Twelve Feudal Princes in the Historical Memoirs, Commercial Press, 1943
   Lo Ch'o-han 羅綽漢

T'ai-p'ing-t'ien-kuo shih-kang 太平天國史綱 An Outline History of the *T'ai-p'ing* Heavenly Kingdom Commercial Press, 1947.
   Lo Erh-Kang 羅爾綱

   Within the space of 134 pages, basic problems and crucial events are treated with extensive documentary evidences. These pages cover the background of the revolution, the formative and the immediate causes, fifteen years of bitter struggle, the land system of the *T'ai-p'ings*, causes for failure, and the ultimate consequences of the revolution.

Shih-hsüeh fang-fa ta-kang 史學方法大綱 Principles of Historical Method *Tu-li* Press, 1945 *Lu Mao-te* 陸懋德

Li-shih yen-chiu-fa 歷史研究法 Methods of Historical Study *Yung-hsiang* Book Store, 1945. *Lü Ssu-mien* 呂思勉

Chung-kuo t'ung-shih yao-lüeh 中國通史要略 Essentials of a General History of China Commercial Press, 1944
   Miao Feng-lin 繆鳳林

T'ai-p'ing-t'ien-kuo ko-ming ssu-ch'ao 太平天國革命思潮 Revolutionary Thought of the *T'ai-p'ings*, Commercial Press, 1946.
   P'eng Tse-i 彭澤益

   Limited to an outline. Shows thorough scholarship, considered opinions, and excellent documentation.

Chung-kuo shu-yüan chih-tu 中國書院制度 The Institution of Chinese Academies China Book Company, 1934.
   Sheng Lang-hsi 盛朗西

   Six chapters: Origin of the Academy, Academy of the *Sung* Period, Academy of the *Yüan* Period, Academies of the *Ming* Period, Academies of the *Ch'ing* Period, Abolition of the Academies.

Li-shih chuan-pien-ti nien-tai 歷史轉變的年代   The Epoch-making Years in History   *Chung Wai* Publishing House, 1947
   Shih Hsiao-ch'ung 石嘯冲
   Summaries of international affairs and important political documents of the years, 1945-46.

Li-tai t'un-k'en yen-chiu 歷代屯墾研究   A Study of the Frontier Cultivation in Various Dynasties
   Cheng-chung Publishing Company, 1945.   *T'ang Ch'i-yü* 唐啓宇

Chung-kuo ching-ying hsi-yü shih 中國經營西域史   History of Chinese Expansion and Colonization in *Sinkiang*
   Commercial Press, 1936.   *Tseng Wen-wu* 曾問吾
   The author, seeing the importance of *Sinkiang* to China, made a thorough study of the history of Chinese enterprises in *Sinkiang* and of the Uighur language. One of the best histories of *Sinkiang;* good maps and documentation.

Chung-kuo chin-pai-nien-shih tzu-liao 中國近百年史資料
   Source-materials for Chinese History of the Last Hundred Years
   Part I, 2 volumes, 1926; Part II, 2 volumes, 1933.
   China Book Company.   *Tso Shun-sheng* 左舜生
   One of the first attempts to use primary sources of modern history of China chronologically and topically; covers the problem of opium importation, *T'aip'ing* revolution, foreign wars, 1898 reform, Boxer movement, negotiations over Mongolia and Tibet, and the Chinese revolution. Part II is in the main a supplement to Part I, adding materials of the first five years of the Chinese Republic.

Chung-kuo chiang-yü yen-ko-lüeh 中國疆域沿革畧 Changes of the Chinese Frontiers in the Course of History
   K'ai-ming Book Co., 1946.   *T'ung Shu-yeh* 童書業

Ch'un-ch'iu shih 春秋史   History of the *Ch'un-ch'iu* Period
   The Commercial Press, 1946.   *T'ung Shu-yeh* 童書業
   A good reference for the chronological outline of this period.

Chung-kuo li-tai nien-hao so-in 中國歷代年號索引 An Index to
Chinese Year-(reign) Titles,   *K'ai-ming* Book Co., 1936
Wang Hung-sheng 汪宏聲

Chin-tai erh-shih-chia p'ing-chuan 近代二十家評傳
Critical Biographies of Twenty Scholars of the Recent Past
Hsing-yen Book Hall, 1934.   *Wang Shen-jan* 王森然
Selection of twenty intellectual leaders of modern China; describes the thought tendencies of the period of the collapse of the old institutions and initiation of the new. The geographical representation of the scholars is of value also.

Chung-kuo shih 中國史   Chinese History of Different Dynasties
Peiping Cultural Association, Vol. I, II, III, 1926, Vol. IV, 1928.
 Wang T'ung-ling 王桐齡
Numerous charts and tables in these volumes will aid students.

Chung-kuo shih-hsüeh-shih kai-lun 中國史學史概論
An Introduction to the History of Historiography
Commercial Press, 1942.   *Wang Yü-chang* 王玉璋

Chung-kuo fa-lü fa-ta-shih 中國法律發達史   History of the Development of Chinese Law   Commercial Press, 1930.
 Yang Hung-lieh 楊鴻烈
27 chapters in two volumes cover the entire period of Chinese history from the formative period of legal concepts to the introduction of Western legal principles and procedures. Students of legal studies should find them a store-house for pecialized studies.

Index — General

Academies
  An-ting 124, 127
  Ch'eng-nan 133, 140
  Ching-sheng 122
  Ch'uan-shan 141
  Chung-shan 126
  Hsüeh-hai-t'ang 128
  Li-cheng 125
  Liang-hu 141
  Lien-ch'ih 122, 128
  Lou-tung 126
  Lung-men 144
  Nan-ching 140
  T'ien-chang 127
  Tsun-ching 135, 141
  Tzu-yang 126
  Wen-cheng 122
  Yü-lu 133
  Yüeh-hsiu 127
Agriculture 71
Annotations 51, 66, 68, 76, 79, 83, 85, 86, 88, 95, 96, 123, 125, 136, 143, 148-150, 164
Biographical approach (*Jen-pieh*) 40
Biographies 39, 40, 65, 68, 123, 124, 125, 127, 196, 197, 201, 202, 17
Calligraphy 68, 69
Chronological treatment (*shih-pieh*) 40, 59
Classic of Changes 93, 78, 88, 92, 93, 96, 100, 101
Classic of Herbs 80
Classic of History 182
Classic of Mountain and Ocean 85
Classic of Tea 73
Classic of Waterways 82, 127
Classics 28, 56, 73, 78, 82, 83, 85, 87, 88, 91, 93, 96, 97, 99, 100, 127, 132, 136, 138
Commentary 84, 88, 93, 97, 100, 148
Confucius 19, 39, 163, 168, 183

Construction 74
Currency 72
Customs, folkways 73
Divination 60, 63, 137
Dynastic Histories
  Ch'en-shu 192, 194
  Chin-shih 127, 192, 193, 195
  Chin-shu 55, 149, 192, 194
  Ch'ing-shih-kao 31, 32, 193, 195
  Chiu T'ang-shu 123, 124, 136, 150, 193
  Chiu-Wu-tai-shih 138, 150, 195
  Chou-shu 192, 194
  Han-shu 31, 95, 125, 127, 148, 149, 150, 155, 162, 191, 194
  Hou-Han-shu 31, 125, 127, 149, 191, 194
  Hsin T'ang-shu 123, 192, 195
  Hsin Wu-tai-shih 193, 195
  Hsin Yüan-shih 132, 193, 195
  Liang-shu 192, 194
  Liao-shih 55, 192, 193, 195
  Ming-shih 6, 7, 40, 126, 130, 193, 195
  Nan-ch'i-shu 192, 194
  Nan-shih 134, 136, 143, 192, 194, 196
  Pei-Ch'i-shu 192, 194
  Pei-shih 127, 134, 136, 143, 192, 195, 196
  San-kuo-chih 22, 125, 149, 192, 194, 196
  Shih-chi 31, 39, 82, 96, 97, 98, 127, 155, 191, 194
  Sui-shu 40, 41, 42, 149, 192, 195, 196
  Sung-shih 192, 195
  Sung-shu 42, 192, 194, 196
  Wei-shu 192, 194
  Yüan-shih 43, 91, 126, 141, 142, 193, 195

222 INDEX — GENERAL

Education 66
Foreign relations 71, 124, 128, 130, 134, 142, 144
Geography 64-65
   Fang-chih 9, 175
Government 66
Historical criticism 18, 23, 26, 159
Historical research 10, 147-158
Immortality, three avenues to 25
Imperial Diary *Ch'i-chü-chu* 9, 205, 206, 207, 208
Industry 70
Jurisprudence 68
Kingdoms
   Three 22, 125, 127
   Ten 143, 156
   Sixteen 131
Literary degrees
   Hsiu-ts'ai 121, 135
   Chü-jen 122, 129, 137, 138, 139, 140, 143
   Chin-shih 121, 122, 128, 129, 131, 132, 133, 134, 137, 140, 142, 143, 144, 179, 180
   Hsiao-lien kung-cheng 124
   Po-hsüeh hung-tz'u 121, 143
Local histories 33, 176, 178-180
Maps and records (*t'u-chi*) 39
Medicine 73, 74, 80, 88, 94, 99
Music 69
National geography 129, 176, 177, 178, 182, 183-189
On dynastic histories 76, 93, 123, 124, 126, 133, 134, 138, 192, 193
Oracle bones 1, 29, 170
Painting 69

Political Parties 70, 71
Religion 68
River course and control 81, 82, 87, 129, 133, 139
Schools of thought or learning
   Ch'eng-Chu 24, 25, 125, 166-167
   Chi-i 167
   Ch'iang-hsüeh hui 131
   Chin-shih p'ai or
   Chin-shih hsüeh 28, 167
   Fu-sheh 130, 133
   Han-hsüeh 26, 133, 166, 167
   Hsün-ku 167
   K'ao-chü or
   K'ao-cheng 26, 166
   Kung-yang 168
   Lu-Wang 24, 25
   Sung Hsüeh 167
   Yin-yün 167
Specialized history (*chuan-shih* or *pieh-shih*) 59
Spring-autumn annals 80, 86, 91, 97, 132, 141, 143
Supplements 51, 52, 53, 54, 55, 56, 57. 63, 92, 93, 94, 98, 124, 127, 128, 131, 140, 150-153
Titles of Historians 2, 4, 7, 175, 205-209
Topical treatment (*shih-pieh*) 59
Treatises 40, 60, 126, 127, 128, 131, 132, 149, 150, 151, 152, 153, 158, 196, 197, **200, 201**
Veritable records 8, 9, 94
Year Titles
   Nien-hao 15, 135, 210-212
Zodiac cycle 21

Index — Translated Chinese Book Titles

A Brief History of Chinese Publishing Enterprises 80
A Comparative Study of the New and Old *T'ang* Histories 138
A Comparative Study of Ancient Capitals and Modern Areas 178
A Comprehensive Geography of the Empire 65
A Critical Examination of the Classic of History 100
A Critical Study of the Authenticity of the Classics 131
A Critical Study of the 17 Dynastic Histories 93
A Critical Study of the Seventeen Histories 192
A Critique of the Thirteen Histories 192
A Critique of Types of Calligraphy 68
A Guide to River Systems 81
A History of Chinese Civil Service 67
A History of Education in China 67
A History of Famous Paintings 69
A History of the System of Marking New Eras 125
A History of Weights and Measures 144
A New Angle of the History of Chinese Science 82
A New Revision of the *Yüan* History 84
A Note on the Nestorian Monument 95
A Short History of Chinese Mathematics 84
A Study of Discrepancies in the History of the Five Dynasties 138
A Study of Frontier Colonization Throughout the Dynasties 103
A Study of Six Ancient Calendars 138
A Study of Snuff and Snuff-bottles 84
A Summary of Seven Verified Records 97
A Synoptic View of the Comprehensive Mirror 54
A Record of Uncertain Dates 86
Abridged View of the Comprehensive Mirror 53
Accounts of Administration in the Western Frontiers 94
Aids to the Seventeen Histories 192
An Eclectic View of the Institute of Temples 78
An Encyclopedic History of China from Antiquity to 209 B.C. 137
An Historical and Geographical Study of Manchuria 176
An Historical Source Book of the Northern Regions 91
An Introduction to the Learning of the *Ch'ing* Period 87
Analysis of the Subtle in the Historical Perspectives 164
Annals of Chin 153
Annotations to the Classic of Mountains and Waterways 85
Annotations to the Comprehensive Mirror 51
Annotations to the *Han-shu* 149
Annotations to the New Five Dynasties History 150

224 INDEX — TRANSLATED CHINESE BOOK TITLES

Annotations to the Old *T'ang* History 123
Annotations to the *T'ang* Code 68
Annotations to the Works of Mencius 95
Anthology of Literary Works of *Yangchow* 102
Anthology of *Ming* Poets 99
Appendix to the Archival Records 83
Appendix to the Commentary on *Mo-tzu* 84
Bibliography of Old Books 95
Biographies of Scholars of the *Han* Learning 65
Biographies of the Great Masters of the Unadorned Learning 167
Bibliography of the Literary Productions of the *Yüan* Period 126
Ch'ing History Draft 193
Ch'ing Period General History 100
Chronological Biography of *Ku Yen-wu* 123
Chronological Biography of *Ting Pao-chen* 90
Chronological History of Negotiations with the Kingdom of *Chin* during Three Reigns 55
Chronological Tables of the 21 Dynastic Histories 133
Chronology of the Boxer Affairs as Recorded from Overseas 71
Classic of Tea 73
Classifications of History in the Thirteen Histories 192
Classified Encyclopedia 88
Classified Essentials of Ten Histories 192
Classified Studies of Inscriptions 82
Collated Edition of Rules and Regulations of the State during the *Sung* Period 129
Collectanea of *Tseng Kuo-fan's* Writings 82
Collectanea on *Yüan* History 89
Collected Works on Restored Editions of *Han* Learning Hall 158
Collection of Chinese Place Names 34
Collection of *Ming* Musical Compositions 103
Commentary on the Water Classic 82
Comments on the Comprehensive Mirror 92
Compendium on the *Hanlin* Academy 98
Complete Book on Agricultural Administration 71
Complete Library in Four Classes of Literature 82
Comprehensive Explanations of the Historical Perspectives 164
Comprehensive Geography of the *Ming* Dynasty 177
Comprehensive Geography of the *Yüan* Empire 177
Comprehensive History of Civilization 62
Comprehensive History of Prime Ministers 66
Comprehensive Institutes 60

Comprehensive Institutes of the *Ch'ing* Dynasty 61
Comprehensive Mirror for the Aid in Government 50
Comprehensive Mirror of Narration of Events from Beginning to End 56
Comprehensive Mirror of the *Ming* 53
Comprehensive Mirror of the *Sung* Dynasty 52
Comprehensive Treatises 61
Corrections of Dynastic Histories 81
Corrections of the History of the Three Kingdoms 125
Corrections to the Two *Han* Histories 125
Critical Annotations to the *Han-shu* 92
Critical Notes on Ancient Philosophers 92
Critical Notes on the 22 Dynastic Histories 124
Dates of Births and Deaths of Famous People in Chinese History 143
Deep Mirror Classified Knowledge 64
Deliberations on the School of *Han* Learning 167
Diary of *Shih Ta-k'ai* 87
Diary of Trip between Shanghai and London 134
Discrepancies in National History 87
Discrepancies in the *Tao-te-ching* 136
Discrepancies in the 22 Dynastic Histories 126
Discussions of *Han* Learning 93
Discussion of Mathematics 93
Dissertation on Fevers 73
Draft History of the *Ming* Period 130
Duplications in the Classic of History 138
Epigraphy on Metal and Stone 100
Essential Collection of Atlases 102
Essentials of *Chin* History 153
Essentials of *Ming* History 53
Essentials of the Comprehensive Mirror 54
Essentials of the Three Histories 191
Events of the *Fu-sheh* Political Club 79
Evidence for the Treatise on Literature in the *Sui-shu* 149
Excerpts from *Ming* History 78
Exposition of Natural Resources 73
Fragments of Writings of *Han* Scholars 168
Fundamental Principles of Cultural History 42, 122
Fundamental Principles of Historical Criticism 164
General History of the *Ming* Dynasty 94, 126
Great Peace Imperial Reading 64
Han Philosophical Writings 100
Hidden Meanings in the Historical Memoirs Explained 96

226　INDEX — TRANSLATED CHINESE BOOK TITLES

Historical Filature 57
Historical Geography 177
Historical Geography Illustrated with Maps 177
Historical Memoirs of the Five Dynasties 154
Historical Memoirs of the Mongols 139
History of Archery 70
History of Currency 72
History of Foreign Relations of Modern China 79
History of Frontiers (Mongolia) 71
History of Philosophies during the *Ming* Period 130
History of *Po-hai* Kingdom 156
History of Southern *Sung* 156
History of *Sung* and *Yüan* Dramatic Literature 67
History of the Campaign against the Eluths 83
History of the Lute 70
History of the Struggle of Political Parties in China 71
History of the Ten Kingdoms 143
History of Thought during the *Ming* Period 65, 85
Illustrated History of Ancient Jade 73
Illustrated History of the Manufacture of Bricks 72
Institution of the Censorate of China 66
Introduction to Classical Studies 87
Introductory Search into the Seventeen Histories 192
Joint Text (Chinese-Manchu) on the Music of the Lute 83
List of *Han* Stone Inscriptions 99
Methods of Architecture 74
Methods of Research in Chinese History 34
Ming History Precedents 89
Narrative *Ming* History 91
Narrative on the Boats of the South 72
New Edition of the *Sung* History 154
New History of the *Yüan* Dynasty 132
New Interpretation of the Classic of History 135
Notes on An Ancient Medical Work 94
Notes on Literary Criticism 96
Notes on Research Studies 98
Notes on the History of the Inscriptions on the Stone Drums 136
Notes on the *Kung-yang's* Commentary on the Spring-Autumn Annals 132
Notes on the Mirror of History 98
Notes on the New *T'ang* History 123
Notes on the Tribute of *Yü* 129
Notes on the 22 Dynastic Histories 76

Index — Translated Chinese Book Titles

Officers and Rites of *Han* 148
Official Work on Chinese Turkestan 100
On Knowledge 91
On Salt Administration 103
Outline History of *Sinkiang* 102
Outline of the Nineteen Histories 193
Outlines of the Eighteen Histories 192
Philological Explanations of Terms in the Classics and Commentaries 95
Philosophers of the Confucian School 140
Pleasant Stories of the Four Reigns 86
Pre-Comprehensive Mirror 52
Pronunciations and Meanings in the *Han-shu* 148
Pronunciations in the *Shih-chi* 148
Questions and Answers on the Classics and Histories 127
Reliable Discussions of the Seventeen Histories 192
Research on Ancient Calendars 78
Revised Edition of *Shih-pen* 158
Secrets of Music 130
Separate Records 59
Seven Classifications of Books 60
Seven Records 60
Seven Treaties 60
Similarities and Differences in the 21 Dynastic Histories 134
Six Canons in the Chinese Art of Painting 69
Social Pronouncements of the Three Histories 191
Songs from Contemporary Poems 70
Source Materials for the History of Chinese Foreign Relations 94
Source Materials for the History of the *T'ai-p'ing* Kingdom 157
Southern *T'ang* History 156
Study of Ceramics 72
Study of Confucius as a Reformer 131
Sung-Yüan Comprehensive Mirror 52
Supplement to the History of Tea 92
Supplement to the Southern and Northern Histories 93
Supplement to the *T'ang* History 154
Supplements to the Abridged View of Comprehensive Mirror 54, 55
Supplements to the Comprehensive Mirror 51, 52, 53
Supplements to the *T'ang* History 124
Surnames in the 24 Histories by Syllabary Rhymes 17
Symposium on Ancient Chinese History 35
Synthesis of Books and Illustrations of Ancient and Modern Times 64, 79
Table of Important Events in the Spring-Autumn Annals 91

Ten Proposals for the Writing of Gazetteers 122
Terrestial Maps 177
Textual Criticism of the Old *T'ang* History 136
The *Fan* Family Library Catalogue 90
The Seventh Collation of the Classics of Waterways 127
The Verified and the Doubtful in Histories 127
Thirty Essays on the *Kung-yang* Commentary 135
Topography of Mongolia 78
Treatise on Geography of Later *Chin* 151
Treatise on Geography of the Sixteen Kingdoms 152
Treatise on the Kinship in the *Chin-shih* 153
Union Index of 33 Biographies of the *Ch'ing* Period 103
Verified Record of Three Cities 32, 65

INDEX — ROMANIZED CHINESE BOOK TITLES

An-hui t'ung-chih 178
Ch'a ching 73
Ch'a-shih pu 92
Chan-yüan wei-ting-kao 101
Ch'ang-chou pien-t'i-wen lu 139
Chang Chü-cheng ta-chuan 215
Ch'ang-sha-fu chih 179
Chang-wen-ta-kung i-chi 86
Ch'ao-hsien chi-shih 71
Chao-mei chan-yen 77
Chao-yü chih 133
Che-chiang t'ung-chih 178
Ch'en-shu 192, 194
Cheng Ch'eng-kung 217
Cheng-chüeh-lou ts'ung-ko 99
Ch'eng-huai-yüan wen-ts'un 102
Chi-chai wen-chi 79
Ch'i-chia hou-Han-shu 157
Ch'i-chiao shui-ching chu 127
Ch'i-chih 60
Chi-fu t'ung-chih 178
Chi Han-shu 153
Chi-lin k'an-chieh chi 144
Ch'i-lu 60
Ch'i-lüeh 59
Chi-nan-fu chih 179
Chi-shih-pen-mo 55
Ch'i-shu 200
Ch'i-wen chü-li 82, 138
Chi-yüan k'ao-lüeh 125
Chia-ku-wen pien 37
Chia-ku-wen tuan-tai yen-chiu-li 37
Chia-ting Chen-chiang chih 136
Chia-yu lü-ling 68
Chiang-chai wen-chi pu-i 93
Ch'iang-fa chun-sheng 83
Chiang-hsi t'ung-chih 178
Chiang-nan t'ung-chih 178
Chiang-ning-fu chih 179
Chiao-chi shih-pen 158

Chiao-ch'ou t'ung-i 122, 164, 165
Chieh-ku lu 69
Ch'ien-ch'ing-tang shu-mu 41
Chien-chuang shu-chi 124
Ch'ien-lung Chekiang t'ung-chih k'ao-i 35
Ch'ien-lung fu, t'ing, chou, hsien, chih 131
Chien-yen i-lai hsi-nien yao-lu 52
Chih-i ou-ts'un 123
Chih-ming kuang-li 134
Ch'ih-pei ou-tan 90
Chih-p'ing lüeh 89
Chih-sheng p'ien 135
Chin-chi 153
Chin-ju hsüeh-shu t'ung-hsi lun 167
Chin-lüeh 153
Ch'in-p'u ho-pi 83
Chin-shih 193, 195, 198, 202
Ch'in-shih 70
Chin-shih chi-shih-pen-mo 57
Chin-shih pu 127
Chin-shih shih-tsu-chih 153
Chin-shih tsung-li 100
Chin-shu 192, 194
Chin-shu yin-i 149
Chin-ssu lu 66
Chin-tai Chung-kuo wai-chiao shih-liao chi-yao 79
Chin-tai erh-shih-chia p'ing-chuan 220
Chin-tai Han-hsüeh pien-ch'ien lun 167
Chin ti-li-chih pu-cheng 151
Ch'in-ting Huang-yü hsi-yü t'u-chih 100
Chin-yao ch'ou-pi 81
Chin yüeh-fu 137
Ch'ing-ch'ao ch'ien-chi 157
Ching-chi chih 17
Ching-chi tsuan-ku 99, 124
Ch'ing chien-kuo pieh-chi 157
Ching-chuan shih-tz'u 95

Ching-hsüeh chih-yen 81
Ching-hsüeh ju-men 87
Ching-i shu-wen 96
Ching-k'ao fu-lu 83
Ch'ing-shih-kao 32, 37, 193, 195, 199
Ching-shih ta-wen 97, 127
Ch'ing-shih t'an-wei 214
Ch'ing-shih t'ien-wen-chih k'ao 132
Ch'ing-tai hsüeh-shu-kai-lun 87, 134
Ch'ing-tai k'ao-shih chih-tu 213
Ch'ing-tai p'u-hsüeh ta-shih lieh-chuan 167
Ch'ing-tai t'ung-shih 101, 216
Ch'ing t'ung-tien 61
Ching-tzu i-t'ung 86
Ch'ing wen-hsien t'ung-k'ao 63
Ch'ing-yüan tang-chin 70
Chiu-chia chiu-Chin-shu 158
Chiu-ching ku-i 36
Chiu-ching pien-tzu tu-meng 138
Chiu-huang ts'e 139
Chiu-kuo-chih 138, 156
Chiu-shih t'ung hsing-ming lüeh 141
Chiu T'ang-shu 193, 195
Chiu T'ang-shu chiao-k'an chi 136
Chiu-T'ang-shu shu-cheng 123
Chiu Wu-tai-shih 137, 195
Ch'iu-yüan tsa-p'ei 98
Chou-i cheng-i 78
Chou-i chi-chieh sheng-i 93
Chou-i shih-i 93
Chou-kuan pien-fei 92
Chou-shan hsing-fei 130
Chou-shu 192, 194
Ch'ou-yang ch'u-i 82
Ch'ü-fu K'ung-miao-chih-chien-chu chi ch'i-hsiu-chi chi-hua 74
Ch'u-Han chu-hou chiang-yü k'ao 136
Chu-shih jan-i 127
Chu-shih t'ung-i lu 134
Chu-tzu p'ing-i 92
Chu-tzu yü jih-ch'ao 87

Ch'ü-yü t'u-chih 177
Ch'üan-heng tu-liang shih-yen k'ao 144
Ch'uan-hsi lu 66
Ch'üan-shih 72
Chuang-tzu chieh 80
Ch'un-ch'iu fan-lu 169
Ch'un-ch'iu Ku-liang-chuan chu 132
Ch'un-ch'iu Kung-yang-chuan chan 141
Ch'un-ch'iu Kung-yang-chuan chu 132
Ch'un-ch'iu ming-tzu chieh-ku 80
Ch'un-ch'iu shih 219
Ch'un-ch'iu ta-shih-piao 91, 132
Ch'un-ch'iu Tso-chuan i-shu 86
Ch'un-ch'iu Tso-shih-chuan chieh 148
Ch'un-ch'iu Tso-shih-chuan ta-i 97
Ch'un-hua hsien-chih 131
Chün-chai 46
Chün-chai shu-chih 45
Ch'ün-ching i-cheng 85
Ch'ün-shu chiao-pu 80
Ch'ün-shu shih-pu 94
Ch'ung-chen ch'ang-pien 78
Chung-hsi-hui nien-li pi-chiao-piao 35
Ch'ung-hsiu Nan-Pei-shih 154
Chung-hua-min-kuo cheng-chih shi 214
Chung-hua min-kuo yu-cheng yü-t'u 15
Chung-kuo che-hsüeh-shih ta-kang 36
Chung-kuo cheng-chih-ssu-hsiang shih 216
Chung-kuo chiang-yü yen-ko-lüeh 219
Chung-kuo chiao-yü shih 67
Chung-kuo chin-pai-nien-shih tzu-liao 219
Chung-kuo chin-san-pai-nien hsüeh-shu-shih 215
Chung-kuo chin-tai ching-chi fa-chan-shih 216
Chung-kuo chin-tai shih 214, 215, 217
Chung-kuo ching-ying hsi-yü shih 219
Chung-kuo ch'u-pan-chieh chien-shih 80
Chung-kuo fa-chih-shih 213

Index — Romanized Chinese Book Titles

Chung-kuo fa-lü fa-ta-shih 220
Chung-kuo hsin-wen-hsüeh yün-tung shih 35
Chung-kuo hsin-wen-hsüeh yün-tung shu-p'ing 35
Chung-kuo hui-hua-shang-ti liu-fa lun 69
Chung-kuo jen-ming ta-tzu-tien 21
Chung-kuo k'o-hsüeh-shih chü-yü 82
Chung-kuo ku-chin ti-ming ta-tz'u-tien 15
Chung-kuo li-shih yen-chiu-fa 34
Chung-kuo li-shih yen-chou fa 134
Chung-kuo li-tai nien-hao so-in 220
Chung-kuo lun-li-hsüeh shih 66
Chung-kuo shih 220
Chung-kuo shih-hsüeh-shih 21, 215
Chung-kuo shih-hsüeh-shih kai-lun 220
Chung-kuo shu-yüan chih-tu 218
Chung-kuo suan-hsüeh hsiao-shih 84
Chung-kuo ti-fang-chih tsung-lu 37
Chung-kuo ti-ming ta-tz'u-tien 15
Chung-kuo tsai-hsiang chih-tu 217
Chung-kuo t'ung-shih chien-pien 215
Chung-kuo t'ung-shih yao-lüeh 218
Chung-kuo wen-hua-shih 217
Chung-kuo yü-shih chih-tu 66
Chung-kuo yü-shih-chih-tu-ti yen-ko 10
Ch'ung-pien Ning-po Fan-shih tien-i-ko t'u-shu mu-lu 90
Chung-shan wen-ch'ao 101
Chung-wai chiao-t'ung shih-liao 94
Ch'ung-wen 46
Ch'ung-wen shu-mu 45
Erh-shih-erh shih jih-shih cheng 123
Erh-shih-i shih nien-piao 133
Erh-shih-i-shih t'ung-i 134, 193
Erh-tz'u shih-chieh ta-chan shih-liao 215
Erh-ya 182
Fa-shu yao-lu 68
Fan-pu yao-lüeh 71

Fang-ch'eng shen-lun 93
Fang-chih shu-mu 37
Fang-weng nien-p'u 124
Feng-ya hsiao-chi 84
Fu-chien t'ung-chih 178
Fu-chou-fu chih 179
Fu-sho chi-shih 79
Fu-wu king-tu 88
Hai-kuo t'u-chih 143
Hai-t'ang t'ung-chih 127
Han-chi 162
Han chih-k'ao 66
Han-chiu-i 149
Han-hsüeh shang-tui 93, 167
Han-hsüeh shih-ch'eng chi 65, 166
Han-hsüeh-t'ang chi-i-shu 158
Han-ju t'ung-i 100, 167
Han-kuan-i 148
Han-shih ts'un-mu 99
Han-shu 162, 191, 194, 198, 202
Han-shu chu 149
Han-shu pien-i 92, 149
Han-shu pu-chu 140
Han-shu shu-cheng 95, 149
Han-shu ti-li-chih-chi-i 79, 127, 149
Han-shu yin-i 148
Hang-chou-fu chih 137, 179
Heng-hsüan so-chien so-ts'ang chi-chin lu 144
Heng-yang hsien-chih 141
Ho-chou chih 122
Ho-fang cheh-yao 78
Ho-nan t'ung-chih 178
Hou-Han-chi 162
Hou-Han-shu 162, 191, 194, 198, 202
Hou-Han-shu pien-i 149
Hou-Han-shu pu-chu 149
Hou-Han-shu pu-piao 150
Hou-Han-shu shu-cheng 149
Hsi-an-fu chih 180
Hsi-cheng chi-ch'eng 79
Hsi-ch'ui shih-k'o lu 136

232   INDEX — ROMANIZED CHINESE BOOK TITLES

Hsi-ch'ui tsung-t'ung shih-lüeh 94
Hsi-ch'ui yao-lüeh 102
Hsi-hsia chi 156
Hsi-hsia chi-shih-pen-mo 56
Hsi-hsia i-wen-chih 152
Hsi-hsia shu-shih 156
Hsi-hu chi-lan 79
Hsi-jung hsiao-p'in 126
Hsi-ming chiang-i 80
Hsi-pao hsüan shu-lu 95
Hsi-suan ch'u-chieh 82
Hsi Wei-shu 156
Hsi-yü shui-tao chi 129
Hsi-yuan lu 68
Hsia-hsüeh chih-nan 81
Hsiang cheng 73
Hsiang-chün chih 141
Hsiang-t'an hsien-chih 141
Hsiao-hsüeh k'ai-meng 87
Hsiao-shih-fan t'ing chu-lu 82
Hsiao-tien chi-chuan 157
Hsiao-tien-chi-nien fu-k'ao 156
Hsieh-ch'eng hou-Han-shu chi-pen 158
Hsien-cheng tu-shu chüeh 83
Hsien-ch'in cheng-chih shih 134
Hsien-fa hui-pien 34
Hsin-chiang chih-lüeh 129
Hsin-chiang li-su chih 73
Hsin-chiang t'ung-chih 178
Hsin-chiao Chin-shu ti-li-chih 151
Hsin-chiu T'ang-shu ho-ch'ao 138, 155
Hsin-ch'ou hsiao-hsia chi 143
Hsin-hsüeh wei-ching k'ao 131
Hsin-kiang shih-lüeh 94
Hsin shih-ko-chi 70
Hsin T'ang-shih 164
Hsin T'ang-shu 192, 195
Hsin T'ang-shu ho-ch'ao 123
Hsin T'ang-shu pu-chu 150
Hsin T'ang-shu t'ien-wen-chih shu-cheng 150
Hsin-ts'un-lu 85

Hsin Wu-tai-shih 193, 195
Hsin Wu-tai-shih chu 150
Hsin Yüan-shih 132, 153, 154, 193, 195, 198
Hsiu pu 73
Hsing-lü t'ung-piao 128
Hsing-shih yao-yen 103
Hsing-shui chin-chien 81
Hsing-yin t'u-chih 134
Hsü-chi Sung-hui-yao kao-pen 129
Hsü Hou-Han-shu 153
Hsü Hou-Han-shu pien-i 149
Hsü Ming-chi-shih-pen-mo 57
Hsü T'ang-shu 124, 154
Hsü t'ung-chien-ch'ang-pien shu-pu 53
Hsü t'ung-tien 61
Hsu tzu-chih-t'ung-chien 53
Hsü tzu-chih-t'ung-chien ch'ang-pien 52
Hsü tzu-chih-t'ung-chien chi-shih-pen-mo 57
Hsü Wen-hsien-t'ung-k'ao 63, 100
Hsüan-ho hua-p'u 69
Hsüeh-cheng ch'üan-shu 44, 67
Hsüeh-chin t'ao-yüan 97
Hsüeh-pien 91
Hsui-chih shih-i 122
Hsün-tzu chi-chieh 140
Hu-ch'uan lu 73
Hu-nan t'ung-chih 178
Hu-pei t'ung-chih 178
Hu-pei t'ung-chih chien-ts'un kao 81
Hu-pei t'ung-chih wei-ch'eng kao 101, 122
Hua-hsüeh pi-chüeh 69
Huai-an-fu chih 132
Huai-t'ing tsai-pi 98
Huan-yü t'ung-chih 177
Huang-ch'ao ching-chieh hsü-pien 140
Huang-ch'ao shih-chi lu 138
Huang-ch'ao tz'u-lin tien-ku 98
Huang-ch'ao wu-kung chi-sheng 124
Huang-hua chi-ch'eng 144

INDEX — ROMANIZED CHINESE BOOK TITLES

Huang Ming shih-kai 10, 94, 126
Huang-yü piao 176
Hui-hsi tao-ch'ing 97
Hui-t'ung-chih-tao 49
Hung-fan cheng-lun 130
I-ching t'ung-chu 100
I-chou chih 65
I-chou-shuang-chi 69
I-hsüeh pien-huo 92
I-i pei-lu 91
I kuang-chi 88
I-li jih-chi 131
I-li kuan-chien 88
I Lo yüan-yüan lu 65
I-man an sheng-kao 93
I-nien-lu 86
I-shih 57, 137
I-su chi 73
I-tsung chin-chien 74
I-wen chih 17
I-yü yao-lu 102
Jen-piao k'ao 135
Jen-tsung shih-lu 94
Jih-hsia chiu-wen k'ao 177
Jih-pen ch'i-shih chi 130
Jo-ho chih 126
Ju-lin tsung-p'ai 140
Jung-ts'un tzu-hua pien-o 92
K'ai-feng-fu chih 180
Kai-yü ts'ung-k'ao 99, 124
Kan-su t'ung-chih 179
Kang-chien-i-chih-lu 34
Kang-mu ting-wu 125
K'ao-hsin lu 139, 172
K'ao-hsin-lu t'i-yao 97
Kao-seng chuan 68
Keng-tsu hai-wai chi-shih 71
K'o-lu 56
K'o-she ou-wen 90
Ku-chin t'u-shu chi-ch'eng 64, 79
Ku-chin tao-chien lu 72
Ku-chin hsüeh-k'ao 135

Ku-ching-chieh hui-han 85
Ku-ching-chieh kou-ch'en 87
Ku-ch'üan ching-hsüan 81
Ku-ch'uan hui 72
Ku-chung sui-pi 96
Ku-hua p'ing-lu 69
Ku kuo-tu chin-chün-hsien ho-k'ao 178
Ku-shih hsin-cheng 35, 142
Ku-shih pien 35, 172
Ku-shih p'ing-tso lun 89
Ku T'ing-lin nien-p'u 123
Ku-wen shang-shu k'ao 36
Ku-wen shang-shu shu-cheng 36
Ku-wen yüan-chien 103
Ku-wen yüeh-hsüan 67
Ku-yü hsin-yen 85
Ku-yü t'u-k'ao 73
Kuan-chih-hsün 148
Kuan-ts'un wen-ch'ao nei-p'ien 90
Kuang-chou-fu chih 180
Kuang-hsi t'ung-chih 179
Kuang i-chou-shuang-chi 69
Kuang-tung t'u-shuo 100
Kuang-tung t'ung-chih 125, 179
Kuang-yü t'u 177
Kuei-chou shui-tao k'ao 131
Kuei-chou t'ung-chih 179
Kuei-lin feng-t'u chi 65
Kuei-t'ien so-chi 96
Kuei-yang chou-chih 141
Kuei-yang-fu chih 180
Kung-chou shih-shih 130
Kung-chü cheng-shih lu 127
Kung-shih 124
Kung-tuan ying-tsao lu 74
K'ung-tzu kai-chih k'ao 131
Kung-yang san-shih lun 135
Kuo-ch'ao Chin-ling shih-ch'ao 67
Kuo-ch'ao Han-hsüeh shih-ch'eng chi 125
Kuo-ch'ao hua-cheng lu 69
Kuo-ch'ao shih jen cheng-lüeh 78

Kuo-ch'ao Sung-hsüeh yüan-yüan chi 125
Kuo-shih k'ao-i 87, 137
Lan-chou-fu chih 180
Lan-t'ai kuei-fan 88
Lao-yü hsien-hua 84
Li-ching shih-li 94
Li Ching-wen 125
Li Hsiu-ch'eng kung-chuang 156
Li-shih chuan-pien-ti nien-tai 219
Li-shih yen-chiu-fa 218
Li-tai chü-chan hsü-lüeh 70
Li-tai fu-p'ai lu 136
Li-tai kuan-yin chi-ts'un 136
Li-tai kung-chü chih 67
Li-tai ming-hua chi 69
Li-tai Ming-jen nien-p'u 21, 143
Li-tai ping-chih 70
Li-tai shih-piao 94, 140
Li-tai tang-cheng shih 71
Li-tai ti-li-chih yün-pien chin-shih 178
Li-tai ti-li yen-ko-piao 178
Li-tai tsai-fu hui-k'ao 66
Li-tai t'un-k'en yen-chiu 103, 219
Liang-Han chü-cheng 125
Liang-Han k'an-wu pu-i 149
Liang-Han-shu k'an-wu 149
Liang-Han-shu shu-cheng 127
Liang-huang-ti shih-lu 10
Liang-shu 192, 194
Liao-chin cheng-shih kang-mu 55
Liao Chin Yüan san-shih tung hsing-ming lu 141
Liao i-wen-chih 152
Liao-shih 192, 193, 195
Liao-shih chi-shih-pen-mo 56
Lieh-ch'ao shih-chi 67
Lieh-hsien chuan 68
Lien-yün-i ts'ung-shu 123
Lin-wen pien-lan 31
Ling-hai yü-t'u 65
Liu Hsiang Hsin fu dz nien-pu 46
Liu-li chen-wei 78, 138
Lu-chiang Ch'ien-shih wen-hui 102
Lu Hsin san-shih-nien chi 35
Lü-hsing hsiao-kao 84
Lu-tzu i-shu 86
Lun-yü ku-hsün 124
Ma-cheng chi 70
Man-chou yüan-liu k'ao 176
Mao-shih Lu-shu kuang-yao 88
Mao-shih wen-nan 102
Mei-chuang tsa-chu 98
Men-wu-erh shih-chi 139, 154
Meng-ku yu-mu chi 78, 123
Meng-ku yu-mu chi pu-chu 128
Meng-tzu tzu-i shu-cheng 95
Miao-chih che-chung 78
Min-kuo chün-shih chin-chi 70
Ming-ch'ao chi-shih-pen-mo pu-pien 57
Ming-chi 53
Ming-chi shih-lu 133
Ming-ju hsüeh-an 65, 85, 130
Ming-shih 193, 195
Ming-shih an 77, 130
Ming-shih ch'ao-lüeh 78
Ming-shih chi-shih pen-mo 57, 91, 133
Ming-shih k'ao-i 137
Ming-shih li-an 89
Ming-shih tsung 99
Ming ts'ao-yün chih 133
Ming t'ung-chien 53
Ming t'ung-pao i 72
Ming Wo-k'ou shih-mo 133
Ming-yüeh-fu 103, 140
Mo-chih 73
Mo-ni-chiao ju Chung-kuo k'ao 68
Mo-tzu chien-ku 138
Mo-tzu chien-ku hou-yü 84
Mo-tzu hsüeh-an 134
Mo-yüan hui-kuan 85
Nan-ch'ang-fu chih 180
Nan-Ch'i-shu 192, 194, 200

INDEX — ROMANIZED CHINESE BOOK TITLES 235

Nan-chiang i-shih 86, 156
Nan ch'uan chi 72
Nan-Han-chi 156
Nan-Han-shu 156
Nan-hua-ching fa-yin 68
Nan-Ming-shu 157
Nan-Pei-shih ho-chu 134, 143, 155
Nan-Pei-shih pu-chih 93, 152
Nan-shih 192, 194, 196
Nan-Sung-shu 156
Nan-T'ang-shu 156
Nan-T'ang-shu ho-ting 155
Nan-tu shih-lüeh 138
Nei-ko hsiao-chih 84
Nien-erh-shih cha-chi 77, 124, 193
Nien-erh-shih k'ao-i 126, 193
Nien-i-shih ssu-p'u 138
Nien-wu-shih lung-kang 217
Ning-kuo fu-chih 131
Nü-ko 74
Nü-shih shih-ch'ao 67
Nung-cheng ch'üan-shu 44, 71
Nung-sang chi-yao 71
Ou-mei cheng-chih yao-i 102
Pai-hua wen-hsüeh shih 35
Pan-Ma i-t'ung 155
Pan-t'an-chai t'i-pa 97
Pao-ch'ao t'ung-k'ao 72
Pao-ting-fu chih 180
Pao-yen-t'ang pi-chi 91
Pei-Ch'i-shu 192, 194
Pei-chiao hui-pien 128
Pei-shih 192, 195, 196
Pei-shih ch'ien lang 127
Pei-shih Nan-shih 136
Pei-yang kung-tu lei-tsuan 89
Pieh-lu 59
Pen-ts'ao ching chieh-yao 80
Ping-t'a meng-hen lu 141
P'ing-ting Lo-ch'a fang-lüeh 128
P'ing-ting shuo-mo fang-lüeh 83
Po-hai-kuo chih 156

Po-kuan-piao chu 66
Po-t'ang tu-shu pi-chi 91
Pu Ch'en chiang-yü-chih 152
Pu Chin-ping-chih 151
Pu Chin-shu i-wen-chih 151
Pu Han-ping-chih 150
Pu Hou-Han-shu i-wen-chih 128, 150, 151
Pu Hou-Han-shu nien-piao 150
Pu Liao-shih ching-chi-chih 153
Pu Nan-pei-shih i-wen-chi 152
Pu San-kuo chiang-yü-chih 131, 151
Pu San-kuo-chih 128
Pu San-kuo i-wen-chih 151
P'u-shu-t'ing chi wai-kao 101
Pu Sung-shu hsing-fa-chih 152
Pu Sung-shu i-wen-chih 152
Pu Sung-shu shih-huo-chih 152
P'u-ts'un-ko nung-shu 72
Pu Wu-tai-shih i-wen-chih 152
Pu Yüan-shih i-wen-chih 153
Pu Yüan-shih shih-tsu-chih 153
San-ch'ao pei-meng hui-pien 55, 71
San-fan chi-shih-pen-mo 57
San-fu chüeh-lu 32, 64
San-kuo-chih 22, 192, 194, 196
San-kuo-chih chu 149
San-kuo-chih chü-cheng 125
San-kuo-chih kuan-piao 151
San-kuo i-wen-chih 151
San-kuo pu-chu 127
San-shih ch'ün-yen 191
San-shih lüeh 191
San-shih-san chung ch'ing-tai chuan-chi yin-te 103
San t'ung-k'ao 64
San-yüan pi-chi 134
Shan-hai-ching hsün-tsan 85
Shan-hai-ching kuang-chu 88, 143
Shan-hsi t'ung-chih 179
Shan-shui chüeh 69
Shan-tung k'ao-ku lu 133

Index — Romanized Chinese Book Titles

Shan-tung t'ung-chih 179
Shang-han lun 73
Shang-shu 56
Shang-shu chan 141
Shang-shu chih-i 132
Shang-shu hsin-chieh 135
Shang-shu k'ao-i 28
Shang-shu pien-chih 138
Shang-shu t'ung-chien 100
Shao-Wu cheng-li chi 130
Shen-chou feng-t'u chi 73
Shen-hsi t'ung-chih 179
Sheng-ch'ao i-shih 86
Sheng-ching t'ung-chih 179
Sheng-p'ing pao-fa 91
Sheng-wu chi 143
Sheng-wu-chi ts'o-yao 99
Sheng-yü hsiang-chieh 84
Shih-chi 35, 191, 194, 199, 202
Shih-chi cheng-i 148
Shih-chi chi-chieh 148
Shih-chi chih-i 81, 135
Shih-chi k'ao 122
Shih-chi k'ao-i 127
Shih-ch'i-shih ch'üeh-lun 192
Shih-chi shih-erh-chu-hou nien-piao k'ao-cheng 218
Shih-ch'i-shih meng-ch'iu 192
Shih-ch'i-shih shang-ch'üeh 36, 93, 192
Shih-ch'i-shih tsan 192
Shih-chi so-yin 96, 148
Shih-chi t'an-yüan 97
Shih-chi ting-pu 98
Shih-chi-yin 148
Shih-chi yin-i 148
Shih-chiu-shih lüeh 193
Shih-hsi chi-ch'eng 134
Shih-hsien-chih k'ao 132
Shih-hsing yün-pien 17, 141
Shih-hsüeh fang-fa ta-kang 218
Shih-hsüeh-shih 10
Shih-ku 74

Shih-ku wen k'ao-shih 136
Shih kung-an 88
Shih-kuo ch'un-ch'iu 143, 156
Shih-liao yü shih-hsüeh 213
Shih-liu-kuo chiang-yü-chih 131, 152
Shih-pa-shih lüeh 192
Shih-san-tai shih-mu 192
Shih-san-tai shih po-i 192
Shih-san-tai wei-shu 137
Shih-shih 10
Shih-shih lei-yao 192
Shih-shuo sui-yü 96
Shih Ta-k'ai jih-chi 87
Shih-t'ung 18, 42, 162
Shih-t'ung hsi-wei 164
Shih-t'ung hsiao-fan 164
Shih-t'ung hsün-ku pu 164
Shih-t'ung hui-yao 164
Shih-t'ung t'ung-shih 164
Shina chimei shusei 34
Shina ritai chimei Yoran 16
Sho-shu 70
Shou-shih t'ung-k'ao 71
Shu-fa ching-yen 81
Shu-fa ya-yen 69

Shu-hsüeh t'ung-kuei 101
Shu-ku ts'ung-ch'ao 99
Shu-mu ta-wen 45
Shu-shih 69
Shu-tuan 68
Shui-ching chu 82
Shui-hsi shu-wu shu-mu 95
Shun-t'ien-fu chih 180
Shuo-fang pei-sheng 91, 127
Shuo-fang pei-sheng cha-chi 77
Shuo-wen-hsi-chuan 10
Shuo-wen ku-chou pu 144
Ssu-ch'ao ch'ao-pi t'u-li 136
Ssu-ch'ao i-wen 86
Ssu-ch'uan t'ung-chih 179
Ssu-k'u ch'üan-shu 82

Index — Romanized Chinese Book Titles

Ssu-k'u shu-mu 45
Ssu-ming ts'ung-shu 100
Ssu-shu shih-ti 95
Ssu-shu ta-ch'üan 96
Ssu-shu tien-ku ho 83
Su Pao-chi t'i-pi 97
Su-shu k'an-wu 87
Su-wen shih-i 94
Sui-shu 40, 192, 195, 196
Sui-shu ching-chi-chih 36, 41
*Sui-shu ching-chi-chih
 k'ao-cheng* 149, 158
Sung-chi chung-i lu 140
Sung-chung shih-pen-chu 158
Sung-hui-yao 129
Sung-ling wen-hsien 101
Sung-pi tsou-shu 99
Sung san-ssu t'iao-li k'ao 129
Sung-shih 192, 195, 202
Sung-shih chi 154
Sung-shih chi-shih-pen-mo 56
Sung-shih chih 154
Sung-shih hsin-pien 154
Sung-shih i-wen-chih pu 152
Sung-shu 194, 196
Sung so-yü 96
*Sung t'ung-chien-ch'ang-pien
 chi-shih-pen-mo* 52
Sung Yüan hsi-ch'ü shih 35, 67, 142, 172
Sung Yüan hsü-pien 144
Sung Yüan hsüeh-an 130
Sung Yüan tzu-chih-t'ung-chien 52
Ta-Ch'ing hui-tien 66, 209
Ta-Ch'ing i-t'ung-chih 65, 129, 177
Ta i-t'ung-chih 177
Ta-ju ts'ui-yü 132
Ta-Ming i-t'ung-chih 177
Ta-ming shui-tao k'ao 87, 139
Ta-t'ung shu 132
Ta-Yüan chan-chi kung-wu chi 142
Ta-Yüan kuan-chih tsa-chi 142
Ta-Yüan ta i-t'ung-chih 177

T'ai-ho yeh-shih 42
T'ai-p'ing huan-yü chi 177
T'ai-p'ing-kuo shih-liao 214
T'ai-p'ing-t'ien-kuo chan-chi 157
*T'ai-p'ing-t'ien-kuo ko-ming
 ssu-ch'ao* 218
T'ai-p'ing-t'ien-kuo shih-kang 218
T'ai-p'ing-t'ien-kuo shih-liao 157
T'ai-ping t'ien-kuo shih-wen ch'ao 36
T'ai-ping yü-lan 64
Tai-ting-lu 97
T'ai-wan t'ung-shih 213
T'ai-yüan-fu chih 180
T'ang Ch'ien-an wen-chi chieh-yao 80
*T'ang-tai cheng-chih-shih
 hsü-lun-kao* 214
Tang-tai Chung-kuo shih-hsüeh 217
T'ang liang-ching ch'eng fang k'ao 129
T'ang-lü shu-i 68
T'ang teng-k'o chih-k'ao 129
T'ang tung-hsia liang-chih k'ao 123
T'ao-chai ts'ang-shih mu 89
T'ao-shuo 72
Tao-te-ching k'ao-i 136
T'ao Yüan-ming chi chi-chu 79
Te-shu-lou tsa-ch'ao 98
Ti-li chih 177
T'ien-chin-fu chih 180
T'ien-hsia chün-kuo li-ping shu 133
T'ien-i-ko pei-mu 126
T'ien-kung k'ai-wu 73
T'ien-men hsien-chih 122
*T'ien-ming i-lai shih-ch'ao
 tung-hua lu* 140
T'ien-shan k'o-hua 131
Tien-tu ou-ts'un 90
Ting-chia cheng-hsin-lu 78
Ting wen-ch'eng kung nien-p'u 90
Tsao-ch'iang hsien-chih pu-cheng 92
Tsao-chuan t'u-shuo 72
*Tseng-kai tsui-chin Shang-hai
 chin-jung shih* 72
Tseng Kuo-fan p'ing-chuan 215

Tseng-wen cheng-kung ch'üan-chi 82
Tso-chih yao-yen 103
Tso-chuan chi-shih-pen-mo 56
Tso-chuan chiu-shu k'ao-cheng 136
Tso-chuan pu-chu 93
Tso-chuan shih-wei 137
Tsou-ting hsüeh-t'ang chang-ch'eng 67
Tsui-ch'ing hui-chuan 157
Ts'ui Tung-pi i-shu 35
Ts'ung-shu yao-lu 130
Tu Ching-chiao-pei shu-hou 95
Tu kang-mu t'iao-chi 98
Tu-i t'ung-yen 101
Tu-shih chiu-miu 81
Tu-shih chu-chieh 82
Tu-shih ou-p'ing 90
Tu-shih ou-shih 90
Tu-shu chi-wen 125
Tu-shu tsa-chih 98
Tu t'ung-chien lun 51
Tuan-shih shuo-wen chiao-ting 80
Tui-i ta-chih 96
T'ung-chien 50
T'ung-chien chi-lan 54
T'ung-chien chi-shih pen-mo 40, 56
T'ung-chien chi-shih-pen-mo pu-hou-pien 56
T'ung-chien chu-pien-cheng 51
T'ung-chien hsü-pien 55
T'ung-chien Hu-chu chü-cheng 125
T'ung-chien kang-mu 34, 50, 53
T'ung-chien p'ing-yü 92
T'ung-chien shih-wen pien-wu 51
T'ung-chien ta-wen 51
T'ung-chien ti-li t'ung-shih 51
T'ung-chien tsuan-yao 54
T'ung-chien wai-chi 51
T'ung-chien wen-i 51
Tung-ch'ien wen-kao 102
T'ung-chih 46, 61, 154
Tung Chin chiang-yü chih 131, 151
Tung-hua lu chui-yen 83

T'ung-k'ao 154
T'ung-ku shu-t'ang i'kao 86
Tung-kuan Han-chi 191
Tung-lin tien-chiang lu 70
Tung-shan wai-chi 101
T'ung-shih 50
T'ung-tien 60, 154
Tung-tu shih-lüeh 147
Tzu-chih-t'ung-chien 34, 50
Tzu-chih-t'ung-chien ch'ien-pien 52
Tzu-chih-t'ung-chien hou-pien 52
Tzu-chih-t'ung-chien kang-mu 53
Tzu-chih-t'ung-chien kang-mu ch'ien-pien 54
Tzu-chih-t'ung-chien kang-mu hsü-pien 54
Tzu-chih-t'ung-chien kang-mu san-pien 54
Tzu-chih-t'ung-chien pu 144
Tzu-chih-t'ung-chien pu-cheng 53
Tzu-chih-t'ung-chien yin-chu 51
Tzu-hui pu 143
Wan-shih hai-p'u 79
Wang-hui p'ien chien-shih 128
Wei-che ts'ung-t'an 100
Wei-ching-wo lei-kao 88
Wei-hsi i-wen 86
Wei-lu so-i 96
Wei-shu 192, 194, 198, 199
Wen-chang chih 67
Wen-hsien t'ung-k'ao 62
Wen-hsing t'iao-li 68
Wen-hsüan p'ang-cheng 90
Wen-hsüeh lun-wen so-yin 35
Wen-shih t'ung-i 42, 49, 122, 164
Weng-shih chia-shih lüeh-chi 89
Weng Sung-ch'an shou-cha 95
Wu-ch'ang-fu chih 180
Wu fu i-t'ung hui-k'ao 85, 139
Wu hsüeh lu 143
Wu-shih-nien-lai Chung-kuo chih fa-lü 68

INDEX — ROMANIZED CHINESE BOOK TITLES 239

Wu-tai liang-Sung chien-pen k'ao 142
Wu-tai shih 153
Wu-tai shih-chi 153, 154, 192, 193
Wu-tai shih-chi pu-chu 155
Wu-tai shih k'ao-i 138
Yang-cheng shu-wu ch'üan-chi ting-pen 98
Yang-chou shui-tao chi 136
Yang-chou wen-ts'ui 102
Yang-chü p'u 92
Yeh-an ts'un-chen 99
Yen-ch'ang ti-hsing chih 123
Yen Chi'en-ch'iu nien-p'u 123
Yen-fa yü-shuo 103
Yen-ko-fang 74
Yen-tzu ch'un-ch'iu 83
Yin-hsien chih 126
Yin-hsü ch'i-wen k'ao-shih 37
Yin-hsü shu-ch'i 10
Yin-hsü shu-ch'i ch'ien-pien 37
Yin-hsü shu-ch'i hou-pien 37
Yin-hsü shu-ch'i lei-pien 136
Yin-jen chuan 73
Ying-tsao fa-shih 74
Yü-ch'uang man-pi 89
Yü-hai 64
Yü-kung chui-chih 129
Yü-kung hui-ch'ien 85
Yü-kung t'u 130
Yu-p'eng shu-wen 95
Yü-shan p'u 73
Yü-shan tsou-tu 99
Yü-shih 73
Yü-t'u chih-chang 81

Yü-t'u yao-lan 102
Yü-yao hsien-chih 137
Yüan-chien lei-han 64, 88
Yüan-feng chiu-yü chih 177
Yüan-hao k'ao 135
Yüan Kao-li chi-shih 142
Yüan-lü tseng-hsiu 35
Yüan mi-shih shan ch'uan ti-ming so-yin 35
Yüan-shih 153, 193, 195
Yüan-shih chi-shih-pen-mo 56
Yüan-shih hsin-pien 84, 142, 154
Yüan-shih i-wen-chih 42, 126
Yüan-shih lei-pien 89, 154
Yüan-shih pen-cheng 91, 141
Yüan-shih shih-tsu piao 126
Yüan-tai ts'ang-k'u chi 142
Yüan-yeh 74
Yüan-yu tang-jen-pei k'ao 70
Yüeh-hsien k'ao 70
Yüeh-hsüan k'ao 125
Yüeh-lü ch'üan-shu 70
Yüeh-lü piao-wei 130
Yüeh-pen chieh-shuo 80
Yün-ch'ing kuan chin-wen 143
Yün-ch'ing-kuan fa-t'ieh 83
Yün-ch'uang man-kao 89
Yün-lang ou-pi 90
Yün-nan-fu chih 180
Yün-nan t'ung-chih 65, 179
Yung-ch'ing hsien-chih 122
Yüng-ch'uang hsiao-p'in 126
Yung-lo ta-tien 129, 137
Yung-lu hsien-chieh 84

INDEX — AUTHORS

A Kuei 179
An Chi 85
Ch'a Chi-tsuo 101
Ch'a Li 86
Ch'a Shen-hsing 98
Cha-ma-la-ting 177
Ch'ai Wen-hsien 7
Chang Chi 74
Chang Chien 56
Chang Chih-tung 41, 67
Chang Chih-wan 86
Chang Ch'un-ling 78
Chang Erh-chi 91
Chang Fang-p'ing 68
Chang Hai-p'eng 97
Chang Hsing-lang 94
Chang Hsing-yüeh 56
Chang Hsü 179
Chang Hsüeh-ch'eng 42, 49, 50, 81, 101, 122, 162, 164, 165
Chang Huai-kuan 68
Chang Huang-yen 100
Chang Hui-yen 91
Chang Hung-en 178
Chang Jo-ying 35
Chang Keng 69
Chang Meng-wen 82
Chang Mu 78, 123
Chang Ping-lin 46, 157, 171
Chang Po-hsi 67
Chang Shou-chieh 148
Chang Shu 37, 46, 158
Chang T'ai-chiao 70
Chang T'ao 153
Chang T'ing-yü 102, 195
Chang Tsung-t'ai 123, 150
Chang Wei-p'ing 78, 84, 86
Chang Wen 191
Chang Wen-chih 72
Chang Wen-t'ao 97

Chang Yen-chang 73
Chang Yen-yüan 68, 69
Chang Ying 64
Chang Yü 180
Chang Yü-shu 83
Ch'ang-sun Wu-chi 68
Chao Ch'i 32, 64
Chao Erh-hsün 37
Chao I 54, 77, 99, 124, 193
Chao Kung-wu 46
Chao Wen-che 54
Chao Yüan-jen 70
Ch'en Chan 124, 154
Ch'en Ching 55
Ch'en Ching-yün 124
Ch'en Fang-chi 178
Ch'en Ho 53
Ch'en Huang 78
Ch'en Huang-chung 125
Ch'en Hung-mou 178
Ch'en Ju-chi 180
Ch'en K'o-chia 53
Ch'en Li 85, 87, 100, 168
Ch'en Meng-lei 64, 79
Ch'en Pang-chan 56
Ch'en Shih-kuan 93
Ch'en Shou 22, 194
Ch'en Shu 153
Ch'en Yüan 27, 35, 68
Cheng Ch'iao 46, 49, 61, 155, 165
Ch'eng Chin-fang 86
Ch'eng Fu-liang 70
Ch'eng Hao 35, 65
Ch'eng I 35, 65
Ch'eng Yen-sheng 157
Cheng Yin 60
Ch'i Chao-nan 54, 100
Chi Ch'eng 74
Chi Ch'ing 179
Chi Tseng-yün 178

Index — Authors

Chi Yün 54, 82, 164
Chiang Ch'en-ying 101
Chiang Fan 65, 70, 97, 125, 166
Chiang K'ai-sheh 14
Chiang T'ing-fu 79
Chiang T'ing-hsi 64
Chiang Yung 68
Chiao Hsün 88, 102
Chiao Hung 40, 87
Ch'ien Ch'i 157
Ch'ien Hsüan-t'ung 27, 35
Ch'ien I-chi 84, 102, 151
Ch'ien Lung 176
Ch'ien Mu 46
Ch'ien Shih-sheng 156
Ch'ien Ta-chao 92, 149, 150
Ch'ien Ta-hsin 40, 42, 51, 86, 126, 153, 193
Ch'ien Wen-tzu 150
Chih Wei-ch'eng 167
Chih Yu 32
Chih Yü 67
Ch'in Hsiang-yeh 53
Ch'in Hui-t'ien 88
Chin Liang 86
Chin Lü-hsiang 52, 54
Ch'in Shih-huang-ti 183
Chin Shou 148
Chou Chi 153
Chou Chia-chou 73
Chou Chia-yu 73
Chou Hu 192
Chou Liang-kung 73
Chou Yung-nien 83, 95
Chu Chang-wen 70
Chu Chih-hsi 21
Chu Hsi 34, 35, 53, 54, 65, 66
Chu Hsü-tseng 67
Chu Ko-liang 22
Chu Kuo-chen 6, 94, 126
Chu Shao-sun 28
Chu Ssu-pen 177

Chu Tsai-yü 70
Chu Yen 72
Chu Yin-liang 88
Chu Yüan-chang 15
Ch'üan Tsu-wang 79, 97, 127, 149
Chuang T'ing-lung 137
Chuang Ts'un-yü 168
Ch'üeh Yin 191, 192
Chung Ku 5
Fa Shih-shan 98
Fan Tsu-hui 50
Fan Yeh 150, 162, 191, 198
Fang Hsüan-ling 194
Fang K'ai 151
Fang Tsung-ch'eng 91, 92
Fang Tung-shu 77, 93, 97, 167
Feng Ch'i 56
Feng Meng-chen 67
Feng Teng-fu 100
Fu Heng 54, 100
Hai Jui 70
Han Yü-shan 34
Ho Ch'ang-ling 91
Ho Ch'o 125
Ho Hsiu 168, 169
Ho Ping-sung 171
Ho Su 83, 103
Hou K'ang 128, 150, 151
Hsia Hsieh 53
Hsia Yün-i 85
Hsiang Chi 181, 198
Hsiang Mu 69
HsiangChih 5
Hsiao Ch'eng 158
Hsiao I-shan 101
Hsiao Te-yen 83
Hsiao Tu-heng 73
Hsiao Tzu-hsien 194
Hsieh Ch'i-k'un 156
Hsieh Chi-shih 98
Hsieh Ho 69
Hsieh Pi 153

Index — Authors

Hsü Ai 66
Hsü Chi-ch'ung 72
Hsü Ch'ien-hsüeh 53, 65, 103, 177
Hsü Kuang-ch'i 44
Hsü Nai 156, 157
Hsü Sung 94, 129
Hsü Ta-ch'un 88, 97, 99
Hsü Wen-ching 85, 93
Hsü Wu-tang 150
Hsü Yeh-min 148
Hsüeh Chü-cheng 137, 153, 195
Hsüeh Fu-ch'eng 82
Hsüeh Ying-ch'i 52
Hsiung Fang 150
Hsün Ch'o 66
Hsün Hsü 40
Hsün Yüeh 162
Hu San-hsing 51
Hu Shih 27, 36
Hu Wei 53, 129
Huang I-chou 53
Huang Jen-heng 153
Huang Kung-wang 69
Huang Liang-tung 180
Huang Shu-lin 164
Huang T'ing-kuei 179
Huang Tsung-hsi 65, 85, 130, 139
Huang Yü-chi 41
Hui Chiao 68
Hui Tung 36, 78, 85, 126, 149, 153, 193
Hung Liang-chi 130, 151, 152
I Keng 83
Juan Hsiao-hsü 41, 60
Juan K'uei-sheng 54
Juan Yüan 65, 99, 124, 125, 128, 179
Jung Keng 30
K'ang Hsi 176
K'ang Yu-wei 14, 69, 131, 135, 169
Kao Ching-sung 179
Kao I-han 66
Kao Shih-ch'i 56

K'o Shang-ch'ien 101
K'o Shao-min 37, 132, 152, 154, 193, 195
Ku Chieh-kang 27, 35, 100, 172
Ku Huai-san 151, 152
Ku Tung-kao 91, 132
Ku Yen-wu 81, 96, 133
Ku Ying-t'ai 57, 91, 133
Ku Yü 70
Ku Yüan 36
Kuan Chieh-chung 180
Kuei Wen-ts'an 100
Kung Ju-heng 73
K'ung Kuang-shen 81
Kung-sha Chung-mu 42
Kung Tzu-chen 169
Kung-yang Kao 168
Kuo Hsiu 99
Kuo Lun 153
Kuo Sung-t'ao 133
Lao Tzu 162
Lei Hsüeh-ch'i 158
Li An 192
Li Chao-lo 98, 178
Li Chen 191
Li Chen-hu 180
Li Ch'eng 74
Li Chin-tsao 95
Li Ch'ing 134, 155
Li Fang 64
Li Fu-sun 93
Li Hsien 177
Li Hsin-ch'uan 52
Li Hsiu-ch'eng 28, 36, 156
Li Hung-chang 178, 180
Li Kuang-ti 92
Li Li 98
Li Mei-shih 180
Li Ming-mo 57
Li O 73
Li Po-yao 194
Li Shih-hsü 81

Li Tang-yang 54
Li T'ao 52
Li Tao-yüan 82
Li T'iao-yüan 100
Li Tou 74
Li Tso-hsien 72
Li Wen-t'ien 77
Li Yen 84
Li Yen-shou 194, 195
Li Yu-t'ang 57
Liang Chang-chü 36, 90, 96
Liang Ch'i-ch'ao 23, 27, 87, 134, 170, 171
Liang Meng-yin 193
Liang Ssu-ch'eng 74
Liang T'ing-nan 156
Liang Yen-nien 84
Liang Yü-sheng 81, 135
Liao P'ing 135
Ling-hu Te-fen 194
Ling T'ing-k'an 94
Liu Ch'ang 149
Liu Chang-shih 149
Liu Chao 150
Liu Ch'eng-kan 81, 135
Liu Chih-chi 32, 42, 162, 163-165
Liu E 36, 37
Liu Feng-kao 155
Liu Feng-lu 135, 168, 169
Liu Hai-su 69
Liu Hsi-chung 51
Liu Hsiang 39, 59, 68
Liu Hsieh 163
Liu Hsin 39, 59, 61
Liu Hsü 195
Liu Hu-ju 18
Liu Pin 50, 149
Liu Shih-p'ei 167
Liu Shu 50, 51, 52
Liu Ts'an 164
Liu Wen-ch'i 83, 135
Liu Yü-i 179

Lo Chen-yü 1, 30, 37, 89, 136
Lo Hung-hsien 177
Lo Ju-fang 75
Lo Tso-nan 80
Lo Tun-jung 157
Lo Yung 36
Lu Chen 156
Lü Hai-huan 71
Lu Hsi-hsiung 54, 82
Lu Hsin-yüan 80, 95
Lu Lung-ch'i 21
Lu Pao-chung 78
Lu Shen 164
Lü Su-kao 179
Lu Wen-ch'ao 40, 43, 94, 152
Lu Yu 193
Lu Yü 73
Lung Kuang-tien 31
Ma Jung 27, 36
Ma Kuo-han 102
Ma San-heng 73
Ma Su 57, 137
Ma Tuan-lin 2, 41, 62, 155
Mao Ch'i-ling 78, 80
Mao P'an-lin 37, 46
Mei Tsu 28, 36
Meng Shen 157
Mi Fei 69
Miao Ch'üan-sun 129, 152
Mo Hsiu-fu 65
Mo Tzu 28
Nan Cho 69
Nan Hsüan 54
Ni Ssu 155
Ni Tsai-t'ien 57
Ni Ts'an 152
Nieh Ch'ung-ch'i 152
Niu Shu-yü 80
Niu Yün-chen 81
O Erh-t'ai 179
Ou-yang Hsiu 153, 154, 164, 195
Pai Huang 178

244   INDEX — AUTHORS

Pan Ku 31, 40, 162, 194
P'an Ch'eng-chang 101, 137
P'an Sheng-chang 87
P'ei Sung-chih 149
P'ei T'ien-hsi 180
P'ei Yin 148
P'eng Chao-sun 51
P'eng P'eng 85
P'eng Shao 68
P'eng Sun-i 90
P'eng Ting-ch'iu 80
P'eng Yüan-jui 54, 155
Pi Yüan 52, 53, 54, 151
Po Lan-hsi 177
P'u Ch'i-lung 164
Shang Lo 54, 177
Shao Chin-han 53, 137, 179
Shao I-ch'en 86
Shao T'ing-ts'ai 89
Shao Yüan-p'ing 89, 154
Shen Chi 72
Shen Ch'in-han 93, 95, 149
Shen Chin-ssu 86
Shen Han-yü 92
Shen Ping-chen 138, 155
Shen Shu-sheng 180
Shen Te-ch'ien 54, 90, 96
Shen T'ung 74
Shen Yüeh 194
Shih Shih-lun 88
Shih Ta-k'ai 87
Ssu-ma Ch'ien 22, 28, 31, 39, 45, 49, 96, 147, 148, 162, 172, 194, 198
Ssu-ma Kuang 50, 54
Ssu-ma Ts'uo 22
Su Shih 20
Sun Ch'i-feng 96
Sun Chih-tsu 158
Sun Hai-p'o 30, 37
Sun Hsing-yen 26
Sun I-jang 30, 36, 37, 57, 78, 82, 84, 138

Sun K'uo-t'u 103
Sun Yat-sen 4, 14
Sung Ch'i 195
Sung Chung 158
Sung Lien 195
Sung Lo 90
Sung, Madam 14
Sung Tz'u 68
Sung Ying-hsing 73
Tai Chen 83, 95, 166
Tai Ming-shih 6, 96
T'an Ssu-t'ung 169
T'ang Ch'i-yu 103
T'ang Chin-chao 36
T'ang Ch'iu 157
T'ang Yen 156
T'ao Hung-ching 72
T'ao Shu 79
Ting Jih-ch'ang 88
Ting Wen-chiang 70
T'o T'o 195
Tou, Madam 19
Ts'ai Hsin 79
Ts'ai Yüan-p'ei 37, 66
Tsang Li-ho 152
Tseng Chi-tse 81
Tseng Ching 87
Tseng Hsien-chih 192
Tseng Kung 165
Tseng Kuo-fan 36, 82
Tseng Pu 151
Tsien Mu — See Ch'ien Mu
Tso Ch'iu-ming 42, 46, 168
Tsou Han-hsün 79, 90, 180
Tsou Po-ch'i 100
Tsou Tan-sheng 148
Ts'ui Chu 5
Ts'ui K'uo 177
Ts'ui Shu 36, 85, 87, 97, 139, 172
T'u Chi 154
T'u Chu 139
Tu Yu 60, 61, 154

Index — Authors

Tuan Fang 89, 102
Tung Chung-shu 169
Tung Kao 176
T'ung Tso-pin 30, 37
Wan Ssu-ta 79, 92
Wan Ssu-t'ung 66, 94, 103, 139
Wan Yen 78, 90
Wang Che-fu 35
Wang Ch'eng 7, 147
Wang Ch'i 63
Wang Chien 60
Wang Chu 154
Wang Fu-chih 80, 93
Wang Hsien-ch'ien 140
Wang Hui-tsu 17, 103, 140
Wang I-jung 81, 99
Wang Jen-tsun 152
Wang K'ai-yün 135, 141
Wang Kuo-wei 1, 27, 30, 35, 67, 142, 171, 172
Wang Ming-sheng 28, 36, 93, 192
Wang Nien-sun 26, 85, 98
Wang Shao-hui 70
Wang Shih-chen 67, 82, 88, 89, 90
Wang Shih-tsen 178
Wang Shih-to 93, 152
Wang Shou-jen 14, 35, 66, 67
Wang Shu-nan 73
Wang T'ing-chen 178
Wang Tseng-fang 179
Wang Tsu-hui 91
Wang Ts'un 177
Wang Tsung-mu 52
Wang Wei 69
Wang Wei-chien 154
Wang Wen-t'ai 157
Wang Yang-ming See Wang Shou-jen
Wang Yao-ch'en 46
Wang Yin-chih 26, 94, 95, 96, 98
Wang Ying-lin 51, 64, 66
Wang Yüan 81, 101
Wang Yüan-ch'i 89
Wang Yün-wu 18, 34
Wei Chao 148
Wei Cheng 40, 195
Wei Ch'eng 14
Wei Chü-hsien 21
Wei Chung 40
Wei Hung 149
Wei Shou 194
Wei Yüan 84, 99, 142, 154, 169
Wen Jui-lin 86, 156
Weng Fang-kang 82, 89
Wu Ch'eng-ch'üan 34
Wu Ch'i 72
Wu Chün 49, 50
Wu Hsiung-kuang 178
Wu I-feng 67
Wu Jen-ch'en 88, 143, 156
Wu Ju-kuang 21, 83, 143
Wu Kuang-ch'eng 156
Wu Lan-hsiu 156
Wu Mi-kuang 86
Wu Ta-cheng 73, 83, **144**
Wu Yen 137
Yang Chung-liang 52
Yang Hsiung 163
Yang Lu-jung 55, 57
Yang Shih-ch'iao 70
Yang Shou-ch'ing 80
Yao Chen-tsung 149, 151
Yao Nai 95, 179
Yao Ssu-lien 194
Yeh Kuei 74, 80, 99
Yen Ch'ang-ming 54, 180
Yen Chih-t'ui 46
Yen Hsiang-hui 78
Yen Jo-chü 53, 95
Yen Yen 53, 144
Yü 182
Yü Ch'eng-lung 99
Yü Chi 93
Yü Hsiao-k'o 87
Yü Huai 92

Yü Ying-lung 177
Yü Yüeh 92
Yüan Chen 14
Yüan Hung 162
Yüan Shih-k'ai 89

Yüan Shu 56
Yüeh Chün 179
Yüeh Hsüan 177
Yüeh Shih 177